CHRONICLES OF THE KING

BOOK 3

THE LORD IS MY SALVATION

A NOVEL

Lynn N. Austin

Beacon Hill Press of Kansas City
Kansas City, Missouri

Copyright 1996
by Beacon Hill Press of Kansas City

ISBN 083-411-6030

Printed in the
United States of America

Cover Design: Ted Ferguson

Cover Illustration: Dave Howard

Library of Congress Cataloging-in-Publication Data

Austin, Lynn N.
      The Lord is my salvation : a novel / Lynn N. Austin.
          p.   cm. — (Chronicles of the king ; bk. 3)
      ISBN 0-8341-1603-0
      1. Hezekiah, King of Judah—Fiction.   2. Bible. O.T.—History of Biblical events—Fiction.   3. Israel—Kings and rulers—Fiction.
      I. Title.   II. Series: Chronicles of the king (Kansas City, Mo.); bk. 3.
      PS3551.U839L67   1996
      813'.54—dc20   96-8396
                                                                         CIP

10   9   8   7   6   5   4   3   2   1

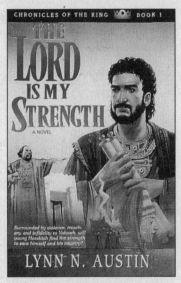

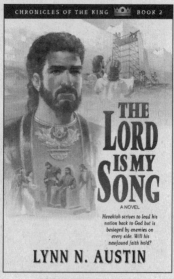

Dedicated to my mother, Jinny Davis,
who taught me to love books

*The L*ORD *is my strength*
and my song;
he has become my salvation.

PSALM 118:14

ABOUT THE AUTHOR

Lynn Austin's penchant for writing emerged gradually, prodded by college professors who recognized her masterful way with the written word.

"I am particularly grateful to a history professor at Southern Connecticut State University who encouraged me to write," she explains. "It was a slow awareness for me, however. Looking back, I know it was something I was always good at, but I didn't fully realize it until those years in college. After college, I left my writing on the shelf for a long time—I was busy with family responsibilities—but it was always in the back of my mind that I would come back to it. I later reached the point at which I decided to get fully into it."

Naturally, an author describing the details of life in King Hezekiah's day must be well versed in Old Testament history. Lynn's knowledge of such details can be traced back to her studies at Hope College, in Holland, Michigan.

"I had an excellent Old Testament teacher there who really fired up my love for the Old Testament," she comments.

Through graduate work in biblical backgrounds and archaeology through Hebrew University and Southwestern Baptist Theological Seminary, Lynn has perpetuated that love.

The author lives near Chicago in Orland Park, Illinois, where she works full time as a freelance writer and speaker. Her husband, Ken, is a Christian musician who has performed with numerous artists well known throughout the Christian music world.

In 1993 Lynn was honored as "New Writer of the Year" at Moody Bible Institute's Write-to-Publish Conference. She is an editor of *Profile*, the journal of the Chicago Women's Conference, and has contributed to a wide variety of Christian periodicals.

The Austins have three children: Joshua, Benjamin, and Maya.

A NOTE TO THE READER

Shortly after King Solomon's death in 931 B.C., the Promised Land split into two separate kingdoms. Israel, the larger nation to the north, set up its capital in Samaria and was no longer governed by a descendant of King David. In the southern nation of Judah, David's royal line continued to rule from Jerusalem.

The narrative of this book centers around events in the life of Hezekiah, who ruled from 716 to 687 B.C.

Interested readers are encouraged to research the full accounts of these events in the Bible as they enjoy this third book in the Chronicles of the King series.

Scripture references for *The Lord Is My Salvation*
> 2 Kings 18:13-37
> 2 Kings 19—20
> 2 Chron. 32
> Isa. 36—39

See also:

> 1 Sam. 4—6
> Isa. 22:15-25
> Isa. 30:12-18
> Isa. 31:1-3
> Isa. 53
> Isa. 54:1

Prologue

Eliakim kissed his fingertips, then touched the mezuzah on the door-post of his house. But unlike most days when he performed the ritual without thinking, today he paid homage to the little box of sacred laws as a tender act of thanksgiving. After his meeting with King Hezekiah, Eliakim couldn't help being thankful.

He pushed open the heavy front door, and a small boy with dark curly hair like his own peeked around the corner at him.

"It's Abba! Abba's home!" the boy shouted.

Eliakim squatted down, and the child hurled himself into his arms, planting a warm, sticky kiss on his cheek.

"Abba, look what I've got!" He opened his fist, revealing two squashed figs stuck to his palm. "Want one?"

"You'd really share your treasures with me?"

"Uh-huh. Here, Abba. Eat one."

"The Proverbs of Solomon say, 'A generous man will himself be blessed, for he shares his food with the poor.'" Eliakim gently tousled his son's curly hair. "But you may eat them, Jerimoth—I'm not hungry." The boy quickly devoured the figs, then licked the sticky juice off his fingers.

Eliakim had named little Jerimoth after Jerusha's father, but with his round face and mischievous brown eyes, he resembled his other grandfather, Hilkiah, more than his namesake. He had been born to Eliakim and Jerusha four years ago, yet Eliakim still found himself studying little Jerimoth in fascination, amazed that God had not only given him Jerusha for his wife but blessed their love with this beautiful child.

"Where's your mama?" he asked.

"Out in the garden with Grandpa."

Eliakim stood, lifting Jerimoth in his arms, and carried him out to their tiny courtyard. He delighted in the familiar warmth of his son's plump arms wrapped around his neck.

"Well, look who's home early," Hilkiah said. "What's the occasion?"

Hilkiah sat on a stone bench, bouncing Eliakim's baby daughter, Tirza, on his knee. "More . . . more . . . ," she begged whenever he stopped.

"That's the only word this child knows," Hilkiah said.

"That's not true—she can say 'Abba.' Can't you, sweetheart?"

Eliakim set Jerimoth down and swung the baby off Hilkiah's knee and high into the air.

"Careful!" Jerusha warned. Eliakim laughed along with his giggling baby. He pushed the dark curls away from her forehead and kissed her. "Ugh—you're sticky too." He set her down and wiped his lips as she toddled back to Hilkiah's knee.

"The early figs are ripe," Jerusha said. "We've been eating our fill of them all morning."

"Do I dare risk a kiss from you, then?" Eliakim bent to kiss Jerusha. "Mmm—sweeter than figs."

Little Jerimoth tugged at his robe. "How come you came home, Abba? It's not dinnertime yet."

"Yes, what's up, Son?" Hilkiah asked as the baby resumed her horsey ride on his knee. "Let's see . . . it's not a new moon . . . we just celebrated Shauvot, so I don't think it's a holiday . . . it isn't the king's birthday, is it?"

"Can't a man come home early to see his family? Do I need to have a reason?" Eliakim spread his hands and shrugged.

Jerusha and Hilkiah exchanged glances and laughed. "Son, the day you leave work early for no reason is the day we'll have snow in the summertime."

"Will you listen to him? My own father doesn't believe a word I say."

"Neither do I, Love." Jerusha pulled him down beside her and tugged playfully on his beard. "Why are you home early?"

"To tell you my good news."

"See? Didn't I say there would be a reason?" Hilkiah said, chuckling.

Eliakim grew serious. "I've been offered a promotion."

"A promotion?" Hilkiah stopped bouncing the baby. "How can you be promoted? You're already the chief engineer. Can you get any higher than that?"

"The king has asked me to serve as his secretary of state."

Hilkiah nearly dropped the baby onto the floor. "God of Abraham!"

Jerusha gripped his hand. "Oh, Eliakim! What will that mean?"

"It means—well, King Hezekiah is the sovereign ruler, of course. Then Shebna ranks second as his prime minister. The third-ranking official is the secretary of state—me."

Hilkiah closed his eyes and tilted his face toward heaven. "God of Abraham! Holy One of Israel! Who am I that You should bless my house and my family like this?"

"I asked Him the same question, Abba."

"My son? The third most important man in the nation? Seated at the king's left hand? Eliakim! It's the fulfillment of Isaiah's prophecy!"

"I know, Abba. I thought of that too. It's funny—I used to dream about being somebody important." He slipped his arm around Jerusha and pulled her close. "But when Jerusha agreed to marry me, all that ended. I honestly don't care about power anymore."

"Son! You didn't refuse the job?" Hilkiah's eyes widened in horror.

Eliakim slowly broke into a grin and held out his right hand. The golden signet ring of the secretary of state gleamed on his finger.

"No, Abba. I didn't refuse it. How could I refuse it? As the psalmist has written, 'Promotion comes from God. He puts down one and raises up another.'"

Little Jerimoth tugged curiously at his hand to examine the shiny ring. "You got a new job, Abba?"

"Yes, Son." He looked at the boy in surprise, proud that he had been able to follow the adult conversation.

"Then you can come home early tomorrow too?"

Everyone laughed, and Eliakim rumpled his son's hair. "I'm afraid not. King Hezekiah had to send me home today because I nearly fainted when he offered me the position. But from now on, I'll have to put in some very long hours at my new office in the palace."

"Are you still gonna build things, Abba?" Jerimoth asked.

"Well, in a way—I'll be building our country."

"Oh."

Eliakim knew by Jerimoth's expression that he had lost interest. He turned to his wife, who had scarcely spoken a word. "And you'll be needing some fancy gowns to accompany the new secretary to formal state dinners."

"You mean—I'll be dining at the palace? With the king?"

"Absolutely."

"Eliakim, I can't! I'm not royalty!"

"That doesn't matter—neither am I."

"But I'm just a poor farmer's daughter. I used to sleep in a loft above the oxen, for heaven's sake!"

He sniffed her neck and hair mischievously. "Hmm—you smell pretty good *now*. Besides, that will make very interesting dinner conversation with the king's wife, don't you think? I'm sure she'd love to hear all about your bed above the barn."

She gave him a playful shove. "Will you be serious?"

"I'm very serious. You'll be the most beautiful woman there, Jerusha. I'd be proud to have you accompany me anywhere in the kingdom."

"Mama, did you really sleep with cows?" little Jerimoth asked. They all laughed again.

A shiver of joy rushed through Eliakim until he could scarcely stay seated. He wanted to dance and leap with happiness. He gazed at his wife and children, then down at the signet ring that still felt strange on his finger.

"I think I know how King David must have felt," he said. "'My cup overflows.'"

*Hezekiah . . . succeeded in everything he
undertook. But . . . God left him to test him
and to know everything that was in his heart.*

—2 Chron. 32:30-31

1

"You may as well return to your rooms, Your Majesty. Lady Hephzibah says it is her time."

"Oh no." The feeling of deep contentment that had filled Hezekiah a moment ago suddenly vanished along with his hopes for an heir. He had walked the short distance to the harem, looking forward to his beautiful wife's company and love this balmy spring evening; he hadn't anticipated being turned away at her door with bad news.

"How's she taking it, Merab?"

"Like she always does, my lord."

Hezekiah looked past Merab into the room and saw Hephzibah sitting before the open window, staring into the darkness. He knew from experience how deeply his wife grieved every month when she learned that she hadn't conceived. He seldom succeeded in consoling her or soothing her bitter tears, but he remembered all the times she had cheered him with her love, her laughter, her beautiful singing, and he wanted to soothe her in return.

"Give us a few minutes alone, Merab."

He pulled up a small footstool beside Hephzibah, but she wouldn't look at him.

"It's a gorgeous evening. Would you like to come up to the rooftop with me?"

Hephzibah shook her head, still staring into the darkness.

"Hephzibah, I'm sorry you're still not pregnant. I know how disappointed you must be."

"Do you know how many years it's been?" she asked. Pain edged her voice, making it brittle.

"I know. It's been a long time."

"Then why do you still refuse to accept the truth?" She finally turned to him, her beautiful face slick with tears, her eyes swollen with grief. "I'm barren, Hezekiah. I'll never give you an heir."

"But you know that Yahweh has promised—"

"He hasn't promised *you* an heir."

He tried to keep his voice gentle, but he needed to convince her of his firm belief in God's word. "Yes, Hephzibah. Yahweh promised that there would always be an heir of King David to reign on the throne of—"

"Oh, why can't you see the truth? I'm never going to have a baby. Never!"

"Because it's not the truth. 'The LORD swore an oath to David, a sure oath that he will not revoke—'"

"Please," she moaned. "You're clinging to a promise that your God never made to you."

"But Yahweh *did* promise me."

"No! He promised *King David!*"

"Hephzibah, it's the same thing. 'One of your own descendants . . . will sit on your throne for ever and ever.'"

She covered her ears. "Stop quoting that to me, and listen! Your brother Gedaliah is King David's descendant, isn't he?"

The mention of his brother's name disturbed Hezekiah. "Well, yes—of course."

"And Gedaliah has four sons, doesn't he?"

His uneasiness grew as she led him down a path he didn't want to explore. He couldn't remain seated. "Yes, but what difference does that—"

"Hezekiah, they're all heirs of King David."

"Yes! So what?"

"Don't you see? If you never have a son, Gedaliah or one of his sons will take your place—but Yahweh has still kept His promise to King David."

Hezekiah saw instantly that she was right. He had been a fool for failing to recognize the truth all these years. The answer to her barrenness was so simple—and so unfair. He sank down onto the window seat beside her and groped for something to say.

"But—how can that be?" he mumbled.

"Do you want a son of your own, or will you be content to let your brother or your nephew inherit your throne?"

The question stunned him. Hezekiah had never considered it before. He couldn't answer.

"If you want your own son to inherit your kingdom, then you'd better renounce me as your wife, because I'm barren." She covered her face and wept, shaking with the force of her sobs.

For the first time, Hezekiah understood her suffering and shared her disappointment. He, too, wanted a son. It wasn't fair. But in spite of his inner turmoil, he knew that right now Hephzibah's suffering exceeded his own. She needed him.

"I can't divorce you, Hephzibah," he said quietly.

"Why? Because Yahweh forbids it?"

"No. Because I love you." Hezekiah gathered her in his arms, ignoring the law that forbade him to touch her. He stroked her soft hair and whispered it again: "I love you, Hephzibah. You mean more to me than having an heir."

She lifted her head, and the desolation in her eyes as she pleaded with him wrenched his heart. "But I want you to have an heir. I want the next king of Judah to be *your* son, not Gedaliah's. I love you so much that I'm willing to give you up in order to make that possible."

"No, Hephzibah. I won't—"

"Then can't you find another way? Isn't there an exception somewhere that allows you to have a second wife if I'm barren?"

"I don't know—I really don't know." He had come to Hephzibah's room tonight filled with faith for the future. But God had snatched the future from his grasp and handed it to Gedaliah.

"It's not fair that you should have to choose between staying faithful to me or having a son. How could a loving God demand such a choice from you?"

"There's a lot I don't understand—," he began, but once Hephzibah had unleashed her bitterness, it compelled her to spew out more.

"Why would Yahweh forbid you to worship Him tomorrow simply because you felt sorry for me and held me in your arms tonight? Why is your God so unfair, Hezekiah? After everything you've done for Him, is this the way He repays you? By making you choose between divorcing me or giving your kingdom to Gedaliah?"

Hezekiah pressed her tightly to himself. "Shh . . . Hephzibah . . . stop."

Her bitterness fed his own, and the force of it frightened him. He knew that God wasn't unfair. But he didn't know how to reconcile his confusion and disappointment with his faith in God's goodness. He needed time alone to think everything through. He couldn't afford to listen as Hephzibah angrily voiced his resentment and doubt.

"Shh—Hephzibah. Listen to me now. A few years ago Shebna tried to talk me into forming a marriage alliance with a foreign king. He was convinced that the Law doesn't prohibit more than one wife, and he insisted that my grandfather's interpretation of the Law was wrong. He tried to show me what the Torah said, but I wouldn't listen to him."

"You mean—you might not have to divorce me? Maybe you can have a son too?"

"I'm not sure. I need to find out the truth. I've put you through a lot of heartache over this, haven't I?—I'm sorry."

Her arms tightened around him. "It doesn't matter—as long as you have a son."

"The priests and Levites are experts in the Law, and if there's a solution to this dilemma, they'll know what it is. I can't believe that God would be unfair to us."

In spite of his words of assurance, Hezekiah's gnawing uneasiness refused to go away. Why hadn't he realized long ago that God had promised David an heir, not him? All these years he had comforted Hephzibah through her disappointment, never doubting God's promise. He had condemned her lack of faith, but she had been right all along. She would never give him the son he wanted.

Like Abraham, he had trusted God to provide an heir, but God had betrayed his trust. After everything Hezekiah had done for Yahweh—all the reforms, all the years of faithfulness to His Law—God would give Hezekiah's throne to Gedaliah, an idolater. He trembled at the injustice of it.

"Don't cry anymore—everything will work out. I'll talk to the priests and Levites tomorrow morning, and by the time I come back tomorrow night I'll have their answer." He held her tightly. "I could never give you up, Hephzibah. Never."

◈

When Hephzibah's servant returned, she found her mistress seated before the window, weeping softly. "Ah, my poor darling. I tried to tell him not to come here. I knew he would upset you."

Hephzibah looked up, smiling as she wiped her tears. "No, Merab. I'm weeping for joy. He held me in his arms tonight. He really held me."

"But the Law says—"

"I know! He finally realizes that Yahweh's laws are unfair. He told me that he would find a way to break the Law so he could have a son without divorcing me."

"The king said that?"

"Yes! Merab, do you know how long I've prayed for this and asked the goddess to change his heart?"

"A long time, my lady."

"Well, tonight it happened. I owe the goddess everything!"

Hephzibah hurried over to the wooden chest beside her bed and opened it, then arranged the sacred vessels for her nightly ritual to Asherah. She lifted the golden statue as a mother would cradle a beloved child and set it on a small table surrounded by several oil lamps and incense burners.

"Merab, where is the incense King Hezekiah gave me?"

"Do you think you should burn that, my lady? He wanted you to take it to Yahweh's Temple."

"I don't care. Bring it to me. The goddess deserves the best I have."

As Merab bustled off to fetch the incense, Hephzibah picked up the small funeral urn. The words of the vow she had made, pledging her firstborn child, were still clearly written on it in charcoal. Maybe now the goddess would answer her other prayers, too, and finally open her womb so she could fulfill her vow.

When she had finished lighting all the oil lamps and incense burners, Hephzibah bowed down with her forehead pressed to the floor and began her prayer of praise and thanksgiving to Asherah.

<hr />

Hezekiah dug through the collection of scrolls he kept in his chambers until he found his copy of "The Instructions to the Kings." Then he drew a lampstand close and sat down to read it carefully.

"He must not take many wives, or his heart will be led astray." He read the words over and over. *"Many wives."* Shebna was right—the Torah didn't say "only one." Would two be considered *"many"?* And what about concubines? Legally, they weren't wives at all. Hezekiah hadn't called for his concubines since he had become king, and they no longer lived in the palace harem. He had moved them to a villa he had built inside Eliakim's new city walls.

When he had studied these instructions years ago, his grandfather had said that if he obeyed these laws, he would never succumb to a king's three greatest temptations: power, pride, and pleasure. But Hezekiah knew he wasn't taking a second wife for pleasure. He simply wanted an heir.

He laid the scroll down and stared into space while his servants moved silently around the room lighting all the remaining lamps. Taking a second wife made sense to his rational mind, yet the thought made him uneasy. He knew he wouldn't rest until he resolved this dilemma. He called his valet.

"Go see if Joah the Levite is still in the palace, or else Eliakim ben Hilkiah. Ask one of them to come here."

While he waited, Hephzibah's question nibbled at the edges of his faith: *"Do you know how many years it has been?"* He understood her bitter accusations toward God—he had waited, trusting for an heir, for more than 10 years.

He looked at the scroll again. *"He must not take many wives."* Why had he stubbornly interpreted the Law to mean something God never intended? Why hadn't he listened when Shebna showed him this passage several years ago? He could have saved Hephzibah years of frustration and sorrow.

A few minutes later his valet returned, followed by Joah and Eliakim. "I found them both, Your Majesty."

"Good. Have a seat, gentlemen." He motioned to his couch, then took a seat opposite them and passed the scroll to Joah. "I need an interpretation of this law. Read the section about kings' wives—here."

Hezekiah pointed to the place, then leaned forward anxiously, his elbows on his knees, watching Joah's face as he read. When the Levite finished, he passed the scroll to Eliakim, who squinted at the tiny letters and tilted the scroll toward the light to read it.

"Now, according to that Law, is the king allowed to marry only one wife?" Hezekiah asked when Eliakim finished reading. "Is that how you interpret this passage?"

Joah pondered a moment. "No—it doesn't say only one. But I think it's important to examine the reason Yahweh gave us this law."

"And what would you say that reason is?"

"I think this particular passage warns Israel's kings that a lack of self-control in their personal affairs can lead to a lack of self-control in other areas of their lives. And this can threaten their relationship with Yahweh."

"I see. And is that how you interpret it, Eliakim?"

"Yes, I think King Solomon's troubles with his wives and the idolatry that resulted is a good example of the dangers this warns against."

Hezekiah stroked his beard thoughtfully, then leaned forward with his elbows on his knees again, his fingers laced together in front of him. "Then if I married a second wife, one I knew worshiped only Yahweh, would I be in violation of the Torah?"

"No, Your Majesty," Joah said after a pause. "I don't think you would be. But again, obeying the purpose of the Law is just as important as obeying the letter."

"Then I want to make my reasons for taking a second wife very clear. I love Hephzibah, but after all these years she is still barren. If the Law allows it, I would marry again to provide an heir to the throne."

"That's a valid reason," Joah said. "But there's another law I should warn you about. It's found in the fifth book of Moses, I believe. It says that if an unloved wife bears a son first, the rights of the first-born belong to him, even if the favored wife has a son later on."

"You mean, once my new wife gives me a son, Hephzibah's son can never inherit the throne of Judah, even if God miraculously opens her womb?"

"That's right, Your Majesty."

This law seemed unfair, and Hezekiah recalled Hephzibah's accusations against Yahweh. But the alternative might be no heir at all.

"I see," he said at last. "Anything else, Joah?"

"Only a word of advice. For the sake of domestic harmony, you'll need to give both wives equal attention."

"I understand." But Hezekiah wondered if Hephzibah would. She had offered to share him so he could have a son, but did she realize that she would have to continue sharing him for the rest of her life?

"Eliakim, would you like to add anything?" he asked.

"No, Your Majesty. Joah knows more about the Law than I do."

"Then I won't keep you. Thank you for coming."

Hezekiah pondered Joah's interpretation for a long time after the two men left. Although the Torah permitted a second marriage, he found it difficult to accept the idea after believing differently for so many years. He knew he could never love a second wife as much as Hephzibah, and it would be hard to treat them equally—even harder to share his time with another woman. And deep inside, he still longed for a son of Hephzibah's to inherit his throne.

As he struggled with these thoughts, he wondered how Hephzibah would react to what the Levite had told him. Would this news cheer her and offer her hope or enflame her bitterness and jealousy? She would have a lot to think about, and Hezekiah would need to talk everything over with her carefully before he made his final decision.

He decided not to wait until tomorrow night. He would go back to Hephzibah's room and tell her tonight.

He quickly walked the short distance to the harem and saw a beam of light shining under her door. He knocked softly. Then, not waiting for the maid to answer, he opened the door and stepped inside.

"Hephzibah, I—"

But Hezekiah never finished what he had come to say. For the shock of discovering Hephzibah kneeling in prayer before a golden statue of Asherah struck him as hard as if the palace walls had tumbled down on top of him.

The floor swayed beneath Hezekiah's feet as he slowly walked toward his wife. He stared at the shrine, then at Hephzibah, unwilling to believe what he saw. He had stepped into a nightmare. This wasn't his wife kneeling before an idol. It couldn't be. He tried to speak, but nothing came out. He fought the urge to be sick.

Please let this be a dream.

But it was real. An agonized cry rose from deep inside him.

"No! Oh, Yahweh . . . please . . . no!"

He grabbed the front of his tunic with shaking hands and tore it down the middle. Then he turned the fabric to shreds, crying out in anguish as he ripped it again and again.

"How could you do this to me? How could you?"

Hephzibah cowered before him as all the blood drained from her face. He seized her by the shoulders, but his hands shook uncontrollably as rage pounded through him, and he quickly let go, afraid he would kill her.

"How long have you had this in my house?" he shouted. "How long have you worshiped an idol?"

"I'm sorry," she sobbed. "I can explain—"

Hezekiah turned away from her in revulsion, and his eyes fell on the shrine she had made. Fine olive oil from his storehouses filled the silver lamps. The royal incense intended for Yahweh's sanctuary burned in the incense stands. The smiling goddess with her swollen belly and heavy breasts gazed back at him with contempt.

This couldn't be happening.

Then Hezekiah saw the urn bearing his own seal. He picked it up and read the deadly symbols of Hephzibah's vow. *Oh, Yahweh, no—not this.* Horror rocked through him. She had pledged to murder his child.

"Hephzibah—you would sacrifice our son?"

"But I made the vow for you—so the enemy wouldn't invade your nation."

"No—," he moaned, fighting tears. "No!"

His father had sacrificed his sons to Molech for the same reason. Hezekiah remembered Eliab's terrified screams as he had rolled into the monster's flaming mouth. He shuddered in horror at the thought of Hephzibah throwing their son into the flames.

He stood paralyzed. Time had frozen, and it seemed he would be trapped in this chilling moment forever. But gradually his blood began to flow through his veins once again, transforming his shock into uncontrollable rage.

With a savage cry, Hezekiah slammed the urn against the far wall with all his strength, shattering it into dust. He saw the obscene goddess smiling at him, mocking him, and he lost all control. He picked up the table as if it weighed nothing and hurled it across the room. When the golden idol crashed to the floor, it broke open, spilling sand from its hollow center. It hadn't been a solid gold statue after all, but a fake, molded from clay and thinly coated with gold.

The overturned lamps and incense burners flew in every direction, knocking over one of the blazing lampstands. The smoldering wicks quickly ignited the puddles of splattered oil, and, before Hezekiah could react, the oil burst into flames. The fire licked across the carpet, engulfed a pile of reed mats, then spread to the silken floor cushions.

He heard a *whoosh* as dried palm branches in an earthenware jar caught fire, then the angry crackle of flames as they jumped to a tapestry banner hanging above the jar. Beside him the woven lattice screen that shielded Hephzibah's bath erupted in flames, and from there the fire quickly leaped up the gauzy curtains that enclosed her bed.

Dimly he heard Hephzibah scream. She had backed into a corner beside the flaming bed with no way to escape. In a daze, Hezekiah tore off his outer robe and used it to beat out the rapidly spreading fire. Hot smoke choked him as he swung the robe into the middle of the flames, over and over again, beating with desperate strength.

The fire spread out of control faster than he could fight it. A wall of flames surrounded Hezekiah, following the arc of spilled oil, and the heat seared his exposed chest where he had torn his tunic. Flying sparks singed his arms and face, but he ignored the pain as he battled on.

"Hephzibah, run! Get out of there!" he cried as he tore the blazing curtains from the bed to clear a path for her. She didn't move. He reached to grab her and pull her out, but a piece of flaming debris suddenly ignited the tassels of his tunic. The oily flames burned off a large patch of skin on his leg. He cried out in agony, wrestling to extinguish his burning clothes.

Dizzy with shock and pain, choking on acrid smoke, Hezekiah fought for his life and for Hephzibah's, desperate to bring the fire under control. When he could no longer use his robe to beat the flames, he bailed water from the bath to soak the carpet. He scooped handfuls of sand from the toppled idol to douse burning puddles of oil. He grabbed the flaming tapestry banner and tore it down so the fire wouldn't spread to the ceiling beams. Then he yanked the curtains off her windows before the fire reached them and used the heavy cloth to smother the flames. After what seemed like many hours, the fire was finally out.

Hezekiah sagged with exhaustion. His lungs ached from breathing smoke. His blistered hands burned as if still immersed in the flames. And the shin of his right leg where his robes caught fire was a throbbing, open wound. But it was better that he suffered, better that he burned in the flames than his firstborn child. The smell of burnt flesh and hair lingered in Hezekiah's nostrils, and it seemed appropriate to him. It was the smell of idolatry.

Hephzibah's shattered Asherah lay among the ashes where it had fallen, its severed head smiling as if nothing had happened. Painfully, Hezekiah scooped up a fistful of sand and walked over to where Hephzibah still cowered beside the bed. He grabbed her hand and forced it open, pouring sand into it.

"Here's your goddess," he said. "Pray to this."

Stepping over the smoldering wreckage, he left her.

◆

Servants rushed into Hephzibah's room from all directions, but she didn't move from where she had slumped in her gutted bedroom.

"What have I done? What have I done?" she sobbed.

Hezekiah was gone. When he walked out her door, Hephzibah knew she had lost him forever. The anguish and bewilderment on his face would haunt her for the rest of her life. She wished she had died in the fire. She knew how much Hezekiah's God meant to him, how hard he had worked for religious reform. Why had she deceived him and betrayed him? Her reasons seemed trivial to her now, beside the enormity of Hezekiah's anger and hatred. He would never forgive her. She wanted to die.

She stared at the handful of sand she clutched and watched it slowly slip away between her fingers. She had lost Hezekiah, her only reason for living, over a handful of worthless sand.

❖

Hezekiah limped down the hall toward his chambers in a daze, coughing smoke from his lungs. The searing pain from his burns slowly penetrated his shock, but the pain of what Hephzibah had done to him was far greater.

Before he reached his door, Eliakim ran up the hall toward him. "What happened? We smelled smoke. Are you . . . God of Abraham! Look at you!"

Hezekiah glanced down at his torn, burnt clothes. "There was a fire in the harem . . . some oil lamps spilled . . . it's out now . . ."

"Your Majesty, you're badly burned! Here—let me help you."

With Eliakim supporting him, Hezekiah stumbled back to his chambers and sank onto his couch. He heard Eliakim calling for servants and issuing orders, but his voice sounded as if he shouted from the end of a long tunnel.

"Fill a basin with cold water. Hurry! You—run to the harem. There was a fire there. Make sure it's out. And you—fetch the royal physicians quickly."

Hezekiah's valet stood over him, wringing his hands. "Get some strong wine," Eliakim told him. "Now!" The servant dashed off, leaving them alone.

Hezekiah's pain surged and expanded like a powerful tide, strengthening every minute. His hands and his chest burned as if still in the flames, but the torture from the burn on his leg made him struggle to stay conscious. He forced himself to talk between labored breaths.

"I guess I was foolish . . . to try to fight the fire . . . myself. But I couldn't call for help . . . I didn't want . . . anyone . . . to see . . ."

Sweat poured down Hezekiah's face into his eyes. His swollen hands were useless to him, and he tried to wipe the sweat away with his forearm. Eliakim grabbed a linen cloth and mopped his face and neck.

"Hold on, Your Majesty. Help is coming."

"My leg—," Hezekiah groaned.

"Yes, I know. God of Abraham—it's very bad."

Hezekiah had to keep talking. He didn't want to pass out. "Eliakim—you're married, aren't you?"

"Yes, Your Majesty. You remember—the Israeli woman who escaped from the Assyrians."

"I remember . . . astounding courage . . ." He leaned his head against the cushions and stifled a moan. "Do you—love her?"

"Yes, I love her as I love my own life. She was a precious gift to me, from God."

Hezekiah closed his eyes and turned away. Eliakim's words stabbed deeper than any of his wounds. Hephzibah had been a gift too. From Ahaz.

"If you love your wife . . . as I loved Hephzibah . . . then you will understand." He opened his eyes again and looked up at Eliakim. "Tonight . . . when I went to her chambers . . . she had a graven image of Asherah. She was worshiping it."

"*What?*" Eliakim paled.

"I tried to destroy it . . . I knocked over some oil lamps. The fire spread so quickly . . . it was out of control . . ."

"Oh, God of Abraham!"

Hezekiah's stomach twisted as he remembered the urn and the vow Hephzibah had written on it in charcoal.

"And she—" But grief choked off his words. He grimaced in pain, hoping Eliakim wouldn't notice that he was trying not to weep.

"Your Majesty, I . . . I don't know what to say . . ."

There was nothing anyone could say. The unimaginable had happened.

The valet hurried into the room with the wine, and Eliakim grabbed it from his hand. Hezekiah heard him pouring it into a cup. A moment later, Eliakim held it to his lips. "Here—it will help ease your pain."

But as he drank the bitter wine, Hezekiah knew it would never ease the pain in his soul. He had never forgiven his father for planning to sacrifice him. How could he forgive Hephzibah for vowing to sacrifice his own child?

Eliakim held the cup for him until Hezekiah had drained it. Hezekiah felt it burn a path to his stomach, but the throbbing, searing pain in his leg grew worse. He moaned in agony, unable to stop himself. Eliakim quickly poured another cup for him.

"No . . . I can't . . ." He was too nauseated to drink more.

Another servant arrived with a bronze basin of water, and Hezekiah plunged his hands into it, longing for cooling relief. But the relief lasted only an instant, and he fought to keep from fainting as pain shuddered through his body.

He looked up at Eliakim again and forced himself to talk. "Even if I had found her . . . with another man . . . it would have been better than what she's done. She betrayed me . . . and everything I believed in. She brought that . . . into my own house!"

As Eliakim held the cup out to him again, Hezekiah saw deep sorrow in his friend's eyes. "Your Majesty, what would you like us to do with her?"

Idolatry demanded the death penalty. Hezekiah and Eliakim both knew it. But even in his anger, Hezekiah couldn't pronounce the death sentence on Hephzibah.

"I can't do it, Eliakim," he said faintly. "I can't."

Eliakim nodded in understanding.

"But she is no longer my wife. Have Shebna prepare divorce papers. She is dead to me. Never mention her name again."

One by one, the court physicians arrived. "You must lie down, Your Majesty," one of them said after seeing his leg. "We can tend you better that way."

The servants helped Hezekiah to his bed, and the movement initiated another wave of pain and nausea that nearly overwhelmed him. He lay flat on his back, panting as he struggled to keep from crying out.

The physicians examined his arms and face and chest, spreading thick balm made with aloe on his numerous burns. Then they plastered his swollen hands with balm and loosely wrapped them in gauze. Finally they turned their attention to his leg. All the flesh on his shin had burned away except for a few blackened shreds still lying in the open wound.

"The tassels and the gold threads from your robe have melted into the wound," one physician said. "And there seems to be dirt, or maybe sand . . . ?"

"Yes . . . probably sand." Hezekiah remembered the hollow idol. "I threw sand on the fire."

"I'm sorry, but we'll need to clean the wound thoroughly. It'll be very painful."

He would welcome the pain if only it would help him forget what Hephzibah had done. He fought back bitter tears at the irony of her betrayal. He had remained faithful to only one wife so he wouldn't be tempted by idolatry—yet she had secretly worshiped idols all along. He had never known the evil hidden in her heart. He had confided in her, shared his life with her, loved her as he had loved no other person. But she had lied to him, pretending to serve God while keeping a secret part of herself, an evil part, hidden from him. All these years.

"We have special drugs we can mix with your wine, Your Majesty—for the pain."

Hezekiah shook his head, remembering his father.

The physician motioned to the servants. "Get ready, then. You'll have to hold him still." They gripped his shoulders and ankles. Hezekiah clenched his teeth, reciting to himself as he braced to endure more pain.

Hear, O Israel! . . . Yahweh is our God—Yahweh alone! . . . You shall love Yahweh your God with all your heart and . . .

The first agonizing stab sliced through him. Hezekiah cried out, then felt nothing more as he lost consciousness.

3

Hours later Hezekiah awoke to agony. He tried to sit up and moaned as pain overwhelmed him. One of the physicians appeared beside him in the darkness.

"Lie still, Your Majesty. Don't try to move."

"I'm so thirsty." His mouth and tongue felt dry. He could scarcely speak.

"Here. Take a drink of water."

Hezekiah's hands were useless—swollen and blistered beneath the bandages. The physician gently raised Hezekiah's head and held the cup to his lips. Some of the water rolled down his throat; the rest dribbled down his chin into his beard. Hezekiah cursed his helplessness.

"Do you want something for the pain?"

"No." Hezekiah could scarcely stand the pain, but he refused to admit his weakness. "How long will I be like this?"

"In the morning we'll examine your burns again and—"

"No. Tell me now."

"Surely you realize that you've received numerous burns and—"

"How serious . . . are they?"

"Your hands and part of your chest are badly blistered."

"And my leg?"

"Your skin was completely burned away. The wound is very deep. And it's been contaminated with sand and bits of cloth. We did our best to cleanse it, but—"

"How long until I'm healed?"

How long would he suffer this unspeakable agony, this maddening helplessness?

"We can't be certain, but you must rest for at least a week, and then—"

A week. Lying helplessly with water dribbling down his chin. "No. Never."

"But rest is the best cure, my lord." He offered Hezekiah another drink, then wiped the water off his face as one would for a child.

"Leave me now."

"But—you might need—"

"I'll call you."

"Yes, Your Majesty."

Hezekiah heard the door close. He was alone. He shut his eyes again, but the pain prevented him from sleeping.

He had found Hephzibah worshiping a pagan idol.

Hezekiah had never forgotten the vivid images of his brothers burning to death in Molech's flames. Now he would never be able to erase the image of his wife bowing before Asherah, pledging to sacrifice his child. He had fought the fires of idolatry all his life; tonight they had defeated him.

Alone in the darkness, Hezekiah didn't try to stop the tears that rolled down his face and disappeared into his beard. Hephzibah, his love, had deceived him. How long had she worshiped idols? One year? Ten years? What did it matter if it was a day or a lifetime? He could never forgive her for what she had done.

Man and woman—God's presence will dwell in their midst. Hezekiah had thought he had shared that kind of love with Hephzibah. In his happiness he had thought God's presence had blessed their marriage. But he had believed a lie. He covered his face with bandaged hands and wept.

By the time the sun rose in the morning, Hezekiah had vowed never to shed another tear over Hephzibah. He buried deep in his soul his love for her and his sorrow over losing her, locking them away in a place he vowed never to search. Two emotions commanded all his attention: the agonizing pain of his burns and his unrestrained anger.

During the night he had allowed the anger to build until it overshadowed everything, even his pain, and as his room began to grow light, he shouted for his valet. The man hurried into the room, followed by the three court physicians.

"Help me up. It's nearly time for the morning sacrifice."

The men didn't move. "Don't gape at me like that—I said help me up!" He struggled to sit, and his valet finally hurried over to help him. "That's it. Now swing my leg over the side."

Hezekiah moaned involuntarily as the blood raced down his injured leg. One of the physicians stepped forward, his eyes wide with fear.

"Your Majesty, I don't think—"

"I didn't hire you to think," he said through clenched teeth. "I hired you to make me well. Find Shebna and tell him to bring the divorce papers. The rest of you help me get dressed."

Hezekiah struggled into his clothes, each movement intensifying the pain. The servants slipped his tunic over his head, and when the linen fabric brushed against his chest, he nearly fainted. The edges of his wounds, where blistered flesh met uninjured skin, hurt the most.

"Shall we order a sedan chair, Your Majesty?"

"What for?"

"Well, to carry you up to—"

"I don't need to be carried." Hephzibah's idolatry would not turn him into a cripple.

Hezekiah stood and took a step forward. The room whirled, and his vision narrowed to a tunnel. The physicians rushed forward to catch him.

"No! Leave me alone. I can walk by myself."

Hezekiah put one foot in front of the other, ignoring his agony and the bizarrely tilting floor, until he reached the couch in his sitting room.

"Thank you for your services," he told his physicians. "You may go home."

"But you can't—"

"Yes, I can. And I will. Good day."

As he waited for Shebna, Hezekiah tried to calculate how far he would need to walk to get to the Temple, how many stairs he would have to climb.

"Pour me some of that," he told his servant, indicating the flask of strong wine Eliakim had made him drink the night before. The warm wine burned all the way to his stomach, but he drained the cup, hoping the drink would numb the pain enough to get him to the Temple—and back again.

"Now bring me something to eat."

A few minutes later, Shebna arrived carrying a parchment scroll.

"You look terrible, Your Majesty! Do you really think you should be out of bed?"

"Obviously I do! I'm sitting here, aren't I? Where are my divorce papers?"

"I have them." He held up the scroll, then let his hand drop to his side again.

"Did Eliakim explain why?"

"I have heard the story. I am very sorry."

"The entire nation has probably heard the story by now. That's why I'm going up to the Temple. Nothing, no one, is going to stop me from setting an example for my nation."

"Do you think it is wise to let the people see you like this?"

"What do you mean?"

"Have you looked in a mirror, Your Majesty?"

Hezekiah stared at his bandaged hands and sighed. "I shouldn't have fought the fire. I should have let everything burn."

"I saw the damage this morning. The fire destroyed her room."

"Good. Have it rebuilt some other way. For my new wife."

His stomach twisted as he said the words. The divorce would be final. He would never see Hephzibah again. He wondered how he would learn to love another woman—or to trust her. But maybe love and trust didn't matter. Maybe having a son would be enough.

"Show me those papers, Shebna."

"Are you certain? A more suitable punishment would be to—"

"I've never been more certain!"

Reluctantly, Shebna passed him the scroll. Hezekiah tried to take it between his bandaged hands, but he lost his grip. The scroll tumbled to the floor.

"I curse her for what she's done to me! And Yahweh has cursed her too. Now pick it up and let me sign it."

"But how can you possibly sign?"

"I'll find a way. Take these miserable bandages off me."

"I am not a physician—"

"Take them off!"

Shebna opened his mouth to speak, then closed it again and carefully lifted Hezekiah's right hand. He found the end of the bandage, untied it, then gently unwound the dressing. Hezekiah tried to hold his hand steady as Shebna worked, but it shook with his rage and his pain. Beneath the gauze, huge pulpy blisters covered his swollen palms.

"Good heavens!"

"It looks worse than it is," he said, lying. But Hezekiah realized that he would never be able to grip a writing instrument or sign his name. He held out his left hand. "Take the other one off too." When Shebna finished, his dark face looked pale. "Now slide my signet ring off."

"But it will never come off. Your finger is too badly swollen."

"Coat it with oil first. There's some over there, in the lamp."

While Shebna obeyed, Hezekiah silently wondered how long it would take him to grow accustomed to the constant, relentless pain.

Would there ever come a time when he would be free from it? He vowed to pretend that he was fine, but when Shebna rubbed the oil on his finger and tried to pull the ring off, Hezekiah cried out, unable to stop himself.

Shebna shrank back. "I am sorry, my lord!"

"I'm all right. Try it again."

"No. I will not do this."

"Shebna, I'm ordering you to slide this ring off my finger!"

"I would sooner resign than inflict any more pain on you."

His eyes met Hezekiah's and held them defiantly. In a battle of wills, Hezekiah knew Shebna's stubbornness matched his own.

"I've brought your breakfast, Your Majesty." The valet broke the tension as he entered with a tray.

"You're excused, Shebna," Hezekiah said. He refused to allow Shebna to watch as the valet fed him as he would a child.

When they were alone, the valet picked up a spoon, fingering it hesitantly.

"You will tell no one that I had to be fed, do you hear me? Or you will pay for it with your life."

"Yes, Your Majesty."

Hezekiah had only managed to choke down a few humiliating bites when the shofar sounded from the Temple.

"Fetch my prayer shawl," he said. "It's time to go."

The Temple seemed a hundred miles away, but he would make it somehow. He would offer his sacrifice. He would confess the sin of allowing an idol into his palace, the sin of loving an idol worshiper. He would ask God for forgiveness.

Hezekiah stood, but he took only a few steps toward the door. The valet couldn't catch him in time, and the king collapsed to the floor, unconscious.

❖

Eliakim walked up the hill to the Temple with his father, worrying about King Hezekiah, remembering the nauseating sight of his burned flesh.

"You got in awfully late last night, Son," Hilkiah said. "And you've been unusually quiet this morning too."

"I know. I wanted to talk to you about it, but not in front of the servants."

Hilkiah stopped walking. "Something happened, then? Something terrible?"

"I'm afraid so."

Crowds of worshipers streamed past them, buffeting them where they stood in the middle of the walkway. Eliakim drew his father aside.

He wondered if he should tell him about Hephzibah's idolatry. He could trust Hilkiah with any secret, but Eliakim ached inside from carrying the terrible knowledge of what she had done, and he hesitated to unload such a burden on anyone else. Hephzibah's actions were unforgivable, an outrage that mocked everything King Hezekiah believed in and worked for. The fact that he loved her so deeply made her deception unspeakable.

"Abba, there was a fire in the harem last night."

"Was anyone hurt?"

"The king's wife inhaled a lot of smoke, and she was badly shaken, but she's all right."

"Thank God!"

"But King Hezekiah fought the fire himself, and his clothes caught on fire—"

"Dear God—"

"I was the first one to help him afterward, and I could tell he was in a lot of pain. The physicians said his burns are very serious."

"We need to pray for him, then."

"Yes, Abba. We need to pray."

They rejoined the crowd of worshipers hurrying up the hill, but neither of them spoke again. When they reached the inner courtyard, Hilkiah tugged on Eliakim's arm and motioned toward the royal dais with a tilt of his head. King Hezekiah wasn't standing in his usual place.

"He never misses a morning sacrifice," Hilkiah whispered.

Eliakim winced. "I know. He must be in bad shape. Pray for him, Abba." He hurried to take his place on the dais, alone.

When the service ended, Eliakim quickly walked down to the palace, dreading what he would find. As he had expected, the corridors bustled with confusion and whispered rumors. Hezekiah was not on his throne. When the courtiers spotted Eliakim, they crowded around him.

"What's going on, Lord Secretary?"

"Where's King Hezekiah?"

"Is something wrong with the king?"

"King Hezekiah won't be holding court today," Eliakim said. "Come back tomorrow."

Eliakim ignored their frantic questions and elbowed his way past them. When he reached the king's private chambers, Shebna answered the door. For a moment the two men stared uncomfortably at each other; then Shebna motioned him inside.

"I just came from the morning sacrifice," Eliakim said, running his fingers through his hair. "Everyone's wondering why King Hezekiah wasn't there. How is he?"

"Not good."

"Worse than last night?"

"Yes."

"Can I talk to him?"

"No."

"Is he awake?"

"He was."

Getting information out of Shebna was going to be like lowering a bucket into a deep well and raising one drop at a time. His eyes glittered with anger, and Eliakim knew that he would probably bear the brunt of Shebna's worry and frustration. Eliakim wasn't looking for a fight, but he wouldn't run from one either. He took another step closer and faced Shebna squarely.

"Tell me what's going on."

Shebna paused a long time before answering. "The king woke up shouting orders. He insisted that he would walk up to the Temple, but—"

"Walk! Didn't someone order a sedan chair?"

"He refused it. When he tried to walk, he collapsed. The physicians are in with him now."

"Have they given you a report?"

"They say he must rest. He cannot get out of bed again."

"Then let's make sure he doesn't."

"How? You have not witnessed his stubbornness! Or his rage!"

"No, but I'm witnessing *yours*. Stop your shouting—I didn't come here to argue with you."

Shebna didn't respond. He turned to stare out the window, his jaw thrust forward defiantly. It wouldn't be easy to deal with him in the king's absence, but Eliakim determined to try.

"Let's get to work," Eliakim said after a moment. "Everything is in a state of confusion downstairs. What needs to be done?"

"I have prepared the divorce papers the king requested. He has not signed them yet. He is not able."

"His hands?" Eliakim remembered Hezekiah's swollen, blistered palms and shuddered.

"Yes. But I do not understand why he is divorcing her. She should be stoned to death."

"I asked the king what he wanted to do last night. And as angry as he was, he said he didn't want Hephzibah executed."

"That makes no sense. It is what your Law demands."

"I know. But he loves her."

"Love does not matter! We must convince him to put her to death. You know the Law. You will help me convince him."

"I can't do that."

"She deserves to die."

"Yes—according to the Law, that's true. But love allows room for mercy." He could see by Shebna's scornful expression that he hadn't convinced him. Shebna didn't believe in a loving God. How could he grasp the concept of mercy?

"She must be executed. The king must set an example of what will happen to people who practice idolatry."

"The king doesn't want people to worship God because they fear the death penalty. And God certainly doesn't want that kind of worship either. Faith in God involves more than outward ceremony. It's a heartfelt belief." *And that's why I never liked you*, he wanted to say. *You're a hypocrite and as much of an idolater as Hephzibah.*

"Since King Hezekiah will obviously not be holding court today, you may as well return home," Shebna said suddenly. "I will remain here with the king."

Eliakim knew Shebna would take advantage of Hezekiah's illness to do whatever he wanted. Eliakim couldn't allow that to happen. Their eyes locked, and Eliakim saw that Shebna hated him as much as he hated Shebna. Perhaps more.

"No, Shebna. I'm staying too."

<hr />

When Hezekiah awoke, a dark figure hovered over his bed. He focused his eyes and recognized Shebna, staring down at him with a worried frown.

"All right, Shebna—you win. I'll take the sedan chair." He smiled weakly, but Shebna's dark face remained somber.

"Where do you want to go, Your Majesty?"

"To the Temple. For the morning sacrifice."

"The sacrifice is over."

"It is? How long have I been out?"

"Several hours, Your Majesty," Eliakim said from the other side of the bed. "It's past midday."

"That late?"

Hezekiah felt much weaker than before. His anger had drained away while he was unconscious, and now he feared the pain would consume him. For the first time he understood the seriousness of his injuries and realized he had to fight to live.

"Help me sit up."

"Please," Shebna begged. "No more heroics. You need to rest. You are only making matters worse for yourself."

"What are you talking about?"

"Even your valiant ancestors were not afraid to admit their weaknesses." Shebna's somber expression frightened Hezekiah, and he knew it could prove fatal to give in to fear.

"Since when are you an expert on my ancestors?"

"Help me convince him," Shebna said to Eliakim.

"'Be merciful to me, O LORD, for I am in distress,'" Eliakim quoted. "'My strength fails because of my affliction, and my bones grow weak.'"

"That was written by your ancestor King David, I believe."

"Very good, Shebna. You're becoming quite a Torah scholar. Now help me sit up. I'd do it myself, but 'my strength fails.'"

Eliakim suppressed a smile.

The two men gently lifted him to a sitting position, propping cushions behind his back. Hezekiah gritted his teeth and blinked back the sweat that poured down his brow, careful to conceal any suffering that the movement caused him.

"Now then, don't we have work to do? Is the kingdom running on its own? Or have I been dethroned while I was unconscious?"

"Do you want to work?" Shebna asked in alarm. "Now? Here?"

"Well, since I can't seem to walk more than two steps without falling on my face, I have no other choice, do I?"

"Wouldn't you rather rest?" Eliakim said. "Shebna and I can—"

"I know you can, but that's not the point. I'm in too much pain to rest."

"I will call the physicians."

"No, Shebna. I don't want their drugs. At least not until I can't stand it any longer. What I need is a distraction."

"I understand. I will bring your work here." Shebna headed for the door.

"Shebna," Hezekiah called after him.

"Yes, Your Majesty?"

"I will sign those divorce papers now."

"Do you want me to read them aloud, Your Majesty?" Shebna asked when he returned a short while later. He had brought the certificate of divorce along with an armful of work.

"No. I don't even want to hear her name. Just give me the papers. I think I can seal them without taking my ring off."

"You are going to make your wounds worse."

"They can't get any worse! Now, put something under the scroll to support it, like that tray over there. Then put the clay in place and bring it here." He would sign the papers if it killed him.

He positioned his hand, palm up, above the scroll, centering his signet ring over the lump of clay. "Now, push down on the back of my ring."

"No. I refuse."

"Eliakim! Do as I say! Push it hard so it seals."

Eliakim obeyed, and in a moment it was over, his official seal firmly imbedded in the soft clay. His marriage was over as well. Hezekiah no longer had a wife.

Memories of Hephzibah washed over him suddenly, surprising him, and he lost his footing, nearly drowning in their vividness and strength. He remembered the night, shortly after his coronation, when he first went to Hephzibah's chambers. Her beauty took his breath away, bewitching him, and he had fallen under her spell. Even after she had admitted worshiping idols, he had abandoned all his concubines for her alone. He remembered her soft scent, the way her voice entranced him when she sang, the sweet taste of her kisses, and a cry of despair swelled inside him like a tidal wave.

"Are you all right, Your Majesty?" Eliakim asked. "Did I hurt you?"

"No. What else do I need to take care of?"

Running his kingdom distracted Hezekiah for the remainder of the afternoon. But that night his sleep was shallow and fitful as the pain pushed into his dreams. He awoke weak and unrested.

For the next few days Shebna and Eliakim brought his work to him, diverting him for most of the day, seldom leaving his bedside. Hezekiah no longer tried to get up or to argue about going to the Temple, but he had little appetite for the food his valet tried to feed him, and he grew weaker and weaker each day.

By the end of the week, Hezekiah's work could no longer distract him from his agony. The torment in his leg had spread like a raging fire throughout his body until every joint and muscle ached and throbbed with it.

For a moment or two someone or something might divert his attention, but the pain always returned to its place of prominence in his every waking thought. Sometimes it seemed to lessen slightly, but it was always there. Sometimes it would build and strengthen until it became excruciating and he couldn't stifle his moans.

Hezekiah could no longer hope that it would ever stop. He thought of nothing else, for the pain became his tyrant, more terrifying than any Assyrian overlord. It pushed everything else from his consciousness and took control. It held his will and his body captive. He couldn't break free.

Lying in the same position grew intolerable, but changing positions brought agony. The servants left the oil lamps burning all night, for he could sleep only a short time before the torment roused him once again. Strong wine made him nauseous but did little else. He begged for distractions until Shebna and Eliakim were exhausted from their efforts, but the diversions worked for only a brief moment.

Hezekiah wondered how much longer it would be until he went mad.

Late in the afternoon of the sixth day as Shebna read to him, Hezekiah's mind began to wander into delirium. He struggled to concentrate as if Shebna read in a foreign language, forcing him to translate. Before long, Hezekiah could no longer keep up. He began to slide down a long, steep slope, away from Shebna and Eliakim, away from his agony and confusion.

"Shebna . . . please . . ." His temples throbbed. He turned his head on the pillow, and the room swirled as if the hand of God had shaken the entire palace. He closed his eyes to make the dizziness stop.

"Yes, Your Majesty? What is it?"

"Did you feel that? It's moving . . ." The two men sprang to their feet, but their abrupt movements triggered another wave of dizziness. "Don't! Don't move—you'll make it fall."

"What's wrong, Your Majesty?" Eliakim said. "What's falling?"

Hezekiah tried to focus on him but couldn't. "Can't you feel it, Eliakim? Why is everything moving?"

Eliakim rested his hand on Hezekiah's brow, and his fingers felt wonderfully cool, like stones from a mountain stream.

"Ah—leave your hand there."

"God of Abraham—he's burning up!"

"No . . . ," Hezekiah said, ". . . there was a fire but it's out, now . . . I put it out."

"He's delirious. Call the physicians."

"I'm thirsty; that's all . . . water . . ."

41

Eliakim held a cup to his lips, and he drank greedily. But why had they given him salt water? It only increased his thirst.

Movement and activity suddenly swirled around his bed. So many people. They made the room tilt again.

"Stop . . . ," he moaned. "You'll make everything fall."

"What are those for?" he heard Shebna asking. "What are you going to do to him?"

"Cold compresses will bring his fever down." Hezekiah didn't recognize the voice.

Now Hezekiah felt a cooling sensation all around him. It felt so good, so cold. But, no—he was too cold. He couldn't get warm. He began to shiver, trembling all over. He couldn't stop. And the pain, the pain—whenever he moved!

"Take them off! You are killing him!" Shebna shouted.

"We have to bring his fever down, my lord, or he will die of the convulsions."

Was he going to die? Hezekiah didn't want to die. Once again Uriah held him in a death grip. The high priest choked off his life. In another moment he would die. He had to fight!

"What is happening to him?" Shebna cried.

"The poison from his leg is spreading through his body." Hezekiah heard the unfamiliar voice again.

He was so thirsty. Water. Why didn't they give him a drink? Then he remembered. He had hidden the spring underground. Eliakim knew where to find it.

"Eliakim . . . listen . . ."

"Yes, Your Majesty?" He heard Eliakim's frightened voice, but he couldn't see him.

"The spring . . . inside the tunnel . . ." How could he make him understand?

"We have to change the dressing on his leg. We must cleanse it again."

Someone touched his leg, and Hezekiah cried out. They were taking the bandage off. No, they were taking his *leg* off.

"Stop . . . stop!" Somebody make them stop!

"Get away! You are going to kill him!" Shebna cried.

"We must cleanse the wound, my lord. The poison will kill him if we don't."

Shebna, help me! I don't want to die!

"Lord Shebna, you'd better wait in the other room until we're finished."

"No, I must stay with the king."

"Lord Eliakim, please take him out of here."

"Come on, Shebna. There's nothing more we can do."

Hezekiah saw a hand in the darkness, slender and cool and white. It beckoned to him to come away into the darkness, away from the pain. The terrible pain.

Yahweh . . . help me . . .

He heard someone screaming. He couldn't fight anymore. He was too tired. Too weak. He wanted to stop fighting, to give in and float away from the agony—into nothingness.

Hezekiah reached out for the ivory hand and clasped it in his own.

"Merab, why is everything so quiet?" Hephzibah asked. "The court-yard, the hallways—the entire palace is like a tomb." She sat before the open window in her new quarters, a musty, cramped room that had once belonged to one of Hezekiah's concubines.

"You're shivering, my lady. Come sit by the fire."

"No—listen a moment." Hephzibah paused, listening. "It's too quiet; don't you see? The silence scares me."

"Let me close those shutters. You'll catch a chill sitting by the win-dow." The handmaiden started to swing the wooden shutters closed, but Hephzibah stopped her.

"Wait. Look down there, Merab. That courtyard usually crawls with activity this time of day. But what do you see?"

"I see that it's empty, my lady. Now come. The fire is nice and warm." Merab closed the shutters firmly and latched them. She nudged Hephzibah closer to the charcoal brazier, sensing her fear.

"But where are all the noblemen and petitioners? They usually come and go all day long. Something's wrong."

"Nonsense."

"Then why hasn't the king gone up to the Temple? It's been more than a week. I've watched for him every day. He has to pass this way, but he hasn't left the palace."

"Don't be silly. The palace has more than one door. He's probably using another one."

"No, he wouldn't do that. I know he wouldn't."

Hephzibah edged closer to the brazier. The coals glowed crimson beneath the grate. She remembered what she had pledged to do, re-membered vowing to throw Hezekiah's child into the flames, and she began to tremble.

Merab wrapped a woolen shawl around her shoulders and rubbed her arms. "You should crawl into bed, my lady. This room must be colder than your old one. You're always shivering."

"I'm scared, Merab. I'm so scared—"

"Hush, now, Baby. You don't need to be afraid."

"But I've lived in this palace for 10 years, and I know something is wrong!"

Merab wouldn't meet her gaze. She plucked lint off Hephzibah's shawl and muttered to herself. "Just look at this thing—how did it get to be such a mess?"

"Merab, if you know what's going on, you've got to tell me."

"Let me find you another shawl. This one—"

"Tell me!"

Merab clutched Hephzibah to her bosom and held her tightly.

"All right, Baby. Shh . . . calm down. King Hezekiah isn't holding court, because he's sick."

"What's wrong with him?"

"I don't know. No one will tell me. When I asked—one of the servants spit on me."

"I have to see him. I have to help him."

"They'll never let you near the king, my lady. They'll spit on you too—everyone blames you for what happened to him."

For days Hephzibah had relived the terrible moments just before the fire, remembering the anger and pain in Hezekiah's eyes when he discovered her betrayal. Now, prodded by Merab's words, the picture lurched forward, and she recalled the next scene. Hezekiah had stood in the middle of the flames, battling to save her life. His clothes had caught fire. She'd heard him cry out in pain. He had been burned! And the fire in the harem had been her fault.

"Merab, you've got to distract the chamberlain long enough for me to slip out."

"My lady, you know you can't leave the harem."

"I have to see my husband. I don't care what they do to me."

"Come. Lie down for a while. You'll feel better—"

"No! You have to help me! I'm *ordering* you to help me!"

She had never shouted at Merab before, and the little servant's eyes filled with tears.

"Yes, my lady."

Hephzibah waited until Merab drew the chamberlain away, then crept out of her room and through the palace hallways to Hezekiah's chambers. But when she reached his door, it opened suddenly, and she faced Shebna.

"What are you doing here?" he cried.

"I—I came to see my husband."

"King Hezekiah no longer has a wife!"

"But I'm—"

"The king has divorced you. I drew up the certificate, and he sealed it the day after the fire."

"You're lying. I never received any divorce papers." But she remembered the revulsion and anger on Hezekiah's face and feared it was true.

Shebna took a step closer to her. Hatred filled his voice. "That is because I did not have the divorce recorded yet. If King Hezekiah dies, you will become the property of the next king. I cannot think of a more suitable punishment for you than to see you claimed by Prince Gedaliah on the palace rooftop in front of the entire city."

"He's not going to die!"

Shebna grabbed her shoulders, and his fingers dug into her. "You should have been stoned to death for what you have done. But that would have been too merciful. Now get out of here!"

He shoved her roughly down the hallway toward the harem, then strode off in the opposite direction. Shebna's horrible words stunned Hephzibah. She turned and ran down the hallway, stopping the first servant she met. "Please help me! Where can I find Lord Eliakim?"

She knew he was kinder and more compassionate than Shebna. He would help her. He would tell her the truth. As the servant led her to Eliakim's office, Hephzibah struggled to calm down, to put her thoughts into focus. She had to plan what she would say to him. But she couldn't think past her fear.

Eliakim sat behind a huge table, sifting through piles of correspondence and official records. He looked up as Hephzibah entered; then his mouth froze in a hard line. The unfamiliar chill in his dark eyes frightened her more than Shebna's hatred.

"What do you want, Hephzibah?"

"Please, my lord—I need to see my husband."

"That's impossible. He's not your husband anymore."

Shebna had told the truth. She stared at Eliakim, horrified.

"According to the Law, the king has the right to divorce you because of your idolatry."

"Listen, please—I know Hezekiah hates me, but you have to believe me! When that statue broke open . . . and all the sand poured out of it . . . I knew that it wasn't really a god. I knew . . ." But Hephzibah couldn't finish. She covered her face and wept. "I'm sorry . . . so sorry."

"Look—you're not supposed to be here. I'll call a servant to take you back to the harem." Eliakim walked around the wide table toward the door, but she blocked his path.

"Please tell me—is Hezekiah going to die?"

Eliakim stared past her without answering, as if she had no right to know. She fell to her knees in front of him.

"I have to know—please!"

At last he answered, but his words filled her with dread. "King Hezekiah is gravely ill."

"From the fire?"

"Yes."

"Please let me see him . . . I just want to see his face again . . . I just want to explain . . ."

"Hephzibah, don't beg. Stand up."

"No. Not until you answer me, my lord. Please!"

At last Eliakim looked down at her. The anger in his eyes had softened. "I wish before God that none of this had happened, Hephzibah. But the truth is, you sealed your own divorce papers the day you chose to worship an idol. There's nothing I can do to help you. I'm sorry."

He rang for his servant, then pulled Hephzibah to her feet. "Take her back to the harem." He closed the door in her face, and the servant led her away like a prisoner.

Before they reached the harem, Hephzibah stopped. "Wait. Don't take me back."

"I have orders, my lady. Come on."

"Listen—I will give you a fistful of gold if you help me."

"Sure you will."

"I mean it! A full shekel of gold. I'll swear it!"

He eyed her with suspicion. "Show me this gold."

"I can't. It's in my room, and if I go back to the harem, they won't let me leave again. But I swear I'll give you as much gold as you want if you'll take me into my husband's room."

Hephzibah saw the greed in his eyes. "What happens once you're inside? What do you want to do?"

"Nothing. I just want to see him—that's all."

"And for that you'll give me a shekel of gold?"

"Yes. I swear by my life." Hephzibah's heart pounded wildly as she watched him consider the idea.

"I'll see what I can do," he said.

Hephzibah followed behind him, hurrying to keep up with his long strides. When they got to the king's chambers, he stopped.

"Wait here," he commanded; then he disappeared inside.

Hephzibah tried to stay calm as she waited for the servant to return, but she couldn't stop thinking of Eliakim's words. At last the door opened, and the servant came out.

"The king is asleep."

Hephzibah went limp. Hezekiah never slept in the middle of the day.

"Swear to me you won't wake him," the servant demanded. "You have to stay hidden behind me. You can't make a sound."

"I swear."

"I must be crazy for doing this," he told her, but he led the way inside. "And you'd better not get me into trouble, or you'll owe me a lot more than a shekel."

Hephzibah recognized the three men huddled in the sitting room. They were the royal physicians who had attended her the night her baby died. She kept her head down and followed the servant into the next room.

The stench in the darkened bedchamber halted her. The rotting smell of sickness filled the stale air, and she couldn't breathe in the oppressive heat. Hephzibah wanted to throw open the heavy curtains and shutters and let light and air into the room, but she cowered behind the servant and waited for her eyes to grow accustomed to the dark.

When she could finally see the shrunken figure in the bed, Hephzibah backed away. This wasn't her husband. This was someone else. But then the stranger moaned and turned his face toward her. It was Hezekiah.

He was impossibly thin, as if all his flesh had melted away, and his face looked gray beneath his dark beard. As he tossed in a delirium of fever, his random thrashing caused him great pain, and he moaned in agony. The burn on his leg was the source of the stench, a blackened, oozing sore that turned Hephzibah's stomach.

He was dying. There could be no doubt.

"Hezekiah! *No!*"

She pushed the servant aside and sank to her knees beside the bed, seizing Hezekiah's hand in both of hers.

"Please don't die hating me. Please let me explain . . ."

His hand felt hot with fever. His waxy blue nails and fingertips looked like a dead man's. The servant clutched her around her waist, trying to pry her away from him.

"Please, my love—please! You can't die. You can't!"

Hezekiah's eyelids slowly opened, and a dazed look of pain filled his unseeing eyes.

"So . . . thirsty . . . ," he mumbled.

With a surge of desperate strength, Hephzibah freed herself from the servant and grabbed a cup of water from the table beside the bed. She held it to Hezekiah's lips. They were tinged with blue around the edges like his lifeless fingers.

"Hephzibah . . . ?" he whispered.

"Yes, my love. It's me."

"Hephzibah . . . I . . ." Then Hezekiah's face twisted in pain, and he let out a terrible moan. "O God . . . help me . . ."

He began to shiver, the spasms shaking his body convulsively, and Hephzibah never felt so terrified or so helpless in her life. If she could have seized the life in her own body and forced it into his, she would have done so.

Someone grabbed her and hurried her out of the room. The terrible sound of Hezekiah's moans followed her into the hallway. Eliakim stood outside the door.

"What have I done? What have I done?" she sobbed. "He's dying—dear God, he's dying!"

"Hephzibah, stop it," Eliakim said.

"Is he going to die? Please don't let him die!"

"The physicians will do everything they can to save him."

"Let me help . . . let me do something . . ." The servant had to support her, or she would have collapsed to the floor.

"Take her back to the harem," Eliakim told him. "This time make sure she stays there."

"I want to take care of him—he's my husband."

"No. He isn't your husband. Not anymore. And don't try to come here again. There's nothing more you can do for him."

Nothing more she could do. She would never see Hezekiah again.

Hezekiah drifted into consciousness, slowly becoming aware of his surroundings. Instantly the relentless pain overwhelmed him, and he wanted to slip away again, but if he did, he might never wake up. Was he dying? Was this what dying felt like, growing weaker and weaker each day while the pain grew stronger and stronger? The sickness that had spread through his body consumed his life like fire licking up straw.

In spite of his agony, Hezekiah fought to stay conscious. He turned his head and saw Eliakim sitting beside the bed with his elbows on his knees, his face buried in his hands. Hezekiah licked his dry lips and tried to speak.

"Eliakim . . ."

Eliakim bolted to his feet. "You're awake?"

"I'm so thirsty."

Eliakim put his hand behind Hezekiah's neck and raised his head to help him drink. The water tasted good and surprisingly cold. How did they keep it so cold when the room felt so hot? He drank all that he could, even though most of it ran down his beard and soaked the bandages on his chest.

"I dreamed that Hephzibah came," he murmured when he finished. "I dreamed she gave me a drink." How long would it take until he could forget Hephzibah completely and erase from his mind the memory of what she had done?

"Can I get you anything else?" Eliakim asked.

"No—sit down. Talk to me."

"All right." He sat down hesitantly, as if poised to run for help. He looked distraught.

"Where's Shebna?"

"He left to eat dinner. Would you like something to eat, Your Majesty?"

Hezekiah couldn't remember when he had eaten last, but he wasn't hungry.

"Just more water." Eliakim gave him more.

"We've been so worried, Your Majesty. I'm glad you're awake. You seem a little better."

No, Hezekiah knew how weak he felt, how hard he struggled to hang on to consciousness. He had lost all track of time as day and night ran together in a haze of pain. Was it just a moment ago that Shebna had read to him?

"How long have I been sick?"

"Your fever started two days ago."

Two days had passed without his awareness. The thought terrified Hezekiah. This was a rehearsal for death, the end of conscious thought. He licked his lips again and tried to talk.

"Once . . . when I was traveling through the Negev I spent the night in a shepherd's tent . . . a sturdy little thing . . . protecting me from rain and sun. But in the morning the shepherd yanked out all the stakes . . . one after the other . . . and just like that, all the life went out of it, and it collapsed in a heap. It wasn't a tent anymore . . . only a pile of lifeless cloth. Then he folded it up and packed it away . . . and only a square of flattened grass could prove it had ever existed." He tried to swallow, but his mouth was too dry. "Is that all there is to life, Eliakim? When our lives suddenly end and we're gone . . . is there nothing left to show that we ever lived?"

"You've accomplished a great deal, Your Majesty. You've restored Judah's covenant with Yahweh and brought great prosperity to our nation and—"

"But what happens when we die?"

"The Torah says we are gathered to be with our fathers and—"

"No! Not with my father."

"I'm sorry, Your Majesty. I . . . I meant father Abraham and Isaac and . . ." Eliakim fell silent.

"Do you want to know what it feels like to die, Eliakim? Like a lion has me in her jaws. She's broken all my bones, and now she's toying with me. I'm waiting for her to finish me off. But I don't want to die. Not now. I'm in the prime of my life . . . and I don't have a son to take my place . . . to finish all that I've started."

Hezekiah burned with fever. Sweat poured off his body and made the bedcovers stick to his skin, but he was too weak to lift his hand to wipe the sweat out of his eyes, too weak to kick the stifling covers aside.

"You aren't going to die, Your Majesty."

"I wish I could believe that. But every hour it feels as if I'm slipping closer and closer to Sheol's gates and there's nothing to grab onto to stop my fall."

He remembered his brother falling into the flames. Eliab had tried to grab Molech's shining arms to stop himself, but the metal had been too hot, too slippery, and he had fallen to his death.

"You will fight this sickness, Your Majesty. Yahweh won't let you die."

"Yahweh seems very far away, Eliakim. I'm watching the horizon, waiting for Him to come, longing to see Him, but my eyes are tired of looking for Him . . . and still He doesn't come . . . doesn't help me . . ."

"God has never left your side, Your Majesty. He's always been right here with you. Sometimes when He seems the farthest away from us, He's really the closest. He uses these breaking experiences to strengthen our faith, and the difficult times to draw us nearer to His side."

"'. . . I will never leave you nor forsake you . . .'"

"Yes—that's right, Your Majesty."

"My grandfather showed me that verse the day he died," Hezekiah mumbled. "But I don't want to die."

Suddenly he went cold, as if someone had opened a window, bringing in a blast of wintry air. He began to shiver.

". . . for you, Your Majesty?"

He realized that Eliakim had asked him a question, but he didn't know what it was. The delirium tried to take control again, leaving him confused and disoriented.

"What's happening to my kingdom? Don't I have work to do?"

Eliakim's answer was a jumble of random words, disconnected from each other.

"Nation . . . officials . . . daily . . ."

Hezekiah closed his eyes, feeling weary and cold. Eliakim piled more blankets on him, but they didn't help. He needed to rest, to sleep, to escape from the pain, but he was afraid.

He opened his eyes again, and a dark stranger stood over his bed. His beardless face was shiny, and he wore an unusual robe that wasn't Judean.

The angel of death.

"Who are you?" he shivered.

"This is your new physician," Eliakim said. "He's trained in the Egyptian healing arts. Shebna sent for him when the boil appeared."

The Egyptian lifted Hezekiah's arm and pinned it tightly between his own arm and body. "I must drain some of your blood now, my lord. It is filled with poison."

The stranger's mouth moved, but Shebna's voice came out. Something sharp stabbed Hezekiah. The physician had slit his arm open, and blood pumped out of the wound. Hezekiah thought of the sacrifice at the Temple as he watched his own blood pouring into a basin. Would they sprinkle it around the altar? Would Yahweh accept this offering and heal him?

"Don't . . . ," he moaned.

Pagans performed these rituals. They shouldn't do this to him. Blood was sacred. *"Whoever sheds the blood of man . . ."* *"I will demand an accounting . . ."* Life was in the blood. They were draining his life away.

"Stop . . ."

No one listened to him.

When he had filled the bowl, the Egyptian tied a tight bandage around Hezekiah's arm. "Now I must drain the poison from the boil and change the dressing on your leg," he said.

"No! Don't touch my leg!"

Whenever they touched his leg it brought agony, then nothingness. He didn't want to return to the darkness. He didn't want to die. Hezekiah tried to move away from him.

"Hold him still," the Egyptian said.

"No! I order you to keep him away from me!" He was the king. They had to obey him. But a moment later he felt strong hands gripping his shoulders and ankles. He struggled to break free, just as he had struggled as a child to break free from the soldier's grip. But he was helpless, just as he had been helpless back then.

Hezekiah felt a stab of pain in his leg, the worst pain he had ever known. It shuddered through his entire body, and he cried out. Then darkness fell once again.

Shebna sat alone in his room, his supper untouched in front of him, when Prince Gedaliah arrived. He hadn't seen the prince in several years—since the night Gedaliah had planned to assassinate his brother—and he wished he didn't have to see him now.

"I received your urgent summons, Shebna. What's so important that I had to drop everything and run up here to Jerusalem?" The prince looked gritty and ill-tempered after his long journey from

Lachish. He stood in the doorway with his hands on his hips, glaring angrily.

"Close the door, Gedaliah, and sit down."

"It must be awfully serious if I have to sit down."

Shebna watched him sink onto the pile of cushions and wished, as he had wished for days, that Hezekiah had an heir. Any son, no matter how young, would be preferable to this arrogant prince. Why had the king been so stubborn about taking another wife? It was obvious to everyone that Hephzibah was barren. Shebna cursed Yahweh's laws for leading to this impossible situation.

"Where are all your servants?" Gedaliah asked, looking around. "I could use a drink."

"I sent them away. I did not want anyone to hear our conversation." Shebna got up and poured Gedaliah a drink, then set the flask of wine on the table beside him. "Here. Drink all you want."

"Aren't you having any?"

"No." He wanted to get this meeting over with. He had already delayed it as long as he dared. "I summoned you because your brother is gravely ill."

Gedaliah swirled the wine around in the goblet, studying it. "Oh? What's the matter with him?"

"I will be blunt. The king is dying."

Gedaliah sat up, suddenly showing interest. "Dying? Really?"

Shebna watched several emotions play across Gedaliah's face, but as they transformed from surprise to slow comprehension to delight, he had to look away.

"Well!" Gedaliah said after a long pause. "Well! I don't know what to say. This is quite a surprise. My brother's dying, is he? Why didn't you send for me sooner? I could have used more time to—"

"We did not believe he might die until a few days ago when the boil appeared. His condition has deteriorated very rapidly since then."

"I'm sorry to hear that." But Gedaliah's face betrayed him. He was overjoyed. Shebna lost control.

"Curse you, Gedaliah! How dare you sit there and pretend you are sorry. You have waited all your life for this opportunity!"

"All right, Shebna. You don't have to shout at me. I'll admit it. I'm delighted." Gedaliah smiled, and Shebna fought the urge to slap his face. "But wouldn't any man be pleased to hear that he's about to become king?"

"Perhaps some of your joy will be tempered when you see what an agonizing death your brother is suffering."

Gedaliah poured himself another drink. "Mind if I help myself?"

"No. But try to refrain from celebrating for another day or two."

"Only a day? Is it that close?"

Shebna's fists tightened. "Yes."

"You still haven't told me what's wrong with him."

Shebna took a deep breath and let it out slowly. "There was a fire in the harem. The king was badly burned trying to put it out."

"Was anyone else hurt?"

Shebna read Gedaliah's thoughts. "No. Hephzibah was unharmed. You will be able to inherit your brother's wife along with his throne."

Gedaliah broke into a broad grin, which he tried to disguise by lifting his glass and draining the remainder of his wine.

"This is good stuff, Shebna. Are you sure you won't have some?"

"I must also tell you that King Hezekiah has not named a successor."

"Which means . . . ?"

"It means that any of Ahaz's sons has a right to claim the throne."

Gedaliah sat up straight, his brow creased in a frown.

"Have you notified my brothers that Hezekiah's dying?"

"Not yet."

"Well done, Shebna, my faithful steward!" Gedaliah relaxed against the cushions again. "Does this mean you're supporting my claim to the throne?"

"For the good of the nation, I want to make sure there is a smooth transition of power."

Gedaliah laughed out loud. "What a cunning mongrel you are, Shebna. You want to make sure you hang on to your precious job—am I right?"

Shebna didn't answer. He didn't dare open his mouth for fear of what he might say.

"All right, all right—we can work something out," Gedaliah said, laughing. "I suppose I owe you that much for not gathering all the grieving heirs to the dying king's bedside. Let's talk about what else needs to be done, to ensure a smooth transition of power, as you put it."

Shebna sighed deeply. "What do you want to know?"

"To begin with, who are my enemies? And sit down—will you? You get on my nerves pacing back and forth like a caged lion."

It was exactly how Shebna felt. Trapped. "No thank you. I prefer to stand."

"Start with the Royal Council. Do I have any enemies there?"

"The only enemy you need to worry about on the council is Eliakim ben Hilkiah. He is intelligent, resourceful—"

"And as cunning as you are?"

"Perhaps. If anyone could successfully rally support behind another heir, it would be Eliakim." It galled Shebna to admit the truth.

"He's a threat to me, then?"

"Yes. He has very close ties to the priests and prophets."

"What do you suggest I do about him?"

"Nothing, for the moment. I have buried him under a mountain of worthless paperwork. He believes he is faithfully running the nation during the king's illness, and I have given him little time to think of starting a rebellion. I assigned someone to watch him in case he tries to contact one of your brothers, but so far he has not even accepted the fact that the king is dying. With luck, he will not realize what is happening until it is too late."

"Clever, Shebna. Very clever."

"Your other major concern is the military."

"General Jonadab?"

"Yes. He is fiercely loyal to King Hezekiah. I also believe he would take orders from Eliakim sooner than from you or me."

"Do you think Jonadab will cause trouble?"

"Possibly. That is why I sent him to Beersheba this morning, along with a large contingent of the king's army. For the sake of security, I chose a few ambitious young army officers to remain behind, men who are looking to advance themselves."

"You sly fox," Gedaliah laughed. "You realize, of course, that I am deeply in your debt. You've handed me the crown on a silver platter! Come on, Shebna. This calls for a toast."

Gedaliah poured himself another drink and raised his glass. Shebna didn't move. "You will have to excuse me, but I am in mourning. My king—my friend—is about to die."

"Have it your way, then." Gedaliah raised the glass to his lips and sipped noisily. "Naturally, you'll want to plan a lavish and fitting funeral for my dear brother. He was a pretty good king, all things considered, and very popular with the people. I think he should be buried in the tombs of David's descendants. Let's lay him to rest with great honor, Shebna. Too bad he never had a son." He drained his glass. "We should also begin preparations for my coronation, don't you think?"

"You would be wise to stay out of the public eye until after the funeral."

"Is there a sympathetic priest we could persuade to perform my coronation at the Temple, or do they all hate me?"

"I will have to give it some thought."

"Let's see—what else do I need to worry about? City elders? Court judges? Any troublemakers among the nobility?"

"None of them know how seriously ill the king is. He was running the kingdom from his bed until a few days ago."

"Good, good. I'm glad you kept things quiet. By the time everyone recovers from this shock, I'll be king."

"Yes. You will be king. It is what you have always wanted."

Gedaliah refilled his glass and raised it high, once again. "Long live King Gedaliah!" He laughed before draining it.

Shebna turned away, his eyes burning. Finally Gedaliah hauled himself to his feet. He was in high spirits from the news of his good fortune and from the wine. He was beginning to slur his words. "Well, if that's everything, why don't we go pay our last respects to my brother?"

Shebna couldn't look at him. "I am sorry, but I cannot go."

"Why not?"

"Because I cannot bear to watch him dying inch by inch."

Gedaliah shrugged. "All right, Shebna. After everything you've done for me, I guess the least I can do is excuse you." He moved toward the door. "Is Hezekiah in his bedroom?"

"Yes, but for the sake of mercy, do not visit your brother unless you are prepared to show him some compassion."

"What's that supposed to mean?"

"It is immoral to gloat in the face of a dying man."

"What would you know about morality, Shebna?" Gedaliah let the door slam on his way out.

Shebna felt filthy after his conversation with the prince, and he had the urge to wash his hands. Gedaliah was right. If he had any moral integrity at all, he would resign rather than help the prince destroy everything that King Hezekiah had accomplished. But in Gedaliah's eyes only traitors resigned, and Shebna valued survival more than integrity. It was too late. He had already cast his lot with the prince.

Shebna turned to stare out of the window, wishing the fire in the harem had never happened. Bitter tears rolled silently down his cheeks.

Eliakim sat in his palace office and read through one of the petitions stacked on the huge pile in front of him. When he saw Shebna's note approving the request, it made him angry. Shebna knew that his decision contradicted the Law. What was he trying to get away with?

Arguments with the haughty Egyptian had become daily events since Hezekiah's illness, and as much as Eliakim dreaded another one, he couldn't avoid it. He headed down the hallway to find Shebna. After a long search, Eliakim found him in the royal archives, deep in conversation with someone who stood in the shadows. When Shebna spotted Eliakim, he stopped midsentence.

"Now what do you want?"

"We need to discuss this petition. Your decision contradicts the Law."

The other man stepped forward, and Eliakim's stomach rolled over in revulsion. Prince Gedaliah.

"Well, if it isn't the busybody engineer, King Hezekiah's faithful messenger boy. I've heard that you're a big man now—secretary of state!" Eliakim ignored him and held the petition out to Shebna.

"Do you have a minute to discuss this in private, or should I come back later?"

"There is nothing to discuss. It is a simple decision. The man owes a debt, and he will have to pay it."

"Yes, but you can't take away his land without leaving him the right of redemption. According to the Torah—"

"Here we go again," Shebna sighed. He and Gedaliah exchanged glances.

The prince took a few steps toward Eliakim. "You really enjoy forcing your outdated Torah laws on everyone, don't you? But I'll bet if we checked into your personal life, you wouldn't be so holy and perfect. What about your lovely wife from Israel, for example? Maybe she didn't escape from the Assyrians at all. Maybe she was sent here to be their eyes and ears."

Surprise and anger swept through Eliakim. "My wife doesn't concern you."

"She does if she's an Assyrian spy."

Eliakim rushed toward Gedaliah, angry enough to punch him. Shebna stepped between them. "Perhaps the prince could give us his opinion on the petition."

"No! That's the king's business, and the prince has no right to see it."

Gedaliah gazed at him evenly. "Well, it will become my business shortly, in a matter of days, or maybe even hours."

Suddenly Eliakim realized why Gedaliah had come from Lachish, and his stomach rolled over again. "As long as King Hezekiah is alive, he's the king—not you." He turned to leave.

"If you're going to ask my brother his opinion on that petition," Gedaliah called after him, "I don't think you'll find him very talkative today."

The thought of the corrupt, idolatrous prince inheriting the throne made Eliakim sick. But when he walked into the king's bedchamber and saw Hezekiah, he nearly wept.

The king no longer tossed feverishly, moaning in pain as he had for days. Instead, he lay deathly still, his eyes closed, his breathing shallow and uneven. His face had the colorless pallor of cold ashes. Eliakim touched his shoulder.

"Your Majesty . . . ?" Hezekiah never moved or opened his eyes.

Eliakim shook him, crying louder, "Your Majesty . . . ?"

Hezekiah didn't respond. The Egyptian physician sat beside the bed with his head in his hands.

"How long has he been like this?" Eliakim asked.

"Since last evening when I lanced the boil."

Eliakim stared at the man, afraid to ask the question.

Finally the doctor looked up. "We're losing him, my lord."

"No," Eliakim moaned. "God of Abraham, no."

He remembered Hezekiah's plea, *I don't want to die,* and he had the urge to shake him harder, to rouse him from the edge of death, shouting, "Fight, my lord! Fight to live!" But he rolled the petition tightly in his trembling hands and backed out of the room. Shebna and Gedaliah waited for him in the hallway.

"Would you like me to take care of that petition now?" Gedaliah said, holding out his hand.

"You miserable vulture!"

"Is that any way to talk to the next king?" Gedaliah's anger smoldered dangerously.

"You'll destroy everything he's accomplished!"

"Does that mean you'd like to resign, Lord Secretary, rather than work for me?"

"No one works for you yet. And as long as King Hezekiah is still alive, I'm still his secretary of state."

"Well, when he dies I have a word of advice for you from those holy books you're so fond of quoting: 'A king's wrath is a messenger of death, but a wise man will appease it.'"

Eliakim walked away.

"Not very wise, is he?" Gedaliah said behind him.

Eliakim wandered back to his office and dropped into a chair, staring sightlessly. Piles of documents covered his worktable, but he shoved them aside with a sweep of his arm, then leaned his elbows on the table and covered his face. He wanted to give up fighting and go home, but he knew he had to keep working. He had to make sure Shebna ran the nation according to the Torah. He finally bent to retrieve the scattered papers. But as he pored over them, he found that nearly every one of them contradicted the laws of God. He recognized Gedaliah's touch on them like a blight on summer fruit.

Hezekiah must live. He must. Eliakim could never support Gedaliah's reign. He hated everything about the prince. Suddenly Eliakim remembered the proverb Gedaliah had quoted, and a chill trickled through his veins. *A king's wrath is a messenger of death.* When King Hezekiah died, Gedaliah would execute him!

Eliakim leaped from his seat, his heart galloping wildly. He hurried from the palace, up the hill to the Temple, fighting the urge to run. He had to find the high priest. He had to claim sanctuary in the Temple before the king died.

But as he neared the Temple courtyards, he realized his plan would never work. Gedaliah wouldn't respect the sanctity of the Temple. He would kill Eliakim there as readily as anywhere else. Nor could he go into hiding and leave his family at risk. Gedaliah knew all about Jerusha.

Eliakim hurried through the gates into the inner courtyard and sank to his knees in front of the altar. The more he thought of how hopelessly trapped he was, the more he panicked. "O God . . . O God . . . !" He struggled to catch his breath as fear squeezed his lungs. He bowed his forehead to the ground and tried to pray but couldn't find the words. "Help me . . . please!"

Footsteps crunched on the stones, coming toward him. He looked up. A white-robed priest bowed to him. "Good afternoon, Lord Secretary. Can I help you with something?"

"Uh, no. Wait. Yes! Yes, I need to talk to the high priest. Is that possible?"

"Of course, my lord."

Eliakim followed the priest past the storehouses he had built and into the Temple side chambers. He remembered all the other building projects he had overseen for the king: the walls, the fortifications, the garrisons, the tunnel. They had contributed to his rise to power. And now they endangered his life.

The high priest seemed surprised to see Eliakim. "How can I help you, Lord Secretary?" He motioned for him to be seated.

Eliakim remained standing. A sudden thought made him shiver with fear. If Gedaliah launched a purge of the religious faction, the priests and Levites would be included in the purge along with Eliakim. In fact, if Gedaliah found out where he was, he could accuse Eliakim and the high priest of conspiracy—especially after Eliakim had spoken with such contempt.

"Oh, no . . . I'm sorry!"

"What is it, my lord?"

"I . . . I shouldn't be here. My life is in danger . . . and now I'm endangering yours by talking to you."

"Why don't you sit down and tell me what this is all about."

Eliakim battled to control his panic. He sank into a chair.

"You already know that the king is ill."

"Yes."

"The truth is—he's dying."

"Dying? So suddenly?"

"I wish it weren't true, but I just saw him, and his physician told me—" Eliakim couldn't finish.

The high priest closed his eyes. "Ah, Sovereign Lord—what a terrible loss."

Eliakim swallowed his grief and continued. "The king's brother Gedaliah will succeed him. He's as corrupt and idolatrous as King Ahaz. Everyone who supported King Hezekiah's reforms is in danger. That includes me and probably you too."

The high priest's voice remained calm. "What can we do?"

"I don't know . . . I haven't had time to think about it . . . I just wanted to warn you . . . I don't know what to do."

"I see." The high priest stroked his beard thoughtfully. "How strong are Gedaliah's supporters?" he asked after a pause.

Eliakim shook his head. "None of King Hezekiah's other brothers would stand a chance against him."

"Does the military support Gedaliah too?"

General Jonadab. Eliakim saw a ray of hope.

"No, the general hates Gedaliah as much as I do."

"Would he be willing to help us?" the priest asked.

"I'm certain that he—oh no! Jonadab isn't in Jerusalem! Shebna sent him to Beersheba yesterday to see about a disturbance and—they've had this all planned! I've been totally blind!"

The priest sighed and gestured helplessly. "Then we can only wait and pray. King Hezekiah's life and, indeed, our own lives are in God's hands."

"Can you call a special convocation tomorrow? A sacrifice, to pray for the king?"

"Yes, I can certainly arrange that."

"Good. Then if anyone asks why I came to see you, tell them that we were arranging the convocation."

The high priest rose. "It's nearly time for the evening sacrifice, my lord. I've just decided that I will preside over it myself. Why don't you go back to the courtyard and wait? Perhaps God will speak to you and give you guidance." The high priest smiled faintly, then embraced Eliakim. "Shalom, Lord Secretary."

Eliakim wandered back the way he had come, oblivious to the increased activity around him as the priests prepared for the evening sacrifice. He trembled with anger when he thought of Shebna and Gedaliah plotting to take over, and he cursed his own stupidity for failing to recognize it. They had outmaneuvered him. They had sent his only ally, General Jonadab, 85 miles into the Judean desert to get rid of him. Even if Eliakim sent for Jonadab immediately, he would never make it back in time. King Hezekiah couldn't possibly live much longer.

Why did evil always have its way? Why did God reward wickedness instead of righteousness?

Eliakim knelt down on the royal dais, but he couldn't pray. As he waited for the crowds to gather and the evening sacrifice to begin, he carefully examined each of his alternatives and its consequences. But every avenue he explored, from starting a revolution to fleeing the country, led to a dead end. The only way to save his own life was to appease Gedaliah. To do that, Eliakim would have to compromise his faith in God.

The sudden call of the shofar jolted Eliakim from his thoughts. He stood up and looked around. Prince Gedaliah stood on the royal dais, looking pleased with himself.

As he had promised, the high priest came forward to preside over the service, a highly unusual occurrence for an ordinary, daily sacrifice. But when the Levites began to sing, Eliakim recognized immediately that this wasn't an ordinary evening sacrifice. Instead of the scheduled liturgy, the high priest sent a message that Prince Gedaliah couldn't possibly ignore.

> *Do not fret because of evil men*
> *or be envious of those who do wrong;*
> *for like the grass they will soon wither,*
> *like green plants they will soon die away.*
> *Trust in the* LORD *and do good; . . . .*
> *Commit your way to the* LORD; *trust in him.*

The truth of the familiar words slowly calmed Eliakim's fears. He had dedicated his life to God. Whether he lived or died, his life remained in God's hands. Eliakim felt the peace of God filling him, replacing his panic and fear.

> *Be still before the* LORD *and wait patiently for him;*
> *do not fret when men succeed in their ways,*
> *when they carry out their wicked schemes. . . .*
> *For evil men will be cut off,*
> *but those who hope in the* LORD *will inherit the land.*

Eliakim stole a glance at Gedaliah. He appeared less self-assured than before. Eliakim looked back toward the Court of the Gentiles but he couldn't see Shebna in the crowd of worshipers.

> *The wicked plot against the righteous*
> *and gnash their teeth at them;*
> *but the Lord laughs at the wicked,*
> *for he knows their day is coming.*

The high priest sprinkled the blood around the altar as the Levites sang. Then as he made his way up the altar ramp with the sacrifice, he deliberately paused to gaze down at the royal dais, staring long and hard at Gedaliah.

> *The wicked draw the sword*
> *and bend the bow . . .*
> *to slay those whose ways are upright.*
> *But their swords will pierce their own hearts,*
> *and their bows will be broken.*

Eliakim glanced at Gedaliah again, and their eyes met. "This is your doing, isn't it?" Gedaliah said. Eliakim looked away, suppressing a smile.

> All sinners will be destroyed;
>   the future of the wicked will be cut off.
> The salvation of the righteous comes from the LORD;
> The LORD helps them and delivers them;
>   he delivers them from the wicked and saves them,
>   because they take refuge in him.

When the service ended, nothing had changed. Eliakim remained hopelessly trapped. But he knew that the priests and Levites stood courageously beside him. They had made that clear, even though Gedaliah's forces could quickly overpower and destroy them. They had placed their lives in God's hands, their trust in Him. Eliakim would do the same.

He didn't return to the palace after the service. Instead, he hurried home, concerned for his family's safety. Even if he couldn't escape, he determined to find a way to save them.

Jerusha and little Jerimoth met him at the door. "You're home early?"

"I got tired of fighting with Shebna, so I decided not to go back to the palace after the sacrifice."

Hilkiah returned a few moments later, still wearing his prayer shawl. "That was certainly an unusual sacrifice—what on earth is going on?" Eliakim shrugged vaguely and sank down on a bench to remove his sandals. "Why do you suppose the high priest conducted the evening sacrifice?" Hilkiah persisted.

"Ask him. Maybe they drew his lot."

"But that wasn't the usual liturgy, either. It—" Eliakim pleaded silently with his father when Jerusha's head was turned, and Hilkiah stopped midsentence. "Oh . . . when's supper? I'm starved. How about you, Jerimoth?"

"Yeah, I'm starved too." The boy patted his round tummy in imitation of Hilkiah, and Eliakim managed a smile.

It required an enormous effort for Eliakim to enter into the conversation during dinner, knowing this family meal might be one of their last. His mind strayed back to the king, and he prayed Hezekiah would live, certain he would die.

When dinner ended, they all went out to the garden to sit until the sky grew dark and the stars began to appear. As Eliakim watched his children playing, his heart squeezed until he could scarcely breathe. He had to get his loved ones out of Jerusalem. He had to hide them somewhere. Finally, Jerusha announced the children's bedtime and held the baby out for Eliakim to kiss. "Ah . . . bah, Ah . . . bah," she chattered happily.

"Good night, Tirza." He kissed her and stroked her soft head; then his arm tightened around little Jerimoth, nestled on his lap. "How about you, Son? Isn't it your bedtime too?"

"Abba, say prayers with me, OK?"

"All right. Get into bed, and I'll be up in a minute."

Jerimoth climbed off his lap and skipped over to give Hilkiah a loud, wet kiss.

"G'night, Grandpa." He followed Jerusha upstairs.

When they were alone, Eliakim slowly exhaled from the strain. "Abba, we need to talk."

"I could tell you had something on your mind all evening. What is it, Son?"

Eliakim forced himself to say the words. "I think . . . it looks like . . . King Hezekiah is going to die."

"Oh, no. Heavenly Father, no. Are you sure?"

"I'm sure."

In the silence that fell between them, Eliakim heard the laughter of his children through the open windows and Jerusha's sweet voice as she talked to them. The happy sounds didn't belong beside the sorrow in his heart.

"But I didn't think the king's burns were that bad—just the one on his leg. Hasn't he been working with you every day?"

"We worked together at first, but the doctors say the poison in the burn has spread through his body. He's been delirious with fever and only half-conscious for the past couple of days. And he's in such terrible pain, Abba. Last night after I talked with him he fell into a coma."

Hilkiah closed his eyes. "Oh, Holy One of Israel. Help him, I pray. Send him a miracle."

"I've been praying for a miracle too, because that's what it's going to take. I've even asked the high priest to hold a special sacrifice tomorrow to pray for him."

"He's that close to death?"

"Yes, Abba."

"And is this what the evening sacrifice was all about?"

Eliakim nodded. "Listen—I'm going to need your help. As soon as you hear that King Hezekiah is gone, as soon as it's official, you've got to get Jerusha and the children out of Jerusalem."

"Why?"

"King Hezekiah's brother, Prince Gedaliah, is preparing to succeed him and—and the prince hates me."

"He hates you? Why?"

"Lots of reasons. Remember a few years ago when I made so many trips to Lachish to work on their fortifications? Gedaliah and I got into some terrible arguments, and it grew to the point that he wouldn't speak to me anymore. He's a liar, a cheat, and an idolater, Abba, and he makes little pretense of following God's Law. I challenged his fitness to govern many times because of his hypocrisy, and eventually King Hezekiah learned of his brother's idolatry through me. Gedaliah also has close ties with Shebna. He appointed him governor in the first place. And you know how things stand between Shebna and me."

"What are you saying?"

Eliakim ran his hand through his hair. "Abba . . . you know there's always a time of transition between reigns, and there's a good chance Jerusalem won't be safe after . . . after King Hezekiah dies. Promise me that you'll get Jerusha and the children away from here and see that they're kept safe."

"Yes, of course I promise, but where should I take them?"

Eliakim stood and paced in front of his father. "I've thought it all through. I'm going to instruct the servants to have food and clothing packed so you'll be ready to leave on an hour's notice. I think the safest place to stay would be with your cousins near Beth Shemesh. We'll send word for them to expect you, and—"

"What about you?"

"I'm the highest-ranking official to oppose Gedaliah's reign. He'll probably want my resignation and—"

"Will he have you killed?"

Eliakim couldn't look in his father's eyes. "Everyone who supported King Hezekiah's religious reforms will be opposed to Gedaliah. Rather than take a chance that we'll rally behind another heir, he'll . . . he'll probably use any excuse he can find to have us all arrested . . . maybe even executed as traitors."

"Eliakim! Don't wait for King Hezekiah to die! If he's really dying as you say, take your family and get out now! Why wait for Gedaliah to kill you?"

Eliakim shook his head. "I can't run, Abba."

"Why not?"

Eliakim saw his father's fear and anger mounting, and he groped for words to convince him. "Because . . . because King Hezekiah is relying on me to keep the kingdom running while he's sick. Besides, I knew when I accepted this position that I'd have to accept the responsibilities and dangers that came with it, and—"

"That's very noble, Son—and very stupid!"

"Abba, don't you understand—?"

"No! I most certainly don't! If your life is in danger, you should get out of here!"

"Abba . . . shh . . ."

"Jerusha and your children need you."

"Please listen to me." He looked into his father's distraught face and swallowed hard. "I know too much, Abba. I know our military capabilities, treasury accounts, the locations of all the weapons and supplies. I know exactly where the Gihon spring and the entrance to the tunnel are. I built and supplied every fortified city in Judah—remember? Including Jerusalem. I know the strengths and weaknesses of our entire defensive system. Jonadab and I designed it. If I fled, Gedaliah would assume I was plotting against him. He would pursue me to the ends of the earth rather than take a chance that I'd go to an enemy nation with what I know." Hilkiah let out a low moan. "And Abba, if I took Jerusha and the children with me, I'd be endangering them too. Besides, where could we go? What other nation would shelter a fleeing secretary of state? Harboring me would be an act of warfare toward the new king."

"Can't you fight him? Surely General Jonadab—"

"They've already gotten Jonadab out of the way. Gedaliah's been waiting for this opportunity all his life, and he's prepared for a fight. He's too strong, Abba. He has Shebna and all the nation's resources under his control. I have the support of the prophets and the priesthood. It's hopeless—don't you see? Gedaliah will be the next king, and there's—there's nothing I can do about it."

He was caught in a web of political intrigue with no way to escape. As Hilkiah began to comprehend how hopelessly trapped Eliakim was, he groaned and stumbled from his seat to embrace him fiercely.

"Oh, Eliakim, my son. I can't accept this. I can't!"

Eliakim could barely speak. "I'm not afraid for myself, Abba, but I'm worried about my family. Promise me you'll take care of them."

"Yes—yes, of course I promise."

Eliakim held his father tightly, then released him.

"Thanks," he whispered. "Now I'd better go say prayers with my son."

◈

Later that night Jerusha lay beside her husband, with her head on his chest, listening to the steady pounding of his heartbeat. She felt the tension in every muscle of his body and knew that his eyes remained open, staring blindly into the darkness. He had come home that evening deeply distressed, had silently brooded all through supper. She put her hand to his face and gently stroked his beard.

"Eliakim? Can't you talk about what's upsetting you?" she whispered.

He sighed and his arm tightened around her shoulder. When he spoke, his voice sounded tight. "He's dying, Jerusha. King Hezekiah is dying."

"Oh, Eliakim. Are you sure?"

"Even the physicians say so."

"What will happen to you? Will you still be secretary of state?"

"I don't know—it doesn't matter. What matters is that he's such a great man, such an outstanding king. He's too young to die. Do you realize he's a few years younger than I am? And he's done so much good during his reign—I don't understand why he has to die."

Her hand rested on his face, and she felt his jaw tighten with anxiety. "He's suffering so much. You can't even imagine how much."

"Who else knows that he's dying?"

"Not many people—only the servants, a few other officials he's called for. But anyone who sees him can tell that he's dying. And he knows it too." His voice trailed off, and he was silent for a long time. "Jerusha, I haven't told you how the fire started. When the king went to Hephzibah's chambers, she was worshiping a graven image of Asherah."

"Why would she do such a thing?"

"Who knows? But the fire started when he tried to destroy the shrine she'd made."

"That's horrible! Then this is all Hephzibah's fault?"

"What's horrible is that he loved her so much. You've seen them together. He loved her like I love you. The only thing that meant more to him than Hephzibah was his faith in God. What she did must have devastated him."

"Oh, Eliakim. How could you hold all this inside?"

"Hephzibah came to me a few days ago. She begged me to take her to see him."

"I hope you didn't do it."

"No. But after she left I started thinking that she might try to go see him on her own, and sure enough, I found her in his room."

"Did the king see her?"

"He's so sick he thought he dreamed it. But I'm ashamed to admit that I'm glad she saw him."

"Eliakim, why? It's all her fault."

"I know, and maybe that's part of it. Maybe I wanted her to see what she's done to him, how he's suffered because of her."

"What will happen to her now?"

"I suppose she'll be banished to the king's villa with his concubines. She's in bad shape, Jerusha. I feel sorry for her in a way. She has no children, and the king has divorced her. What does she have to live for? But she'd probably rather be banished than become the property of Prince Gedaliah, like she's supposed to. If Shebna gets his way, she'll be executed."

For a moment Jerusha almost said "good." Hephzibah deserved the severest punishment. But for the first time in more than four years, Jerusha recalled her own past, her own sin and unbelief, and knew that if God could forgive her, then he could forgive Hephzibah as well.

"Eliakim, hold me," she whispered. As Eliakim's arms tightened around her, she tried to put herself in Hephzibah's place—to imagine hurting her husband so deeply that he would divorce her, to imagine the horror of knowing that her own sin had caused his death. She shuddered.

"What's wrong, Love?"

"Oh, Eliakim, I love you so much! If anything ever happened to you . . ." She began to cry.

"Shhh . . . don't cry, Love. It's all right . . . I'm right here . . ."

But as Eliakim kissed her, Jerusha felt his tears flowing together with her own.

7

Isaiah pushed through the enormous crowd that overflowed the Temple gates to join Eliakim and the city officials for the special sacrifice. Like the other solemn-faced men who jammed the courtyards to pray, the news of King Hezekiah's critical illness had shocked Isaiah. The immense crowd reminded him of Hezekiah's popularity, how much the people loved this king who had brought renewed prosperity. He stared up at the dazzling, cloudless sky and wished for a bleak, icy day, gloomy and gray to match the heaviness in his heart.

The high priest unsheathed his knife, ready to slay the sacrifice as the Levites began to sing:

> O LORD, *do not rebuke me in your anger*
> *or discipline me in your wrath.*
> *Be merciful to me, LORD, for I am faint;*
> *O LORD, heal me, for my bones are in agony.*

The high priest slit the animal's throat, draining the blood. Then the other priests helped prepare it for the altar. Isaiah closed his eyes, pleading silently with God in prayer.

"O Yahweh, You are merciful and gracious and compassionate. You abound in love and faithfulness. Have mercy on Your servant Hezekiah. He's been faithful to You, Lord, and he's brought Your people back to You too. I pray that You will heal him, Father, according to Your loving-kindness. Spare his life, just as You once spared it when he was a child. Let him live to serve You, O God!"

The high priest ascended the ramp to place the offering on the fire. With one voice, the congregation shouted, "O Lord, hear our cry for mercy; O Lord, accept our prayer."

Then, in the same instant that the pillar of flame soared toward heaven, Yahweh spoke to Isaiah. He seemed to wrap His arms tightly around him, speaking tenderly, as a loving Father to His frightened child. But His words pierced Isaiah's heart.

No, My son. It is not my will to heal Hezekiah. Today I will take him to be with Me.

As the congregation fell prostrate in worship before God, Isaiah sank to his knees, weeping in despair. Yahweh had answered. King Hezekiah was going to die.

Isaiah threw himself prostrate with the others, but he acted in sorrow, not worship. He pleaded with God to change His mind, to have mercy on Hezekiah, but God's answer never wavered.

No, My son.

God's firm reply was as solid and massive as the great altar above Isaiah's head. Isaiah couldn't plead his way around it. He covered his face and wept bitterly, for not only had Yahweh refused to answer his prayers, but Isaiah knew he must go to the palace and tell the king he would die.

When the others stood to join in the song of praise, Isaiah remained prostrate. "Why, Yahweh? Hezekiah has sought to please You in everything he has done. Why must he die?"

But God didn't answer.

When the service ended, Eliakim crouched beside Isaiah and helped him to his feet, anxiously searching Isaiah's face.

"Rabbi? Has Yahweh told you what will happen?"

"Yes, Eliakim. King Hezekiah is going to die."

"No!"

Isaiah rested his hand on Eliakim's shoulder. "I must go and tell him."

Eliakim took a shuddering breath, struggling to compose himself. "Rabbi, your life is in danger, and so is mine. Prince Gedaliah—"

"I know," he said quietly. "I know."

He looked into Eliakim's sorrowful face and remembered another time, years before, when Eliakim had given him a similar warning. Isaiah had fled then, to escape King Ahaz. But this time he wouldn't flee.

"Rabbi, please—I need time to get my family out of Jerusalem. Can you wait a few hours to tell him?"

"Go on. Do what you need to do. There's time." Eliakim nodded mutely and hurried away.

With a sorrowful heart, Isaiah watched the dancing flames slowly consume the offering on the altar. Yahweh had once snatched Hezekiah from Molech's flames, saying, *"I have summoned you by name; you are mine."* Had His purpose for Hezekiah's life already been fulfilled?

"I don't understand, Yahweh," he whispered. "Why does he have to die?"

━◆━

Eliakim left the royal dais and forced his way through the crowded courtyard, searching for his father. When he spotted him in the outer courtyard, he called to him above the noise.

"Abba! Abba, wait!"

Hilkiah stood aside and waited for him to push through the crush of worshipers.

"What is it, Son?"

"Abba, it's time. You've got to take Jerusha and the children out of Jerusalem. Today. Now."

"What will we tell her?"

"I don't know. I'll think of something. Come on."

Eliakim hurried down the hill with his father, frantically making plans to save his family. But gradually the truth about his own life began to penetrate his thoughts. The closer King Hezekiah edged toward death, the nearer Eliakim's own death sentence loomed.

Suddenly he understood how the king felt—knowing he would die, wanting desperately to live. But Eliakim didn't know how he could escape. God had spoken to Isaiah. And Gedaliah would surely order Eliakim's execution.

All of Eliakim's emotions clashed inside him at once; grief at the death of his king, sorrow at the loss of his wife and children, bewilderment at God's refusal to answer their prayers, anger that the godless Gedaliah would inherit the throne, terror as he stood face-to-face with death. The warfare left him dazed.

Swirling around his warring emotions was the urgent need to find the right words to say to Jerusha to convince her to leave Jerusalem without him. And then he had to gather the courage to say goodbye to her forever.

O God, please help me.

When they reached their front door, Eliakim and Hilkiah both stopped. "Abba, take them to your cousin's house in Beth Shemesh as we've planned. I'll instruct Joah the Levite to stay in touch with you. Don't try to come back until it's safe. He'll let you know when—when the bloodshed is over."

Hilkiah nodded grimly, and Eliakim took another deep breath. "Jerusha has already suffered so much sorrow in her lifetime—she's going to need you, Abba. Don't let her become bitter again. Tell her—tell her that everything happens for a reason, according to God's will. And tell my children—" Eliakim couldn't finish.

Hilkiah hugged him fiercely. "My son—oh, my precious son! I can't accept this. I can't!"

At last Eliakim gently separated himself from Hilkiah's embrace. "Come on, Abba. It will be a long journey to Beth Shemesh with the two children."

"Yes, yes—you're right. I'm sorry."

They both kissed their fingertips and touched the little box on the doorpost. God's holy Law. No matter what happened to him, Eliakim vowed never to compromise with Gedaliah or renounce his faith in God.

"I'll go get my things," Hilkiah mumbled and ran upstairs.

Eliakim wandered through the house searching for Jerusha, praying desperately for strength. He found her outside in the garden. The baby napped in a reed basket, and little Jerimoth sat on a mat in the sunshine with Jerusha, learning to count as he shelled dried beans.

"One . . . two . . . three . . . four. Mama, that one had four in it."

"Yes," she smiled. Then she looked up and saw Eliakim watching them from the doorway. "What's wrong?"

"Nothing, Love," he answered, attempting a smile he didn't feel. How he hated to lie to her. "I have a surprise for you."

Little Jerimoth scrambled to his feet and ran to Eliakim, scattering beans and pods all over the mat. "Me, too, Abba? Do you have a surprise for me too?"

"Yes, Son. For you too." He bent to lift him in his arms, certain that any moment his heart would break and his sorrow at leaving his wife and children would spill over as Hilkiah's had. Jerusha came to him, gently brushing the tears from his beard.

"They're tears of joy," he said, trying to smile again. "The king is much better today. He's going to live after all."

"Oh, thank God."

"In fact, that's my surprise. He's sending me to Beth Shemesh on court business, and I'm taking all of you with me."

"Really?" Jerusha cocked her head, gazing at him as if trying to read behind his words. Eliakim knew he wasn't a very convincing liar. He hadn't had much practice.

"Yes. In fact, I've known that this trip was a possibility for some time, and I've already made all the arrangements. Abba has relatives in Beth Shemesh, so it will be a combination of business and pleasure."

"Do you think we should travel that far with the baby?"

"Why not? That child has bounced so many miles on Abba's knee she'll probably outride all of us." He looked down at his beautiful, chubby daughter sleeping peacefully, and he had to turn away into the house. Jerusha followed him.

"When will we leave?"

"That's the best surprise of all. We're leaving today. Right away, in fact."

"Now? I wish you would have warned me, Eliakim. This is so sudden."

"I had Abba and the servants pack everything for you so it would truly be a surprise. You won't have to do a thing."

"Your father's going too?"

"Yes, I even talked Abba into going. Can you believe it?"

"No, I can't—"

"Of course, he's only going because he's afraid he'll miss his grandchildren." Eliakim's stomach churned from the strain of his lies. He avoided looking at Jerusha, aware that she would probably see through him. As he ran out of words, his false cheer sounded forced.

At that moment Hilkiah bounded down the stairs, his face washed and shiny with oil, a beaming smile spread bravely across it. He circled his arm around Jerusha and drew her away.

"Come, come, my dear. Don't look so worried. Think of this as an adventure. You'll love the countryside. And everything's arranged already. We're traveling with one of my caravans. You should like that—eh, little Jerimoth?"

Hilkiah took the boy from Eliakim, and suddenly Eliakim's empty arms ached. But even more, he dreaded releasing Jerusha from his embrace when the time came.

"Are we riding on camels, Grandpa?"

Hilkiah chuckled. "No, I'm afraid not. Only horses."

"Abba, I want to ride on your horse," Jerimoth said.

"You'll have to ride with me on the way back, Son. I'm not leaving yet."

"What do you mean?" Jerusha asked. "Why not?"

"I'm coming later. I want you slowpokes to get a head start. I have some business to finish at the palace first. I'll catch up with you tonight or maybe tomorrow."

"Why can't we wait for you?"

"Well . . . ," Eliakim stammered, "because . . ."

"Because my caravan can't wait around for him all day—that's why," Hilkiah said. "Time is money, you know."

The servants had efficiently put Eliakim's plans into action, and all too soon they had everything ready. Jerimoth fussed because his father wasn't going with them, and much to Eliakim's distress, he had to speak sharply to the boy. The baby whined and cried, awakened from her nap too early. She wouldn't let Jerusha put her down, and Eliakim could only give his wife a one-armed hug and a quick kiss as she struggled with the cranky baby.

"I'll see you later," he whispered. "I love you."

Then his family and the servants climbed into the carts and waved good-bye. Eliakim stood in the doorway, watching numbly until they disappeared around the corner.

The house seemed quiet and still when he finally went back inside, but reminders of his family lay all around him. Hilkiah's prayer shawl, forgotten on the bench near the door. The jar of pink blossoms, the wilted petals beginning to drop. The baby's blanket and basket in the garden beneath a tree. Empty pods and beans scattered on the mat where Jerimoth had left them.

Eliakim wandered through the empty house, battling against the enormous fear that threatened to paralyze him. When he came to his workroom he closed the door, then fell to his knees and cried out to God.

"Heavenly Father, help me accept Your will for my life. Do with me whatever You want, but please give me the courage to face it. I haven't any.

"And, Father, I pray for Abba and my children. They're in Your care now, and I trust You because I know You love them even more than I do. Keep them safe, keep them true to Your laws, and help them to always remember how much I loved them.

"But, Father, most of all I pray for Jerusha. You've brought her through so much—please be with her in this trial as well. And when I die, please don't let her be bitter. Please keep her faith strong. I love her, Father . . . I love her so much . . ."

—◈—

Isaiah waited as long as he dared, giving Eliakim the extra time he had promised. But as the afternoon shadows began to lengthen, he knew he couldn't postpone his task any longer. He walked the short distance to the palace by memory, his vision blurred by grief.

Here am I. Send me!

That was what he had told Yahweh many years ago when he first agreed to be His spokesman. Isaiah had endured mockings and insults and even threats to his life in the years that followed his commission, for Yahweh had warned him from the start that the task he had volunteered for wouldn't be easy. But now he wondered if anything he had done for Yahweh had been as difficult as telling King Hezekiah he was going to die.

Isaiah had lived through the reigns of four different kings: Uzziah, Jotham, Ahaz, and now Hezekiah. None of the others had followed God's Law as diligently or as faithfully as Hezekiah.

"Why, Yahweh?" he asked again, but he already knew God's answer: *"My thoughts are not your thoughts, neither are your ways my ways."*

The royal physicians huddled miserably in the king's outer sitting room. They looked up when Isaiah entered. He nodded slightly in greeting, unable to speak, then walked past them into the bedroom. As he paused inside the doorway, fresh tears filled his eyes when he saw the dying king.

Hezekiah lay gray and still, his eyes closed, his breathing short and painful. The angel of death seemed to hover over his body, little more than skin and bones, waiting for Isaiah to finish his task.

"Give us a few minutes alone, please," Isaiah said to Shebna and the servants. Then he walked to Hezekiah's bedside and laid his hand on his shoulder. After a moment the king's eyes slowly opened.

"Rabbi . . . ?"

"Yes, Your Majesty. It's me."

He saw the unasked question in Hezekiah's eyes and couldn't avoid his task any longer. His voice trembled with emotion as he forced the words out of his mouth.

"This is what Yahweh says. You need to put your house in order, Your Majesty, because you're going to die. You won't recover."

Tears flowed down Isaiah's face in spite of his efforts to control them, and he quickly brushed them aside. He knew from Hezekiah's expression that he had heard, that he understood. The king nodded almost imperceptibly, as if he lacked the strength to do more, then closed his eyes again.

"May you rest in peace," Isaiah whispered. He took a long, final look at King Hezekiah, then turned and left the room.

◆

Hezekiah knew that Isaiah's words were final. The prophet spoke the Word of God, and it could never be changed. Twice before, Isaiah had prophesied Hezekiah's salvation—when his father tried to sacrifice him to Molech, and a few years ago, when the Assyrians threatened to invade his nation. Both times Yahweh had miraculously intervened to save him, just as the prophet had promised. Now Hezekiah would die. He felt his life swiftly draining from him, like water disappearing into the desert sand. Until Isaiah came, Hezekiah had continued to hope. Perhaps he could fight off the poison and the sickness; perhaps the physicians would find a treatment that would cure him. Now Hezekiah knew it was hopeless.

The bitter irony of his death struck him. God had once saved him from an idol's fire, only to let him perish because of another idol's fire. Had he accomplished anything during his lifetime? Would his death have any meaning at all?

How quickly his life had passed! He still wanted to accomplish more. And he had left many things undone. Now in the few remaining moments of his life he needed to get his house in order. He needed to name a successor. The next king of Judah would be an heir of King David, as God had promised. But he wouldn't be his own son.

Hephzibah. How he had loved her!

She had worshiped the fertility goddess, thinking a lifeless idol could grant them a son, but it had led to this; he would die because of her idolatry.

Yet even as he faced the final inevitability of God's Word, even though he would gladly welcome the freedom from the agonizing pain he suffered, Hezekiah's fear began to multiply. He wasn't ready to die. Isaiah had prayed that he would rest in peace, but peace refused to come.

Even though I walk through the valley of the shadow of death, I will fear no evil, for you are with me . . .

Hezekiah tried to pray for the courage to accept death, to embrace it without fear, but he couldn't. He clung desperately to life, even as his strength melted away. Afraid of the unknown, he refused to let go. He didn't want to die.

O God! Where are You?

Hezekiah felt utterly alone, abandoned by God in his pain and fear. He turned his face to the wall, in the direction of the Temple, blotting everything else from his mind as he desperately sought the calming presence of God for his fearful soul.

"O Lord . . . Your Word says that if we follow Your laws and keep Your covenant that You will bless us . . . that You will keep us free from every disease. Remember, Lord, how I've tried to walk before You faithfully . . . and with wholehearted devotion as You have commanded . . . remember how I've tried to do what is good in Your eyes . . ."

But before he could finish his prayer, Hezekiah closed his eyes and wept.

The simple country farm outside Beth Shemesh reminded Jerusha of her father's land in Israel. She'd gradually adjusted to life in the city, but arriving at Hilkiah's cousins' place this morning brought back memories of all that she missed: the smell of hay and oxen, the soft swish of olive branches in the wind, the taste of cold spring water on a hot, dusty day.

She held baby Tirza on her lap and watched little Jerimoth explore the outdoors. At first the open spaces frightened him after the safety of their tiny courtyard garden. But once he had adjusted, he wanted to experience everything at once—watching the servants milk the goats, picking early grapes from the vineyard, playing hide-and-seek among the olive trees. He had already made himself at home.

Eliakim's elaborate story and false cheer hadn't fooled Jerusha. Something was wrong. The lower the sun sank in the sky, the deeper her anxiety grew. All afternoon she listened for the sound of horses' hooves signaling her husband's arrival, but when he still hadn't arrived as the family prepared for supper, the overwhelming fear gripped Jerusha that she would never see Eliakim again. She stared down the deserted road, fighting her tears.

Hilkiah came and stood by her side, gently resting his hand on her shoulder. "Come, my child. Dinner's almost ready."

"Aren't we going to wait for Eliakim?" She watched his face, searching for a clue to the truth as she deliberately spoke her husband's name. The sparkle in Hilkiah's eye was missing, and she thought she detected pain in its place.

"You know what he's like when he's working. No sense of time, that son of mine. It's better we should eat than wait." He turned away from her too quickly. "Come on, Jerimoth," he called. "Time to wash for dinner."

The boy raced up to Hilkiah and hurled himself into his arms. "Is Abba here?" he asked, breathlessly.

"Not yet, Son."

"But I don't want to eat without Abba."

"Shh . . . your Aunt Shoshanna has dinner prepared already. We must eat. It would be rude not to eat."

"Abba isn't coming at all, is he, Grandpa?"

Jerusha froze as her son voiced her fear. She watched her father-in-law carefully, waiting for his answer. She knew that Hilkiah could never tell a lie.

"What did your father tell you, Jerimoth?" he asked gently.

"That he would see us later."

"Well then, if it's within your father's power, I know he will keep his promise."

"Why isn't he here yet? Where is he? It's almost dark."

"How can I know these things, Jerimoth? It's impossible to say for sure where your father is right now."

"Do *you* think he's coming, Grandpa?"

Hilkiah didn't answer right away, and Jerusha saw the uncertainty in his face. She strained forward to hear his answer, knowing it would either calm her fears or confirm her suspicions.

"Jerimoth, your father is a very busy man. A very important man. Only Yahweh can know for certain when we will see him again. Now, come. Aren't you hungry? I know I am."

Jerusha hugged the baby tightly to herself and stared down the road toward Jerusalem again. Hilkiah's words hadn't revealed what he knew, but they lingered in her mind like a prophecy. *Only Yahweh knew when she would see Eliakim again.*

"Grandpa?" Jerimoth asked as they washed their hands for dinner. "Can Abba's horse see in the dark?"

"Such questions he asks! Am I a horse that I should know such a thing?"

The mealtime seemed strained. Hilkiah's cousins carried the conversation while Jerusha ate in silence, her worries and fears multiplying rapidly. Everyone else talked of relatives she'd never met and past events she hadn't been part of. By the time they had cleared the dishes away, the children were yawning from their long day.

"Time for bed," she told Jerimoth.

"I want to stay up until Abba comes."

"We don't know when that will be, Honey. It might be very late." *Or it might be never.*

"But I'm not tired, Mama."

"Then you may lie in bed and listen for Abba, and if you hear him coming you may get up again, all right?"

"But Abba always says prayers with me. Who will say them with me if he's not here?"

"I would be very happy to say prayers with you tonight," Hilkiah said.

Jerimoth considered the offer for a moment. "Abba told me that when he was a little boy you used to tuck him in every night and say prayers with him, just like we do."

"That's right, I did."

"Do you remember when Abba was a little boy, Grandpa?"

"Yes, I remember." Hilkiah's voice sounded strange. "Call me when you're ready for prayers." He turned and quickly fled outside. Jerusha looked at his cousins, but they wouldn't meet her gaze. Instead, they busied themselves with nothing.

After the children were in bed, Jerusha wrapped herself in a shawl and went outside to look for Hilkiah. She found him sitting on the low stone wall of the vineyard with his back to the house, staring at the half-moon lying low on the horizon. She sat beside him.

"Jerimoth is ready to say prayers."

"All right."

Jerusha gripped his arm to stop him as he started to rise. "Abba, wait." She had to know the truth. "Last night Eliakim told me that King Hezekiah was dying—yet today the king was healthy enough to send us here to Beth Shemesh."

She paused, but Hilkiah said nothing. A gentle breeze stirred the leaves of the grapevines. "Abba, if Eliakim knew for weeks that we might be coming here, if the servants knew and had everything packed, why did he rush home to tell us we had to leave right away? And why did we have to hurry if *he* wasn't in a hurry to get here?"

Hilkiah still didn't answer.

"I can learn to live with the truth, but I can't live with uncertainty. I need to know what's happened to Eliakim. If you know, Abba, tell me."

Hilkiah passed his hand over his face and slowly nodded. "My son Eliakim," he sighed. "Not so long ago he was a boy like little Jerimoth, complaining, 'Do I have to go to bed already?' We said prayers together, Eliakim and I, every night. Sometimes he'd try to rush through them—you know Eliakim: always in a hurry—and then I'd have to say, 'Whoa! Slow down, Son! You're not just reciting words; you're having a conversation with the God of Abraham, the Holy One of Israel, blessed be His name.'" He paused, and an owl hooted in a tree beyond the barn.

"But my son Eliakim is no longer a boy. He's a man, now, and Yahweh has seen fit to make him a very important man." He stopped again, and Jerusha felt him shudder. "When your children are little you can hold them close to you, take care of them, protect them. But soon a day comes when you must give them over to the Almighty One's care. I'm sorry for keeping the truth from you, my daughter. But don't you see? How can I tell you what I haven't accepted myself? How can I find the words to say what I don't want to hear?"

Jerusha began to tremble. She felt a sob rising deep in her heart and couldn't stop it. "O God, no . . . please . . ."

Hilkiah drew her into his arms and held her tightly, as if trying to hold her together, as if what he would tell her would cause her to shatter like a broken dish.

"Eliakim sent you and the children here so that you would be safe. King Hezekiah is going to die."

"No . . . no . . ."

"The king's brother will inherit the throne, and Eliakim is afraid that Gedaliah will launch a purge of all the men who supported the king's religious reforms."

"Then why didn't he come with us? Why doesn't he escape before it's too late?" Hilkiah's arms tightened around her. He finally answered in a thick voice.

"Because Eliakim is a man of honor and integrity. He's not a man to run and hide. He's chosen to stay."

"Why didn't he tell me himself?"

"He was afraid you wouldn't leave if you knew the truth, and he wanted you and his two children to be safe."

"He has *three* children, Abba. I'm carrying another child."

"Oh, my sweet daughter. Does Eliakim know?"

"He's been so busy and so upset about the king that I never had a chance to tell him."

They held each other in silence for a few moments; then Hilkiah wiped his eyes. "I must pray with little Jerimoth before he falls asleep. I won't be long."

Jerusha sat alone on the wall, numb and shivering, looking out over the fields and orchards that reminded her so much of home. If only Eliakim had been an ordinary man, a farmer like her father. They could have lived a quiet life, raising their children, growing old together. But Yahweh had made him a very important man, a man of honor and integrity. She must remember those words. Her children may forget their father's face, but they must never forget his faithfulness to God.

◆

Isaiah walked through the palace hallways in a daze of grief. He didn't know where he was going, only that he wanted to get as far away from the palace as possible and be alone. Telling King Hezekiah that he would die had been one of the most painful prophecies he had ever uttered. He had foretold the destruction of entire nations and kingdoms, but they had deserved their fate. What had this good king ever done wrong?

Soon the entire nation would hear the official announcement of Hezekiah's death. Then Isaiah could release his grief and mourn along with everyone else. How he would miss this godly king! But as Isaiah crossed the middle courtyard of the palace, a shout suddenly rang in his ears.

Go back!

Isaiah stopped in surprise and looked around to see who had called to him. The courtyard was deserted.

"Yahweh?" he asked in amazement.

Then the voice of God spoke to him with startling clarity.

Go back and tell Hezekiah, the leader of my people, "This is what the LORD, the God of your father David says: I have heard your prayer and seen your tears: I will heal you . . ."

There was more, but Isaiah's heart leaped inside him, and he didn't wait to hear the rest. He turned around and ran back the way he had come, bounding up the stairs, reaching the king's chambers, panting for breath. When he burst through the door, Shebna and the startled physicians stared at him in surprise. He hurried past them, into the bedroom.

Hezekiah lay alone with his face to the wall. He slowly turned his head, and his ashen face glistened with tears.

"This is what the LORD, the God of your father David says," Isaiah panted. "I have heard your prayer and seen your tears; I will heal you! On the third day from now you will go up to the temple of the LORD. I will add fifteen years to your life. And I will deliver you and this city from the hand of the king of Assyria. I will defend this city for my sake and for the sake of my servant David."

◆

Hezekiah closed his eyes as tears of relief ran down his cheeks. Yahweh was a personal God, his God. Yahweh had heard his prayers. He had seen every tear Hezekiah had shed. And in His great love and mercy, Yahweh had decided to answer his prayers. He was going to live!

At last Hezekiah wiped his eyes and looked up at Isaiah again. The room whirled dizzily as he struggled with the ravages of his fever, and he needed proof that Isaiah was real, not a hallucination. He needed a pledge, a tangible sign, to restore his strength and hope, for he knew he still hovered close to death.

Hezekiah stretched out his hand and touched Isaiah's arm, feeling the coarse fabric of Isaiah's robe, the warmth and life in the prophet's flesh. He wasn't hallucinating.

"What will be the sign that the Lord will heal me? And that I will go up to the Temple three days from now?"

For a moment Isaiah didn't respond. Then he strode across the room and flung aside the heavy curtains, unlatched the wooden shutters, and threw them open as well. Hezekiah winced as painful sunlight streamed into his room for the first time in many days. Gradually his eyes adjusted to the brightness.

Isaiah pointed to Ahaz's tower in the courtyard beyond. "This is the LORD's sign to you that the LORD will do what he has promised: Shall the shadow go forward 10 steps, or shall it go back 10 steps?"

Hezekiah stared at Isaiah in amazement, unable to comprehend his astounding words. He was going to live. It seemed like a feverish dream.

"It's simple for the shadow to go forward 10 steps," Hezekiah said. "Have it go *back* 10 steps." His grandfather had told him long ago that Yahweh could do the impossible.

Isaiah dropped to his knees and closed his eyes in silent prayer. A moment later he fell forward, with his forehead pressed to the floor. Hezekiah concentrated on the shadow that blanketed the tower's winding stairs, not daring to take his eyes off it. The air outside shimmered in the late afternoon heat, but he shivered, still clammy with feverish sweat.

Then slowly, almost imperceptibly at first, the leading edge of the shadow began to do the impossible, retreating up the stairs the full distance it had traveled since noon. By the time Isaiah lifted his forehead from the floor, the shadow had moved backward a full 10 stairs to its noontime position, and the sun blazed with fierce midday heat.

"O God . . . thank You . . . thank You . . . ," Hezekiah murmured. He had exhausted his strength, and he slumped against the pillows again, grimacing in pain. He still felt as if he were dying, but now he knew he would live. God had heard him. *His* God.

—✦—

Shebna burst into the bedroom, followed by the terrified physicians. King Hezekiah lay against the pillows with his eyes closed. He looked as if he were dead.

"The sun!"

"It's an omen!"

"Is the king . . . ?"

"The king will live," Isaiah said. "He will live." He rose shakily to his feet from where he knelt beside the window. "Prepare a poultice of figs, and apply it to the boil—and he will recover." The doctors quickly fled the room to do it.

Shebna remained behind, staring speechlessly, his dark eyes traveling involuntarily from the king, to Isaiah, to the clock tower beyond the open window. He had been gazing idly out of the window a few moments ago and thought he had seen the impossible—the shadow on Ahaz's tower had appeared to move backward. Shebna couldn't believe his eyes. He stared intently at the tower once again, but now the shadow was back where it should be, on the 10th step. In a little while it would reach the bottom step, and the sun would set. Shebna couldn't have imagined it. Some of the physicians and servants had seen it too. They had been filled with superstitious dread, believing it was an omen, believing that King Hezekiah had died.

Shebna hurried over to the side of the bed. Hezekiah's chest rose and fell only slightly. His breathing was shallow and irregular. He didn't look as if he could live much longer.

"He will live."

Isaiah's voice startled Shebna. He turned to stare at the rabbi. Shebna wanted to believe it, but his eyes told him otherwise.

"Are you certain?"

"Yes, I'm positive. In three days he will worship at the Temple."

"That is impossible. Look at him! You are not a physician—why do you make such outrageous claims? The doctors have all said the king cannot live, much less recover in three days' time. It is cruel to raise everyone's hopes."

"I didn't say it—Yahweh did."

Shebna shook his head. "You are bluffing."

He knew that Isaiah had been right once before when he'd prophesied that the Assyrians wouldn't invade Judah, but Isaiah could have had an informant in the North who had sent him advance word of Assyria's movements. This time he had to be guessing. He couldn't possibly know if the king would live or die.

Shebna glanced at Ahaz's tower again. He had seen the shadow move backward. So had everyone else. How could he explain that?

Suddenly Eliakim burst into the room, gasping as if he had run all the way up the hill to the palace. He stared fearfully at the king.

"He's going to live," Isaiah said.

"But . . . I saw the sun . . . I thought . . ."

"It was Yahweh's sign to King Hezekiah that he will live."

"Oh, praise God!" Eliakim slumped onto the chair beside the bed and covered his face.

Suddenly Shebna thought of Prince Gedaliah. If Hezekiah lived, then this would be the second time that the prince had come close to inheriting the throne only to lose it again. He would not weep for joy as Eliakim did.

Shebna knew there must never be a third time. He would never support Gedaliah's claim to the throne again. As soon as King Hezekiah was well enough, Shebna would make certain that he married a suitable wife. The next king must be Hezekiah's son, not his brother.

Suddenly Hezekiah's eyes flickered open. They were filled with pain, but he was fully conscious and aware.

"Shebna . . . ?"

"Yes, Your Majesty?"

"Arrange a thank offering . . . at the Temple . . . three days." He smiled slightly, then closed his eyes again and fell asleep.

─◆─

Millions of stars filled the night sky as Jerusha sat alone in the vineyard. From the open window behind her, she heard her son's sleepy voice, along with Hilkiah's husky one, reciting prayers together.

Blessed are You, Yahweh, King of heaven and earth . . .

She hoped she would never have to go back to Jerusalem, back to a house filled with unbearable memories. She wanted to stay here in the country and raise her children far from the political intrigue of the palace.

The new king would launch a purge, Hilkiah had said. Eliakim might already be dead. As the horrible truth slowly took root in her heart, Jerusha felt a cry of grief swelling inside her. She forced it down, knowing she had to remain strong for her children.

She looked around at the peaceful countryside, trying to draw comfort in the familiar noises of the farm: the sound of hens clucking over their nests, of goats and sheep jostling for position in their pens, the slow clopping of a horse's hooves as its owner led it up the road to the stable for the night.

"Hear, O Israel! Yahweh is our God—Yahweh alone!" her son recited with Hilkiah.

The chirp of crickets and frogs blended with the voices in prayer and with the steady rhythm of a horse's hooves as it plodded up the road toward her. Then suddenly all the sounds disappeared again as the truth dug deeper into her heart. She would never see Eliakim again.

Jerusha didn't notice the horse's hooves drawing steadily louder, closer, as her grief overflowed. When they suddenly stopped in front of her, she looked up. Eliakim stood with the reins in his hand, smiling at her. She stumbled across the grass and into his arms.

"I would have been here sooner," he said, "but unlike our daughter, I never could stay on a horse."

9

The sun hadn't yet risen when Hezekiah awoke on the third day. He was terribly weak, but his fever had broken, and his mind felt as clear as the morning sky after the wind has chased away the rain. He called for his servants, ordering them to light all the lamps in his bedchamber. Then he struggled to sit up.

"Shall I help you, Your Majesty?" his valet asked.

"No. I want to do it myself. I'm tired of being sick. I want to be well again." His joints and muscles ached, but it was a good pain, a healing pain, as if the life flowed back into his body with force.

All his servants hurried to wait on him, and one of them began massaging balm made with aloe into the fresh pink skin on the palms of his hands. It smelled familiar, and he vaguely recalled his servants doing this several times a day while he was delirious. He was grateful that they had, even though it had hurt him at the time, for although his skin felt tight when he opened his palms wide, the burns had healed well. He would regain the full use of his hands.

They brought him his breakfast when the massage ended, and he fed himself for the first time since the fire. He felt ravenously hungry and asked for second helpings of bread with date honey.

"Bring me some parchment and something to write with," he said after the servants cleared away the food. Words of praise to Yahweh raced through his mind, along with vivid images of his ordeal, and he wanted to get them down in writing before they vanished. He held the quill stiffly; his writing looked cramped and sloppy, but he composed his psalm quickly as if trying to capture water from an overflowing spring.

First he wrote of his fear of death and the anguish he'd suffered when he thought God had abandoned him. Eliakim had told him that difficult experiences deepen our relationship with God, and Hezekiah knew it was true.

"Lord, by such things men live. . . . Surely it was for my benefit that I suffered such anguish."

Then came words of praise and thanksgiving. Hezekiah wanted to write a magnificent hymn to God, thanking Him for saving his life once again. But even as he scribbled the words, they seemed inadequate. He envied King David—his soaring songs of thanksgiving seemed to praise God so much better than his own.

When he finished, Hezekiah laid the page aside and slowly swung his legs over the side of the bed, groping for the floor. He flexed his right foot and felt the painful tightness in the new skin that had begun to grow back, replacing his burned flesh. The muscles of his legs trembled, and he wasn't convinced they would hold his weight. But this was the morning of the third day, and, as Isaiah had promised, Hezekiah would worship in Yahweh's Temple. He stood for the first time in days, leaning against the bed for support. His servants helped him dress. He was about to take his first step when Isaiah walked through the door.

"Good morning, Your Majesty. May I join you in worship?" He smiled his familiar, fleeting half-smile and offered his arm for Hezekiah to lean on.

Hezekiah took a step, then another and another. He felt dizzy, weightless, and grateful for Isaiah's rocklike strength. He leaned on him heavily. Hezekiah took two more steps, leaving his bedchamber for the first time in more than two weeks, and entered his sitting room. Shebna bolted to his feet in surprise.

"You are up!"

"Yes, Shebna, and I'm going to the Temple."

Hezekiah's valet followed them from the bedroom, carrying the parchment with the psalm he'd written. "What about this, Your Majesty?"

Hezekiah looked at it a moment, then rolled it up and handed it to Isaiah. "Keep this for me, Rabbi."

The shofar sounded from the Temple wall above them. "We'd better start walking," Hezekiah said. "I don't want to be late."

Hezekiah left the palace and hobbled up the royal walkway to the Temple, gradually gaining his balance after lying in bed for so long. He relied on Isaiah less and less as he climbed stiffly up the hill. His leg tugged painfully with each step he took, but at least the pain remained in his leg instead of spreading through his body. The new skin seemed too tightly stretched, forcing him to favor his left leg. He would probably walk with a limp for the rest of his life. Like his ancestor Jacob, who walked with a limp, Hezekiah had also wrestled with God.

As he hobbled through the gate and took his place on the royal dais, an immense cheer erupted from the crowd in the courtyard. The deafening sound continued for several minutes, and Hezekiah thought it could be heard for miles around.

"Praise the Lord," he murmured aloud, unashamed as tears rolled silently down his face. "The grave cannot praise You, O God. Only the living can praise You, as I am doing today. And I will sing Your praise in the Temple of Yahweh every day of my life!"

⬥

Isaiah sat at the table in his tiny one-room home and reread the words of the king's psalm. Like their ancestor King David, Hezekiah also had a gift for writing songs of praise to God. Isaiah dipped his pen into the pot of ink and wrote across the top of the parchment, *A writing of Hezekiah king of Judah after his illness and recovery:*

> *I said, "In the prime of my life*
> > *must I go through the gates of death*
> > *and be robbed of the rest of my years?"*
> *I said, "I will not again see the LORD,*
> > *the LORD, in the land of the living;*
> *no longer will I look on mankind,*
> > *or be with those who now dwell in this world.*
> *Like a shepherd's tent my house*
> > *has been pulled down and taken from me.*
> *Like a weaver I have rolled up my life,*
> > *and he has cut me off from the loom;*
> > *day and night you made an end of me.*
> *I waited patiently till dawn,*
> > *but like a lion he broke all my bones;*
> > *day and night you made an end of me.*
> *I cried like a swift or thrush,*
> > *I moaned like a mourning dove.*
> *My eyes grew weak as I looked to the heavens.*
> > *I am troubled; O Lord, come to my aid!"*
> *But what can I say?*
> *He has spoken to me, and he himself has done this.*
> *I will walk humbly all my years*
> > *because of this anguish of my soul.*

Lord, by such things men live;
and my spirit finds life in them too.
You restored me to health
and let me live.
Surely it was for my benefit
that I suffered such anguish.
In your love you kept me
from the pit of destruction;
you have put all my sins
behind your back.
For the grave cannot praise you,
death cannot sing your praise;
those who go down to the pit
cannot hope for your faithfulness.
The living, the living—they praise you,
as I am doing today;
fathers tell their children
about your faithfulness.

The LORD will save me,
and we will sing with stringed instruments
all the days of our lives
in the temple of the LORD.

When he had finished, Isaiah rolled the parchment carefully and placed it in the earthenware storage jar with his other scrolls. They contained all the precious words Yahweh had spoken to him over the years and the visions he had seen during the reigns of Uzziah, Jotham, Ahaz, and now King Hezekiah.

Part

2

But Hezekiah's heart was proud and he did not respond to the kindness shown him; therefore the LORD's wrath was on him and on Judah and Jerusalem.

—2 Chron. 32:25

10

King Merodach-Baladan reached the top of the ziggurat first and paused in front of the Temple of Bel to gaze at the city below. Babylon's turquoise canals and broad streets fanned out like a net, snaring mud-brick houses and green patches of park land in their web. Beyond the city's broad protective walls, emerald fields and marshes stretched toward the horizon, nourished by the sluggish Euphrates River as it snaked across the plain. Everything looked remarkably clean and orderly from this height, and Merodach-Baladan loved order.

It was early in the day, and a holiday at that, so the king detected little movement in the quiet streets below. The few people he saw appeared small and vulnerable from this height, like ants he could easily crush beneath his thumb. He liked the lofty view and the feeling it gave him of being above all other men, far removed and supreme.

Merodach-Baladan was in his mid-40s; his wavy black hair and classical Babylonian features didn't stand out in a crowd unless he was clothed in the rich trappings of royalty. But his shrewd political mind sprinted far ahead of the average man's, just as his lean, limber body had outraced his advisers to the top of the monument.

Gradually the other four members of his royal council straggled up the ziggurat's steep stairs behind him, panting and gasping from exertion. They flopped onto the stone benches arranged in a semicircle outside the temple. Even the king's military commander, who trained every day in order to remain fit, had difficulty recovering his breath. Merodach-Baladan smiled to himself as he listened to them, savoring the fact that he'd reached the summit first, without becoming short-winded.

"Take a good look, gentlemen," he said, gesturing to the miniature city below. "You're gazing at the birthplace of the 'New Babylonian Empire.' In fact, you're seated within her very womb, watching as she's being formed." He studied their sweating faces as they surveyed the view, then snapped his fingers to draw their attention back to himself.

"We're closer to that miraculous day of birth now than when we stood here last New Year's Day. And much closer than three years ago when I first conceived my New Babylonian Empire. Soon we will slay the Assyrian beast for good, and Babylon will rise to take her predestined place."

"May almighty Bel, king of all gods, make it so!" the secretary of state shouted, leaping to his feet. He was a handsome, ambitious man with a tongue as smooth as his clean-shaven face. Merodach-Baladan enjoyed the secretary's flattery and admired his zeal, but he kept the man close to his side, wary of what such charm might accomplish behind his back.

"And this time next year," the emperor continued, "when we climb once again to Bel's sanctuary to seek his blessings for a new year, we will be ready to begin the first stage of my master plan—attacking the weakened beast's flank and bringing Assyria to her knees at last."

"May the all-powerful Bel make it so!" the secretary declared again, and the other three men murmured in agreement.

"Civilization, gentlemen! That's what the New Babylonian Empire will offer the world. Look at the order and beauty we have already accomplished here." The king swept his hand in an arc, indicating the city below. "What nation wouldn't gladly embrace such splendor after years of Assyrian brutality? Marching, conquering, oppressing. That's all the Assyrians know. But now their empire is swiftly coming to an end, and Babylon will rise to take Assyria's place with the glory and splendor of Shamash, god of the sun."

The king's military adviser raised his fist and shook it defiantly. "Death to the Assyrians! May they find no rest in the netherworld!"

"Hear! Hear!" the others echoed. The king gave them time to shout and cheer before continuing.

"For the next stage of my master plan, I'll need time as my ally." He pointed to the clock tower in the plaza at the base of the ziggurat. "The new Babylon isn't quite ready to withstand an Assyrian assault, but if we can keep the beast at bay for another year—better yet, two years—we can use the time to make ourselves ready.

"In the meantime, we must continue to fan the flames of rebellion throughout the Assyrian empire." He moved his hands back and forth as if pumping a bellows. "Our enemy has spread across too many fronts. They will never be able to quench a widespread rebellion. Look here . . ." He snapped his fingers again, and the prime minister hurried to produce a map, unrolling it awkwardly. The stiff parchment scraped against the stone as he struggled to spread it out on the bench and to prevent the curling ends from rolling up again.

"Here—let me help," the commander said, pinning down two corners of the map. When it finally lay flat, the king proceeded.

"Emperor Sargon's sudden death wounded Assyria, and she's lying low, licking her wounds as Sargon's son struggles for control. That's the time to destroy a beast, when it's injured and weak."

"But, Your Majesty," the prime minister said, "that's also the time when a beast will fight viciously—when it's cornered and wounded."

"You're always a pessimist," the military commander said. "Why do you have to look for problems instead of solving them?"

"We shall see," Merodach-Baladan said. "We'll see how much fight Sennacherib, son of Sargon, has left in him, especially when the nations he thought were his victims turn on him and become his foes."

The king spread his broad hands over the map, slowly moving them from east to west, claiming the nations beneath them. "Elam will join with us . . . Moab . . . and Edom too. The Philistines have rebelled before at Ashdod and will undoubtedly rally again. But we need Egypt on our side, and these nations in the middle. Syria. Israel. Judah. Is there a spark of nationalism left in any of them that we can fan into rebellion?"

The prime minister shook his head gloomily. "Syria and Israel are shattered. Their populations were deported and have disappeared into the empire."

"And this one?" the king asked, looking down at the map. "Judah?"

"Now there lies somewhat of a mystery, Your Majesty," the secretary of the treasury said, speaking for the first time. He was the youngest of the five men, newly appointed to office. His family controlled a vast international trading empire, and his experience and accounting skills were exceptional for a man his age.

"I enjoy solving mysteries," the king said. "Proceed."

"Well, Your Majesty, for centuries Judah has been a poor half-sister to Israel, living in her shadow. Yet within the last few years, Judah's trade has suddenly blossomed. She's become a major player in regional commerce. Her economy is thriving while many of the nations around her are suffering because of the heavy Assyrian tribute."

"Why is that?" the king interrupted. "Why does Judah thrive while the rest of us suffer?"

"Well, she used to be an Assyrian vassal too, but the current king stopped paying tribute a dozen years ago. Now she's prospering."

"How did he get away with that?" the prime minister asked. "Why didn't Sargon flatten him as he flattened all the other nations who rebelled?"

The treasurer shrugged. "I have no idea. That's the mystery."

"Maybe it's because his capitol sits protected on a steep mountain ridge," the commander said. "Jerusalem isn't as accessible as Babylon." He gestured to the broad, flat plains and grimaced.

"Does Judah have any allies?" the king asked. The advisers looked at each other, but no one seemed to know. "Well, who did they support in the Ashdod rebellion a few years back?" he asked impatiently.

The commander shook his head. "I think they stayed neutral, Your Majesty. I don't think they were involved at all."

"Why not?" The king's voice rose to a shout. "What is their king—a hermit? A coward?"

"He's much too active in international trade to be a hermit," the treasurer said.

"And he's not a coward, or he'd be paying tribute like the rest of us," the commander said.

"What's this king's name?" There was a long pause.

"King . . . Hezi- . . . Hezekiah!" the secretary of state said triumphantly. He looked enormously pleased with himself for being the first to recall the obscure king's name.

"King Hezekiah," Merodach-Baladan repeated. As he said the strange name aloud, he began formulating a plan that excited him. He located the tiny nation on the map and planted his index finger on it as if to hold it in place, under his control, while he mused out loud.

"Babylon is Assyria's number-one enemy. We always have been. But suppose we convinced Assyria that they had another enemy to fear. Suppose Judah became the instigator of a revolution instead of us. If we could trick King Hezekiah into stirring up trouble, he could distract Assyria and buy us the time we need."

"How are we going to do that?" the prime minister asked. "He didn't join the last rebellion."

"We'll appeal to his pride. He isn't *joining* a rebellion this time—he's *leading* one. Babylon will seek his friendship on behalf of all the weaker, tribute-paying nations. We'll send him gifts and ask how he's managed to rebel so successfully, then beg him to help his suffering neighbors do the same."

"A brilliant strategy, Your Majesty," the secretary of state said, smiling broadly. "Cunning and brilliant."

The prime minister frowned. "It won't be an easy task to flatter an unknown king."

"Then we'll have to find out more about him, won't we?" Merodach-Baladan said.

The young treasurer suddenly leaped to his feet. "Wait a minute, Your Majesty! I have the answer! My brother sends caravans along those western trade routes. He's the one who told me how prosperous Judah has become in the last few years. He traveled to Jerusalem last month and told me a long, elaborate story about how Judah's king was deathly ill and nearly died—"

"King Hezekiah was ill?"

"Yes. My brother said the entire city shut down for half a day so everyone could pray to the gods to heal him. He swears that not only was this king miraculously healed, but the gods gave him a sign of their divine favor—the sun moved backward across the sky!"

"The sun? That's preposterous."

"I know, Your Majesty. But my brother was there, and he swears he saw it. He said it was late in the afternoon and the shadows were growing long—then all of a sudden it was as bright as noonday and just as hot. And yet there wasn't a cloud in the sky. The effect only lasted a few moments; then it was afternoon again. The whole city saw it, and the people started going crazy, wondering what the omen meant. He wanted me to check with your astrologers and see if they had observed it."

"And had they?"

The treasurer shrugged sheepishly. "I never asked them. I didn't want to sound like a fool. I would have dismissed the story altogether, except that my brother isn't usually superstitious or quick to believe in omens. But he's convinced he saw it. And so is everyone else in Jerusalem."

"It's too ridiculous," the prime minister said. "We can't use something so—"

"Shut up," the king said. "I don't care if it's true or not. The treasurer's right. If the Judeans believe it happened, then this miracle is the excuse we're looking for. Babylon's interest in heavenly signs is famous throughout the world. And what if our astrologers had seen it? Wouldn't it be natural for us to pay homage to the man who caused it? Why wouldn't we send gifts and request the friendship of such a wondrous king?"

"I like it!" the secretary of state said. "Do you think he'll fall for it?"

"You have the smoothest tongue in all of Babylon," the king said. "It will be your job to make sure he does. You'll head up the delegation as my royal ambassador. But be careful how you approach him. Remember—we're going as astrologers and diplomats. He mustn't suspect our political motives. He must be the one to stir up trouble by proposing an alliance." He turned to the treasurer. "I want you to accompany him as deputy ambassador. Check out this king's resources and wealth."

"Your Majesty, I'd like to go along as an envoy," the army commander said. "I want to see what kind of military power he has that gives him the guts to rebel against Assyria."

"Good idea. But go in civilian clothes, as an attaché. Make sure this king perceives us as friends and not as a threat. Assign some of your best scouts to pose as your servants, but have them take careful note of everything Hezekiah allows you to see—his fortifications, his armories, his personnel. Because when Assyria finally collapses after expending all her energy on a western rebellion, I may want to add Judah to my New Babylonian Empire—if there's anything left of it."

Merodach-Baladan scooped up the map, and it rolled into a scroll by itself as soon as the two men let go of it. "That's enough business for one day." He gestured for his advisers to follow him into the temple. "Gentlemen, let's celebrate the New Year with the gods. May they bring about the final downfall of Assyria and, with the help of King Hezekiah, the birth of the New Babylonian Empire!"

11

Hezekiah heard about the mysterious Babylonian envoys and their caravan long before they knelt in front of him in the throne room. Messengers had raced to Jerusalem with news of their arrival as soon as the Babylonians crossed the border into Judean territory. By the time the procession passed through Jerusalem's gates, the entire city had come to a standstill as people left work to gaze at the peculiar strangers.

The three diplomats, adorned with golden bracelets and earrings, wore magnificent fur-trimmed robes and rode in brightly painted chariots. Even their horses' bridles were trimmed in purple and silver. Dozens of servants led the heavily laden caravan of camels. But the two men riding in the last chariot attracted the most attention; they wore the embroidered blue robes and strange conical caps of Babylonian astrologers.

Late in the afternoon Hezekiah sat on his throne awaiting their arrival. He was dressed in his finest robe and the heavy, ornate crown of Judah.

"I'm intrigued, Shebna. I can't imagine why these Babylonians would make the long journey to our nation."

"Nor can I, Your Majesty. We will have to wait and see."

But waiting made Hezekiah restless. Dozens of nobles and court officials crammed into the throne room to watch the spectacle, and his servants glistened with sweat as they fanned palm branches to cool the air. At last the chamberlain announced the Babylonians' arrival.

The ambassador entered first, a handsome, clean-shaven man in his early 50s. His two assistants and the two Babylonian astrologers trailed behind him as he approached Hezekiah's throne. They lowered their eyes in respect, as if unworthy to gaze at him, then fell prostrate at his feet, waiting for him to extend his scepter.

"You may rise."

"Thank you, most gracious Majesty," they murmured. The ambassador rose to his feet, but the other men remained on their knees before him.

"Your honorable Majesty, King Hezekiah of Judah, we thank you for receiving our delegation. I am Nebo-Polassar, the king's ambassador. We bring you a message from King Merodach-Baladan of Babylon and also these gifts to honor you."

The ambassador motioned to his waiting servants, who entered the throne room with arms laden. More than a dozen men piled goods at Hezekiah's feet, then bowed prostrate. Hezekiah stared in amazement, unwilling to believe his eyes. Had his tiny nation gained such worldwide fame that Babylon, one of the three great world powers, would send representatives to bow before him? Usually they paid no attention to his nation except as a possible vassal state or tribute-payer. Now Hezekiah knew beyond a doubt just how far he had brought his nation in the dozen years he had reigned.

"You may state your petition," he said, working hard to conceal his amazement.

"My king asks for nothing except your friendship, Your Majesty. We've come because of the miraculous sign that occurred in your land and to present you with these gifts as a very small token of our esteem."

The ambassador signaled his servants again, and they rose to open their bundles, spreading the contents across the carpet in front of Hezekiah. They unwrapped dozens of golden cups and bowls, stacks of embroidered cloth and garments trimmed in jewels and fur, ivory chests and alabaster flasks filled with myrrh, calamus, nard, saffron, and other spices. The exotic fragrances filled the throne room as the servants opened each container for him to glimpse.

"This is only a small portion of the tribute we offer you, Your Majesty. King Merodach-Baladan also sent a gift made especially for you." Two more servants entered, carrying a wooden crate suspended between poles. The other servants quickly cleared a space, and they set it on the floor at Hezekiah's feet, then bowed low. "Open it," the ambassador said.

They pried the lid off and drew out a dazzling golden box, two feet by three feet square. The lid and all four sides were covered with elaborate engravings. It took two servants to lift it out of the crate, and when they opened it Hezekiah saw why. It contained dozens of bars of pure gold. He thought of all the wealth the Assyrian monarch had once forced his nation to send, and he gazed at this gift, stunned.

"Your Majesty, as our royal astrologer will explain, the pictures on this box tell your amazing story." The ambassador turned to one of the astrologers kneeling before Hezekiah, and the man touched his forehead to the floor three times in reverence.

"Oh, most worthy king!" he murmured. "All the stars foretold your death. The god Nebo, scribe and herald of the gods, had written your name beside the death star. Then reports arrived in our nation that you journeyed close to the gates of death. But suddenly an even greater sign appeared in the heavens. Lord Shamash, god of the sun and of justice, saw the injustice of your untimely death and rolled backward across the sky, erasing your name with his shadow." The astrologer touched his forehead to the floor again and said, "We pay you honor, O Blessed One!"

The blasphemous box gave Hezekiah a start, as if the Babylonians had dashed cold water in his face. He stared uncomfortably at the images of foreign idols, knowing he should never accept such a gift. Yahweh's Law forbade making images in the form of anything in heaven or on earth. Of course, their Gentile king didn't know Yahweh's Law; God had entrusted it to His chosen people. Yet if he refused the gift, Hezekiah would have to reject Babylon's offer of friendship as well.

"Please convey my compliments to your craftsmen," he finally said. "Tell them their work is extraordinary."

"King Hezekiah, favored one of Lord Shamash," the ambassador said, "you have commanded the blessing of the gods, and our King Merodach-Baladan seeks to pay you homage and to humbly request your friendship."

The entire delegation bowed, pressing their foreheads to the floor once again. The throne room fell silent. Hezekiah glanced briefly at Shebna and Eliakim, seated on either side of him. The Egyptian's mouth hung open slightly, and his dark eyes couldn't hide his astonishment. But Eliakim stared at the floor, as if trying to avert his eyes from the golden box.

Hezekiah looked down at the chest filled with gold. Less than 30 years ago, his father had stripped every last ounce of gold from Judah's treasuries to pay tribute to Assyria. Now, after reigning only a dozen years, Hezekiah was receiving tribute from other nations! But the respect and honor the king of Babylon offered amazed him even more than the small fortune in gold. What a triumph!

Once again, Hezekiah extended his scepter. He had made his decision. "You may rise," he said. "Babylon is an ancient and honored land. Tell King Merodach-Baladan that I thank him for his generous gifts and I accept his offer. I am pleased to grasp his hand in friendship."

A spontaneous cheer arose from the Judean nobles crowded along the rear walls of the throne room. This momentous occasion called for a celebration.

"And now, Ambassador, please allow me to extend my hospitality to you and the members of your delegation. My palace administrator will host a state dinner tonight in your honor, and you will be my guests here in the palace for as long as you care to stay."

"Thank you, Your Majesty," the ambassador said, bowing. "We accept, although we're not worthy to stay under your roof."

"My servants will show you to your rooms now. Please let Shebna know if you need anything else."

The ambassador bowed and moved toward the door, then suddenly turned back. "If I may be so bold, Your Majesty, I would like to ask one small favor. King Merodach-Baladan wants to know which one of Judah's gods granted your miraculous healing so that he can offer a sacrifice to that deity."

A feeling of deep uneasiness crept over Hezekiah again at this reminder of the Babylonians' idolatry. "My nation acknowledges and worships one God, not many. It will be time for the regular evening sacrifice at Yahweh's Temple very shortly. If you wish, you may accompany my palace administrator to the Court of the Gentiles. He will explain the laws regarding sacrifices to you."

The Babylonian entourage had scarcely left the throne room when Shebna leaped from his seat in excitement. "Do you realize what an extraordinary opportunity this is, Your Majesty? They say they are asking only for your friendship, but with a little persuasion on our part it should be very easy to convince them to sign a formal treaty with us!"

"They're idol worshipers," Eliakim said, pointing to the golden box. "How can we sign an alliance with pagans?"

Shebna waved him away irritably. "What difference does their religion make? We are not obligated to worship their gods. We want their military support."

"We don't need their military support," Eliakim said. "We can trust Yahweh—"

"Maybe we do not need it at the moment, but if the new Assyrian emperor proves to be weaker than his father, then now would be the ideal time to take the offensive. With strong allies backing us, we could win back some of the farmland of the Jordan Valley."

Hezekiah sat back and listened in silence to the two men. He had grown used to their incessant arguing a long time ago and had even learned to appreciate it. They represented the two sides of himself: Shebna, the bold, analytical, problem-solving side; Eliakim, the more cautious side that weighed each decision according to Yahweh's Law. Giving them freedom to argue and discuss issues helped Hezekiah reach balanced, thoughtful decisions.

"Are you forgetting that Sennacherib commanded his father's military forces?" Eliakim said. "I don't think he'll hesitate to send his army into battle at the slightest hint of rebellion."

"Well, we were lucky the last time the Assyrians marched westward—"

"It wasn't luck—it was God!"

"If all the vassal nations united and rebelled at once, we could defeat the Assyrians."

"Never! Besides—we're not a vassal nation."

"All the more reason to jump into the fight," Shebna said. "We could lead the other nations. We have a trained military, fortified cities, a thriving economy. If we went to war, we could expand our territory and take back Galilee, maybe all of Israel."

"How can we take back Israel? It's an Assyrian province! You saw how swiftly the Assyrians quenched the Philistine rebellion a few years ago. Rabbi Isaiah warned us to stay neutral, and it was good advice. We need to remain neutral now too."

"This is different."

"No, Shebna. It's exactly the same."

"Only cowards stay neutral, cowering behind the walls of their fortresses. Now is the time to step forward as a leader, Your Majesty. Do you see all of this?" Shebna gestured to the gifts spread out on the carpet. "This proves that you have risen to a position of leadership and respect among the other nations. Babylon is paying you homage! We must take advantage of this opportunity, or we may never get another chance like it. We cannot stay neutral forever. We must take our rightful place as leader among the nations."

"No. It's too dangerous to sign a treaty with Babylon. Assyria is far from dead. An alliance with Babylon is a declaration of war against Assyria. Don't risk it!"

"You are wrong, Eliakim. The Assyrian Empire is finished. They have not gone to war in several years. Besides, what if our neighboring nations successfully rebel against Assyria? If we refuse their friendship now, what will stop them from attacking us once they gain their freedom? We need to be allied with our neighbors—"

"Our neighbors are too weak to help themselves, let alone help *us!* Listen—"

"Enough." Hezekiah held up his hand for silence. He had heard both sides, and now he needed to make a decision. He leaned back on his throne, stroking his beard. "I don't like the idea of barricading ourselves behind Jerusalem's walls while the nations around us carve up the world among themselves. If the Assyrian Empire is really crumbling, then I want my fair share of the spoils. I've already rebelled against Assyria by not sending tribute all these years, so I'm already allied to any other nation that rebels. Shebna is right. I want to be part of the rebellion, not a neutral nation for the victors to claim as spoil. Do you think we can persuade the Babylonian ambassador to sign a treaty of alliance with us?"

"They are already honoring you and paying tribute to you," Shebna said. "It should not be difficult to convince them to sign a formal agreement."

"Good." Hezekiah lifted the heavy crown off his head and studied its glittering stones for a moment. "Let's show them everything we have—our fortifications, our treasuries, the military garrisons. Let's convince them that we're a strong ally, worth having on their side . . . What's wrong, Eliakim? Why are you shaking your head?"

"If you show them your strengths you're also revealing your weaknesses. Besides, I don't think we should—"

"How can it hurt to take them on a tour of our fortifications?" Shebna interrupted. "These men are diplomats and astrologers, not spies. They are our guests. They will hardly be taking notes."

"I agree," Hezekiah said. "It can't hurt. If they sign a treaty with us, it will strengthen our nation. We won't have to rebel against Assyria alone."

Shebna's eyes danced with excitement. "Your Majesty, it has long been my dream to forge an alliance of nations with you as the leader. Working together, this alliance could end the Assyrian threat for good."

Hezekiah looked at the engraved box full of gold and thought of the arsenal he could purchase with so much wealth. Shebna was right—this alliance with Babylon would be only the beginning. It could ensure their independence from Assyria forever. Maybe Yahweh had provided this opportunity in order for Judah to emerge as a leader among nations. Hezekiah felt poised on the brink of greatness and power.

"Shebna, draft a proposal for a treaty of alliance with Babylon. We must convince them to sign it before they leave. And Eliakim, prepare an itinerary for our guests. Tomorrow I want you to give them a tour of our resources."

Eliakim didn't try to hide his distress. "How much do you want me to show them, Your Majesty?"

His reluctance irritated Hezekiah. He wanted bold, decisive men beside him, not overly cautious and conservative ones. This opportunity may never come again. "Show them everything! Your fortifications and defenses, the armory, my treasury. And show them your storehouses and the water tunnel too. That should impress them." Eliakim nodded grimly. "But before you get started on that, I want you to go up to the Temple and talk to the high priest. Explain about our guests, and tell him he must preside over the evening sacrifice tonight. Tell him I want all the musicians to take part and as many priests as he can round up. Do it right away."

"Yes, Your Majesty." Eliakim skirted around the golden box and hurried from the throne room.

◆

As King Hezekiah stood on the royal dais at the Temple a short time later, he tried to watch the ceremony through his visitors' eyes and to imagine what they would report to their king. He had heard descriptions of the immense Babylonian ziggurats that climbed to the heavens, and he knew that Yahweh's Temple couldn't compare with one of those. Nevertheless, the view from the top of God's holy hill would take their breath away. Rolling green mountains embraced the city on all sides, and on a clear evening like tonight they might even glimpse the Dead Sea and the Judean wilderness many miles to the east. The setting sun glittered off the Temple's golden roof, and everything seemed to sparkle and shine like new—the golden doors to the holy place, the bronze pillars Jakin and Boaz, the shimmering water in the brazen laver, the priests' silver trumpets. Even the priests' garments looked whiter than Hezekiah had ever seen them, and the precious stones in the high priest's ephod gleamed impressively. As he had requested, a full antiphonal choir of Levite singers and musicians filled the packed courtyards with magnificent praise.

Hezekiah preferred the Temple's clean lines and simple, unadorned beauty to the gaudy embellishments of idolatry. He imagined Shebna explaining its symbolism to his guests, and he beamed with pride. He remembered what the Temple had looked like when he inherited the nation from Ahaz—the gold pried off the doors, the bronze pillars and laver stripped and lopsided, the altar shoved askew to make room for idolatry—and he felt tremendous satisfaction at all he had accomplished. He'd restored Yahweh's Temple to its original splendor—perhaps he'd made it even more magnificent than in Solomon's day—and as Hezekiah looked around, it seemed every bit as impressive as a mud-brick Babylonian ziggurat.

Later that night he recalled his many accomplishments once again as he sat down to a lavish dinner with his guests. Torches in the palace banquet room blazed with light, and the sound of lively music filled the air along with the smell of rich food and roasting meat. He remembered his coronation banquet and felt satisfied, for now his nation prospered, and Hezekiah could eat off the fat of the land, not the backs of his people.

"I must tell you, Your Majesty," the ambassador said, leaning close, "the offering to your gods—pardon me, your *God*—was absolutely magnificent! As was your Temple!"

"Thank you. Did Shebna tell you that my ancestors built it more than 300 years ago?"

"Yes, and it's the envy of many nations, I assure you. The talent and skill of your Temple musicians is also well known in Babylon, but truly the half hasn't been told! I would steal them away from you and transport the entire ensemble back to my own land if I could." He laughed heartily. "Shebna tells me that only the men from one tribe of your people may serve as priests."

"Yes, the tribe of Levi. The Temple musicians must also be descendants of Levi."

"I will never forget that magnificent music as long as I live! Such talent to be concentrated in one family line!"

Hezekiah beamed at the lavish praise. "In fact, ambassador, I'm related to the tribe of Levi myself," he said. "My father was a descendant of the royal house of David from the tribe of Judah, but my mother was from the tribe of Levi. Her father was a Levite musician."

Hezekiah knew his grandfather would be proud of him. Zechariah had predicted that one day he would accomplish great things as king of his nation, and these envoys from Babylon certainly confirmed that vision. A Judean king hadn't been honored like this since the golden age of Solomon.

"I can't help wondering, Your Majesty—is this marvelous wine we're drinking grown here in Judah?" the ambassador asked.

"Yes. Do you like it?"

"It's better than the wine served in our king's palace, isn't it?" He turned to his deputy, seated beside him.

"I have never had better!" the young man said.

The Babylonians' smooth faces glowed with pleasure, but they still looked strange to Hezekiah, seated among the thickly bearded men of his nation. For the first time he noticed how out-of-place Shebna looked, even though the Egyptian had been beardless for as long as Hezekiah had known him.

"If I could meet with your trade minister before I leave," the deputy said, "perhaps I could persuade him to export some of this wine to my country."

"My secretary of state will see to it," Hezekiah replied, nodding at Eliakim. The dinner was an enormous success, and Hezekiah felt proud of the excellent impression he had made on his visitors. But during a pause in the conversation he overheard the deputy ambassador talking to Eliakim.

"Those beautiful women seated over there—are they King Hezekiah's harem?" The deputy gestured to the women's table across the room, where the wives of Judah's leading officials and nobles were seated. Eliakim's wife and Shebna's concubine sat among them, but Hephzibah's place at the head of the table was vacant.

In an instant, a towering wall of grief collapsed on Hezekiah, leaving him stunned and broken. He had managed to push his loss aside during the excitement of the day, but it had taken only the slightest reminder of Hephzibah to bring his sorrow crashing down on him with an intensity that devastated him. When would it go away? When would he be able to forget what she had done?

"No, they are the women of the court, not the king's harem," Eliakim answered quietly. "Would you like some more wine, Lord Deputy?"

For a painful moment, Hezekiah imagined Hephzibah sitting in her place at the head of the women's table. Her extraordinary beauty and elegance would cause the Babylonians to stare, as most men did when they saw her. He remembered how he would catch Hephzibah's eye across the room and their deep love for each other would pass between them without words. She could convey so much with her smile, her eyes, the tilt of her head, and she would flirt with him shamelessly, tantalizing him until he could scarcely stand to be separated from her. Later, when he finally held her in his arms as he had longed to do all evening, they would laugh as they shared all the things they hadn't been able to say to each other.

But tonight Hephzibah's place was empty, and he felt a gnawing, helpless anger at her for destroying the love they had once shared, anger at having to return to his rooms alone, his arms aching and empty. He turned away from the women's table, promising himself not to look that way again.

"Tomorrow I want to take your delegation on a tour of my palace and armory," Hezekiah said to the ambassador. "I want to show you how I've fortified Jerusalem against the Assyrians."

The ambassador bowed his head deeply. "It would be a great honor, Your Majesty."

12

"Magnificent! Absolutely magnificent," the ambassador said. He stood inside the armory with Hezekiah, gazing at row after row of polished swords and shields and spears. The armory beneath the guard tower was cool and quiet after the heat of the day and the bustle of activity they had observed from the city wall above them.

"This is only a small portion of my weaponry," Hezekiah told him. "I've built many fortified cites throughout my nation, each one garrisoned and well-stocked with food supplies and weapons just like these."

"Most impressive! Jerusalem is quite a fortress, Your Majesty. No wonder you alone of all the nations have dared to shake off Assyria's yoke. I bow to you."

Hezekiah exchanged glances with Shebna as the ambassador and his entourage of servants bowed to him once again. Excitement pulsed through him. He had seen the respect in the Babylonians' eyes as they had surveyed the thick double walls around the new city and listened to Eliakim explain how he had built it with rubble from the tunnel. He'd heard the Babylonians gasp when he led them inside the new storage buildings and they saw pyramids of jars bearing his seal, filled with grain, oil, and wine. They had been silently awestruck by his trea-sure-house beneath the palace and the stacks of pure gold, shining white silver, and precious stones that he'd accumulated, filling the rooms that he'd inherited empty. The tour had reminded Hezekiah once again of all that he'd accomplished since his father's death and of how he'd brought his nation from the edge of poverty to renewed prosperity.

"Your Majesty, you are a magnificent example to all the nations, the first king to rebel successfully. The omen we saw in the sky did more than announce your healing. It confirmed your leadership as one who is favored by the gods. Our king longs to gain his freedom from Assyria as you have done. Perhaps someday you might help us, but in the meantime we look to you with honor and respect."

Hezekiah saw the opportunity he had waited for all morning. He casually folded his arms across his chest, holding back his mounting excitement. "Do you have the authority to speak for King Merodach-Baladan?" he asked.

"In most matters, yes."

"Then let me ask you this, Ambassador—how badly would your king like his freedom? Badly enough to sign a treaty with his neighboring nations and risk a rebellion?"

Nebo-Polassar appeared worried as he considered the question for a moment. "We would dare to take such a risk only if a stronger nation such as yours were to lead that rebellion."

Hezekiah glanced at Shebna. "Then if I assumed leadership and proposed a treaty, would you be willing to sign it on behalf of King Merodach-Baladan and Babylon?"

The ambassador's eyes grew wide with surprise. "You would be willing to accept us as your allies, Your Majesty?"

"Yes, I would."

"Then we would be honored to sign your treaty!"

Hezekiah wanted to shout in triumph, but he held back. "Good. Let's go to my palace, and you and Shebna can negotiate the details."

⬥

Hezekiah stared at the Babylonian seal on the treaty he held in his hands. "You did it, Shebna!" he said, thumping him on the back. "This is unbelievable!"

"And it is only the beginning. As head of the alliance, you will soon take your place as a world leader."

"When I remember the mess I inherited—well, I never dreamed this day would come."

"None of your forefathers since King Solomon has signed a treaty of alliance with a great world power like Babylon. And you signed as equals. You will owe Babylon no tribute."

"Unbelievable! Listen, I'm too excited to sit still! I'm dismissing court for the day so we can celebrate this—" A shout by the throne room door interrupted him. Suddenly Isaiah pushed past the chamberlain and strode into the room unannounced. Shebna leaped to his feet.

"Just a minute. You do not have permission to—"

"What did those men say? Where did they come from?" Isaiah cried.

Shebna planted his hands on the prophet's chest, pushing him backward toward the door. "You cannot barge in here asking questions. Get out!"

Isaiah's face displayed a mixture of bewilderment and fear, and it unnerved Hezekiah. "Shebna, wait. Let him come in. We have no reason to hide the truth from him. The men came from a distant land, Rabbi, from Babylon."

Isaiah moaned as if in deep pain. All the excitement that had crackled through the throne room a moment ago suddenly vanished. Isaiah looked up at Hezekiah, his face pinched with sorrow.

"What did they see in your palace?"

"They saw everything I own. The armory, the storehouses—I didn't hide any of my treasures from them."

Isaiah closed his eyes, a look of despair written across his face. But when he opened them again, they flashed with anger. "I have some very hard words for you, King Hezekiah. You might prefer to hear them in private."

"Who do you think you are, talking to the king like this?" Shebna dragged him toward the door again. "Get out!"

"Let him go, Shebna."

The prophet walked back toward the throne, his eyes never leaving Hezekiah's. "Early in your reign you asked me to speak Yahweh's Word, didn't you, Your Majesty?"

"Yes, I did, but—"

"Then *hear* the Word of God, King Hezekiah! Alone or in front of all these people!"

"Alone."

Isaiah's slim body trembled with the effort of restraining himself until the last of Hezekiah's officials had left the room. Then his words poured out with a fury that left Hezekiah shaken.

"You showed the Babylonians *your* treasures, *your* great riches, but did you acknowledge the Source of all your wealth? When you took them through your storerooms, were you praising God for all that He's given you, or was Yahweh far from your thoughts? Did you tell the Babylonians that Yahweh is your greatest treasure, not your gold and jewels, or did pride silence you?" The prophet's voice grew louder with each question.

Hezekiah cringed as he recognized the truth of Isaiah's accusations, but he tried to defend himself. "I didn't invite the Babylonians to come here. They heard about my illness, and they came—"

"They came to marvel at your miraculous healing! But did you give God the glory for your renewed health? Did you testify to His unearned mercy and grace in restoring your life? Or did you let their flattery convince you that you must be a very important man since God listened to your prayers?"

Hezekiah remembered how he had let the Babylonians bow to him, calling him "favored one," and he turned away from Isaiah's probing gaze and piercing words.

"'Pride goes before destruction, a haughty spirit before a fall!' Pride says, 'I did it! I accomplished everything by *myself!*' Pride leaves out God!"

Hezekiah groped behind him for his throne and sank down. He knew how many times in the past few days he had marveled at all that he had accomplished during his reign. At the Temple, during the banquet, in the armory and storehouses—he had forgotten God and never once acknowledged that He was the One who had brought renewed prosperity to his nation.

"*God* should have been glorified in the Babylonians' eyes, not *you*, King Hezekiah! What do you have that He didn't give to you? What do you own that wasn't a gift from Him?"

"Nothing, Rabbi."

"Yes, nothing. And God can take everything away from you again in an instant, leaving you just as you started. Would you like proof of that?"

"No."

"If you truly understood the holiness of God, you would have a proper attitude about yourself!" A shudder passed through the prophet's body, and Hezekiah lowered his head, gripping the armrests as Isaiah continued. "Hear the word of the LORD Almighty: The time will surely come when everything in your palace, and all that your fathers have stored up until this day, will be carried off to Babylon. Nothing will be left, says the LORD. And some of your descendants, your own flesh and blood who will be born to you, will be taken away, and they will become eunuchs in the palace of the king of Babylon."

Hezekiah never doubted that every word of Isaiah's sobering prophecy would come true. But two thoughts filled him with quiet hope—it would take place in the future, not during his reign; and God would give him descendants, sons of his own flesh and blood. "The word of the LORD you have spoken is good," he said quietly. "I've done wrong. I should pay for my sin." He looked up and saw the prophet brushing tears from his eyes.

"I don't think you realize what you've done," Isaiah said. "When the Babylonians come back someday . . . I don't think you understand what they'll do to this holy city . . . they'll . . ." He stopped, unable to finish, then turned and strode from the throne room.

13

Praise the LORD, O my soul;
  all my inmost being, praise his holy name.
Praise the LORD, O my soul,
  and forget not all his benefits.

Jerusha stood in the Women's Court, listening as the Levites sang her favorite psalm. She wished she was a Levite so she could sing glorious songs of praise to God; for when He had spared King Hezekiah's life, He had spared her husband's as well. Now she and Eliakim could go on as before, sharing their love, watching their children grow.

God had given them such beautiful children, so bright and strong. And now a new one would be born next spring. She touched her stomach, which already showed signs of the baby she carried, and thanked God again for all the happiness He had given her.

Who forgives all your sins
  and heals all your diseases,
who redeems your life from the pit
  and crowns you with love and compassion.

The crowd in front of her parted slightly, and Jerusha caught a glimpse of Eliakim standing beside the king on the royal platform. She couldn't help feeling proud of him, standing there so tall and handsome. That important man was her husband! How could she ever thank God for such a miracle?

Jerusha lost sight of Eliakim when someone stepped in front of her, but now she had a clear view of King Hezekiah. His illness had left him paler and thinner than before, and she saw a few streaks of gray threaded through his hair and beard. But even more noticeable than the limp in his step was the lingering sadness in his eyes and in the slant of his broad shoulders. It seemed as though his spirit had died even though his body had recovered.

Jerusha shook her head. It was obvious that the king still mourned for his wife. How could Hephzibah worship a pagan idol? How could she deceive her husband, knowing how hard he had fought against idolatry, how hard he had worked for reform? Without warning, Jerusha found herself thinking that Hephzibah deserved to die.

> The LORD is compassionate and gracious,
> slow to anger, abounding in love. . . .
> He does not treat us as our sins deserve
> or repay us according to our iniquities.

"O God—forgive me," Jerusha prayed. She knew she deserved to die as much as Hephzibah did, but God had forgiven her. She wondered if Hephzibah had found God's forgiveness. Eliakim had told her how the king had banished his wife to the villa with his former concubines. Hephzibah would live out her days there, childless and forsaken. Jerusha remembered her desolate existence as an Assyrian slave and knew the hopelessness and despair that would fill Hephzibah's life.

"May the Lord make his face to shine upon you . . . and give you peace."

As the high priest pronounced the benediction, a feeling of peace rested on Jerusha. God had forgiven her sins. But suppose she had never made peace with God. Suppose she still lived with the guilt of her sins, unrepentant, unforgiven, unloved. Jerusha shuddered.

"What's wrong, my child?"

Jerusha looked up as Hilkiah came to meet her.

"I was watching King Hezekiah during the sacrifice, Abba. He looks so lonely and depressed." She took Hilkiah's arm, and they started walking home together. "It made me think of Hephzibah, what she must be going through."

"And you knew exactly how she must feel," Hilkiah said, nodding in understanding.

"Do you think Hephzibah will ever find forgiveness as I did?"

Hilkiah stopped walking. He turned to face Jerusha, taking both her hands in his. "Our Heavenly Father never gives up on any of His children. But He needs people who are willing to be His voice and His hands to reach the lost."

"You don't mean me?"

"Hephzibah will never hear that God forgives her unless someone tells her."

"But I'm still learning about God myself, Abba. I can't talk to Hephzibah. I wouldn't know what to say."

"On the contrary, my dear girl. You would know exactly what to say. You've lived through the same hopelessness she's probably experiencing, and you know firsthand what God can do. Yahweh will give you the words, just as He gave you the words to say to Eliakim when he was suffering. God used you in my son's life. Maybe now He wants to use you in Hephzibah's life too."

"I don't even know if she'll talk to me."

"All Yahweh asks is that you try. 'God has turned your mourning into dancing. He's removed your sackcloth and clothed you with joy.' Why? So that 'your heart may sing to him and not be silent.' Give it careful thought, my child."

Jerusha thought of little else for the rest of the morning. She was afraid to go see Hephzibah, yet afraid not to go. Suppose she had refused to do what Hilkiah asked the last time? What would have happened to Eliakim? Was God really asking her to be His spokesperson to Hephzibah? She would learn the answer only if she went to see her.

That afternoon Jerusha settled the children for their naps, then left them with the servants and walked down the hill from her house. She easily found the king's villa near the new western gate; it was a magnificent house made of dressed stone and cedar, surrounded by a high wall.

"I'm here to see Lady Hephzibah," she told the gatekeeper.

He blinked in surprise. "Lady Hephzibah?"

"Yes. I'm the wife of Lord Eliakim, King Hezekiah's secretary." Her voice shook. She expected the man to slam the door in her face, but, much to her surprise, he motioned her inside.

"Follow me."

He led the way along a covered walkway past an open courtyard where bees buzzed among the flowers and doves called to each other in the treetops. It was a peaceful setting, but it seemed too quiet to Jerusha, as if something was missing. Then she remembered—none of the king's concubines had children. Without the sound of their laughter, the courtyard resembled a graveyard.

The gatekeeper stopped beside the last door along the walkway. He knocked, then opened it without waiting for an answer.

"Lady Hephzibah? Someone to see you." He motioned for Jerusha to enter, then closed the door behind her and left.

Hephzibah sat alone in front of a window, looking out on a narrow alley and the back wall of the villa. All the other windows of the dark, airless room were tightly shuttered. The tiny cubicle looked as though it had been built for a servant, not for a king's wife. A coarse sheet covered the narrow bed and a pallet of straw. No mirror or tapestries hung on the walls, no perfumes or lotions lined the tabletop—only a tray of untouched food. Jerusha wondered why the king would punish Hephzibah like this. She gazed at the starkly furnished rooms for a moment before she understood—Hephzibah had chosen it to punish herself. She had made the room into a prison cell in which to serve her life sentence.

The oppressive atmosphere of hopelessness and despair reminded Jerusha of the Assyrian camp, and she wanted to run out. What was she doing here? She didn't know what to say to Hephzibah. She had decided so abruptly to come that she hadn't had time to rehearse any words.

"Lady Hephzibah?" she said shakily. "I don't know if you remember me or not—my name is Jerusha? I'm Eliakim's wife, the king's secretary?" Her words seemed to come out all wrong and sounded like questions. Jerusha waited for a response, but Hephzibah didn't turn around.

Hephzibah had always been petite and delicate, but now she looked frail and haggard, as if she hadn't eaten in weeks. She wore a tunic of plain cloth with her hair unpinned as if she were in mourning. She stared sightlessly out the window. Jerusha thought of Marah, who was still a slave in the Assyrian camp. Except for the grace of God, Jerusha would still be held captive too, and she knew in that moment that she had to help Hephzibah find release. She took another step closer.

"We've met before, Lady Hephzibah, at several state banquets? Maybe you remember, we sat together at the women's table?" It seemed cruel to remind Hephzibah of the life she had lost and would never live again. Jerusha recalled the tender longing in the king's eyes as he would gaze at Hephzibah across the crowded banquet room, and she shuddered at the terrible consequences of Hephzibah's sin. *O God—please don't ever let me destroy Eliakim's love like this!* she prayed.

"It doesn't matter if you remember me or not, my lady. I just thought . . . I mean, I've come to . . ." Jerusha stopped. Why had she come? She felt so helpless. The room fell silent. Then, as Hephzibah slowly took her eyes from the window and turned around, Jerusha felt a jolt of shock. It was like looking at a corpse. Hephzibah resembled one of the lifeless severed heads Iddina used to bring home as trophies. Her beautiful features with her delicate nose and full lips had no life or color in them. Her eyes were past sorrow, past grief, as if forever washed dry of tears. In fact, she showed no emotion at all, and suddenly Jerusha wondered if there was even a woman inside this shell for God to reach. Jerusha groped for the edge of the cot and sat down.

"Why?" Hephzibah asked suddenly. Her low voice sounded dry and raspy, like an unused hinge. "Why did you come here?"

"Because you were once so kind to me when I was new at the palace. I wasn't the daughter of a nobleman like you, but you never made me feel inferior. You helped me learn everything and . . . and made me feel as if I belonged." Before she could stop them, tears filled Jerusha's eyes. Hephzibah had no hope. Her life would continue like this until the day she died. This punishment was more cruel than stoning.

"I—I'm sorry," Jerusha said, wiping her tears.

Hephzibah turned back to the window again. "If you came here to pity me, you can go now," she said. "I don't need your pity."

"No, that's not why I came. You were once a good friend to me when I needed one, and I want to be a friend to you."

Hephzibah didn't reply. She held her body so still she might have been carved from stone. Jerusha knew Hephzibah would force her body not to feel, knowing she would never be held or loved again. She wanted to gather Hephzibah into her arms and comfort her like a child, but Hephzibah would never accept consolation.

"No." Hephzibah said without turning around. It sounded more like the rattle of dead leaves than a word. "You won't ever come back."

"But I'd like to—"

Hephzibah turned swiftly, cutting off Jerusha's words. "Didn't they tell you what I did?"

"Eliakim told me about the fire. About how—about why it started."

"You can't even say the words, can you? I was worshiping an idol."

"Yes, I know." Jerusha reminded herself that she had also been a sinner and that she needed to extend God's love and forgiveness to Hephzibah. "But I still want to be your friend."

"Then I'm sure they didn't tell you all of it," Hephzibah said, looking past Jerusha. Suddenly Jerusha didn't want to know any secret that horrible. She wanted to run back to her home and her children and forget this tortured woman.

"You can tell me, Hephzibah," she forced herself to say. She sensed Hephzibah's inner struggle, needing a friend but also wanting to punish herself by driving away any chance of friendship. Jerusha steeled herself for some terrible revelation, but she wasn't prepared for the truth when Hephzibah finally blurted it out.

"I pledged my child—King Hezekiah's child—as a burnt sacrifice to Asherah. If I hadn't been caught, I would have burned our baby alive."

The memory came back to Jerusha with dreadful strength; the warmth of her newborn daughter nestled beside her and her horror and helplessness when Iddina snatched her baby from her arms. She had fought with desperate strength to stop him, to prevent him from burning her child alive, but she hadn't been able to save her. Jerusha couldn't comprehend why Hephzibah would willingly allow her child to die such a horrible death. She shuddered as her own wound ripped open afresh; then she began to cry.

"Now do you still want to be my friend?" Hephzibah asked.

The knowledge of what Hephzibah had done would always remind Jerusha of her own pain and loss, and she didn't want to be reminded. But Hephzibah was manipulating her emotions, trying to drive her away, and it angered Jerusha.

"The Assyrians raped me. I had their child, a little girl. But they took her away from me before she was even a day old, and they sacrificed her to their gods. I'm weeping for her!"

"Then go home and weep for her there. I don't need your friendship."

What God had asked her to do was too hard. Hephzibah would have to find forgiveness through someone else. Jerusha couldn't do it. Still crying, she stood and walked to the door. But as she closed the door behind her, she heard Hephzibah's final words: "You won't ever come back."

On the long walk home, Jerusha's ragged emotions had a chance to knit themselves together. She had handled the visit poorly, allowing Hephzibah to manipulate her instead of taking the lead. By the time Jerusha reached home, she knew that Hephzibah's final challenge meant she must return to see her again, even though she didn't know where she would find the courage to do it. She entered her front door deep in thought and hung up her shawl. When Eliakim walked into the hallway carrying little Jerimoth on his shoulders, he startled her.

"Eliakim! You're home early—what's wrong?"

He slid Jerimoth down to the floor, then spread his palms in the air and smiled. "You always say that! Does it take a tragedy to bring me home early once in a while?"

He looked so handsome with his boyish grin and tousled hair. She thought of Hephzibah losing her husband's love, never seeing him or holding him close again, and she rushed into Eliakim's arms, clinging to him.

"Remind me to come home early more often!" He said, laughing. But as he bent to kiss her, he noticed her tears. "Jerusha? You're crying! What's wrong?"

"I—I love you so much!"

"Is that such a sad state of affairs? Am I that difficult to live with?"

"If you ever stopped loving me—I don't know how I could live."

He held her tightly. "Now, you know that could never happen. Why would you even think such a thing?"

"Because sometimes it *does* happen."

He held her away from him and studied her troubled face; then he gave little Jerimoth, who was clinging to his leg, a playful swat. "Go see where all the servants are, Son. Ask one of them to give you a date cake. Your mama and I need to talk."

Jerusha watched him toddle off and silently thanked God for blessing her with children. Again she thought of Hephzibah, who had no children, no husband, and she couldn't stop her tears.

"Jerusha, you're crying again. What's wrong?" Eliakim brushed away her tears with his fingertips.

"Oh, Eliakim! I'm so thankful for all that I have. I—I went to see Hephzibah today, and she—"

"You *what?*" Eliakim's smile suddenly vanished.

"I went to see Hephzibah—"

"Not King Hezekiah's wife?" The shock on Eliakim's face surprised her.

"Well, yes—I—"

Eliakim grabbed her by the shoulders. His face had turned as pale as ashes. "Jerusha! You didn't!"

"Yes, Eliakim—I went—"

"But *why?*" he shouted. "Why would you do such a stupid thing?"

His reaction stunned her. For a moment Jerusha couldn't think, couldn't remember exactly why she had decided to visit Hephzibah. Nor could she understand why her husband was so upset with her.

"I—I felt sorry for her. She was once so kind to me, and I thought she needed a friend—that's all."

"That's *all?* God of Abraham! Didn't you stop to think about *me?*" Eliakim had never shouted at Jerusha before, and the sound made her knees shake.

"But it has nothing to do with you."

"It has everything to do with me! Jerusha, *think!* I'm the king's secretary of state. Hephzibah betrayed him—no, it was worse than that; she nearly killed him! And now my wife is befriending her? Making social calls? *My* wife?"

"I . . . I didn't think . . ."

"No, you certainly didn't! Jerusha, please. You can't ever go back there again, all right?"

"But she's all alone. I was only trying to—"

"She's *supposed* to be alone. She's been banished. She's in exile. According to the Law, she should have been stoned to death."

"Hephzibah's punishment is worse than stoning. Listen, Eliakim—I didn't go to pay her a social visit. I went to help her find God's forgiveness."

"She doesn't deserve forgiveness." Jerusha had never seen Eliakim so angry, and she barely recognized him. His gentle brown eyes were no longer warm, but glittering with hatred. His face looked rigid and cold as he spoke each word with barely controlled fury. "Jerusha, I was there the night King Hezekiah discovered his wife worshiping an idol. I will never forget how he suffered! His skin was burned off! It hung on his leg in shreds, and he was ready to pass out from the pain when I found him. But the pain in his soul—God of Abraham—I will never forget it as long as I live! His physical suffering was nothing compared to the anguish of his soul. She deceived him. She made a mockery of his God. She doesn't deserve forgiveness."

"None of us do, Eliakim! *Not one* of us! You know my past better than anyone. But God forgave me. I don't deserve all of this." She made a sweeping gesture with her arms. "My sins are just as great as hers, and if she deserves to be stoned to death, then so do I."

She had startled him, and for a moment he couldn't reply. Then his features softened, and the gentleness returned to his eyes. "I'm sorry," he said quietly. "You're right—we've all sinned." He took her hand in both of his and squeezed it tenderly. "But Hephzibah will have to be reconciled with God some other way. You can't become involved with her. You won't."

If Jerusha wanted an excuse for staying away from Hephzibah, Eliakim had provided one. Yet she couldn't shake the conviction that she had to return. "But what if God asks me to go back?"

"That's ridiculous."

"Look—this wasn't my idea, Eliakim. I felt the same way you did about her. But this morning when I went to the Temple and I saw the king standing there all alone, God reminded me of my own past, and I knew that this was something I had to do."

Instantly Eliakim grew angry again. "And suppose King Hezekiah hears about it? Don't you understand what a difficult situation you're placing me in? How will it look to him? He hates Hephzibah! He has every right to hate her!"

"How can the king go to the Temple and stand before God with hatred in his heart?"

"That's none of my business, and it's none of yours either."

"If you're his friend, it *should* be your business."

Again, she saw Eliakim's face turn white as the coldness and hatred crept back into his eyes. "When I took office I swore an oath of allegiance and loyalty to the king. I can't have you compromising my integrity by socializing with his idolatrous wife! Stay away from her!"

Jerusha recalled Hephzibah's parting words and knew that regardless of what Eliakim said, she had to return one more time. She had to explain to her that God could forgive any sin, even one as shocking as Hephzibah's.

"All right," she said softly. "I'll go to her tomorrow and tell her why I can't come anymore, and—"

"No, Jerusha, you won't! You won't ever go back there again!"

"Will you help me write a letter to her so I can explain why—?"

"No!"

"But I need to tell her—"

"Aren't you listening to me? Don't you understand anything I've said?"

"But, she'll think—"

"I don't care what she thinks! I'm worried about what the king will think!" He was shouting again, and the baby awoke from her nap and began to cry. "You better make up your mind which you care about more, Jerusha—Hephzibah's feelings or mine!" He pushed past her and stormed out the front door, slamming it behind him.

◆

Late that night Eliakim still hadn't returned home. Jerusha lay in bed in the dark unable to sleep, her mind turning endlessly as she grappled with her dilemma. She wanted to obey Eliakim and never see Hephzibah again, but she couldn't shake the conviction that God wanted her to return. If she disobeyed her husband, she would have to deceive him, just like Hephzibah had deceived her husband. But what if she lost Eliakim's love forever?

As she tossed in bed, she finally heard the front door open. She slipped into her robe and went downstairs, afraid to face her husband. He sat on the bench removing his sandals, but he sprang to his feet when he saw her.

"Eliakim, I'm sorry—," she began, but he pulled her into his arms and held her tightly.

"I was afraid to come home. I was ashamed of the way I treated you, Jerusha. I should have *asked* you not to go instead of shouting at you. I'm sorry."

"I didn't realize that visiting Hephzibah would reflect on you."

"Please, Jerusha. Do you understand now why you can't go back?" He held her away from him and searched her face. She hoped he wouldn't make her promise. She wasn't sure she could.

"Yes, but—"

"Then we won't mention it again."

But as she clung to Eliakim, Jerusha knew she had to return once more to explain everything to Hephzibah. She whispered a silent prayer that her husband would never find out.

For the second time in a matter of months, foreign envoys paraded into Hezekiah's throne room and bowed before him. But as he extended his scepter to Pharaoh Shabako's representatives, Hezekiah experienced none of the elation and excitement of the last visit. Isaiah's rebuke had transformed the Babylonian treaty from one of his greatest successes into a reminder of his sin. He had succumbed to the same temptation as his ancestor, King Uzziah: pride.

"Your Majesty, King Hezekiah, I bring gifts and greetings from Pharaoh Shabako, founder of the 25th dynasty of Egypt. He has asked me to extend the hand of friendship to you on his behalf."

"He is very generous. What is his petition?"

"Pharaoh knows that we have a mutual enemy in Emperor Sennacherib of Assyria. He has heard of your defense treaty with Babylon. Our nation has signed a similar treaty with the kings of Philistia and Tyre, pledging our mutual military support against the Assyrians. Pharaoh invites you to sign as well. Why not join with us?"

Indeed, why not? Hezekiah wasn't allied with Assyria. Why not ally himself with her enemies? And Egypt was one of the three major world powers. Still, he couldn't help wondering if he truly had a choice. What would happen to his nation if he refused Pharaoh's request?

"And what does Pharaoh Shabako expect of my nation in return for this treaty?"

"Only that you will remain an enemy of Assyria. Then we will form a solid block of resistance to halt their advance south."

"I'm sure Pharaoh knows my nation guards his northern border. Assyria would have to attack me before he could get to Egypt. What does he offer me in return for blocking the door to his country?"

"Pharaoh pledges that his army will come to your aid if you or any of our other allies are attacked. We also offer you the opportunity to purchase horses and chariots to bolster your armed forces."

Hezekiah glanced at General Jonadab, aware of the general's eagerness to acquire a cavalry and chariots. The unnamed heaviness that had settled over him after Isaiah's rebuke refused to lift, and he felt old and tired.

"You will be my guests here at the palace while I consider Pharaoh Shabako's generous offer. Please—join me for a banquet tonight in your honor..I will give Pharaoh my answer tomorrow."

Their confident faces told him that they already expected him to join the alliance. He had nothing to lose and an important ally to gain. Why, then, did he feel such a nagging uneasiness?

After the servants had escorted the Egyptians to their quarters, Hezekiah turned to Shebna. "You're the obvious choice to go as my envoy, Shebna. And I imagine General Jonadab will want to accompany you to negotiate for those chariots and horses."

"Yes, Your Majesty. It is an incredible opportunity to—"

Eliakim came out of his seat. "Wait a minute. You can't do this. You can't sign a treaty with Egypt."

"What's wrong, Eliakim?"

"Your Majesty, in the first year of your reign you said you would make all decisions in keeping with the laws of the Torah, didn't you?"

Hezekiah shifted in his seat. "Yes, that's right."

"Well, in the fifth Book of Moses it says, 'The king . . . must not acquire great numbers of horses for himself or make the people return to Egypt to get more of them.'"

Hezekiah knew that verse. It came right before the one that said, "He must not take many wives." Zechariah said the first verse forbade alliances with Egypt. But Zechariah also said the next one forbade marriage to more than one wife, and that misinterpretation had kept Hezekiah from having an heir—and had nearly cost him his life. He felt angry suddenly, and he didn't want to hear these passages of Scripture misused anymore. He was weary of them.

"I know what it says, Eliakim. But it doesn't apply in this situation. We're not returning to Egypt as slaves. We're making a purchase—that's all. A business transaction."

Eliakim kept his voice controlled. "No, Your Majesty, it's more than that. You'll be making a terrible mistake if you sign an alliance with Egypt. And I strongly oppose the purchase of Egyptian horses and chariots for the same reason I opposed the alliance with Babylon, because—"

Shebna interrupted him. "We all remember your foolish opposition, but these alliances will greatly increase our national security. You, your family, this entire city will be safer because of these treaties."

"No. 'Unless the LORD watches over the city, the watchmen stand guard in vain.' We need to put our trust in God, as we did the last time Assyria threatened us."

Hezekiah remembered the Assyrian invasion of Israel and Yahweh's protection of Judah as if it had happened to someone else, not to him. It seemed a lifetime ago . . . before he'd lost Hephzibah . . . before he'd heard Isaiah's rebuke. Right now, God's help seemed far away, Egypt's help much closer and more certain.

"Listen," Eliakim continued, "alliances offer false security. It won't matter to the Assyrians how many nations oppose them. The greater the opposition, the greater the challenge for them. The Assyrians thrive on it! They'll pick our allies off one by one so swiftly they'll never have time to come to each other's defense. Don't you see what a trap we're falling into? Isaiah warned us not to get involved in the Ashdod rebellion several years ago, and we were wise to listen to him. When Assyria took revenge on them, we were spared. Besides, when have the Egyptians or the Philistines ever come to our aid before? Read your history books. They want this alliance for themselves. It's a trap. They'll use us to absorb Assyria's wrath in order to save themselves. Don't fall for their lies. God is our Protector and Ally. We don't need anyone else!"

"We cannot stay neutral," Shebna said. "Look at a map if you do not believe it. We are already in the middle of it all. When war comes, it will be worldwide. The Assyrian empire is crumbling, and it is time to grab our rightful share of it."

"Shebna's right," Hezekiah said reluctantly. "It's too late to decide if we want to get involved; we're already involved whether we like it or not."

His first decision to befriend Babylon had started a chain reaction that he couldn't stop. He wasn't happy about it; he felt trapped, as if he was no longer making sovereign decisions but was having them forced on him. He supposed it was the price he had to pay for having allies.

Hezekiah's uneasiness grew to a deep anxiety that he couldn't quite place. He trusted Shebna's wisdom; Shebna was a man of exceptional abilities who understood current events and international politics. But Hezekiah also trusted Eliakim's judgment, even when he disagreed with him. Hezekiah's mistake with the Babylonians had shaken his confidence in himself and in his ability to make decisions. He could no longer figure out how to strike a compromise between his two advisers' differing opinions. One of them must be wrong. Hezekiah hoped he had made the right choice.

Eliakim returned to his office very troubled and unable to concentrate on his work. The king had made a serious mistake. How could he convince him to change his mind before it was too late?

Hezekiah seemed different since his illness. He still worshiped God, still followed all the rituals, but his zeal for the Lord had withered. Earlier in his reign he would have consulted Yahweh before making such a grave decision as this, but ever since the Babylonians had come, Hezekiah seemed afraid to seek God for answers the way he used to.

When a shadow fell across his worktable, Eliakim looked up. Shebna stood in his doorway. Eliakim returned Shebna's gaze, waiting. He felt at a disadvantage sitting, so he slowly stood. Neither of them would look away. Finally Shebna spoke.

"It is obvious that you do not support King Hezekiah's policies and decisions anymore."

It was a true statement, and Eliakim felt no need to defend himself. He nodded slightly.

Anger flared in Shebna's eyes at Eliakim's refusal to be drawn into an argument. "It is time for you to step down and make room for a secretary of state who supports the king."

Eliakim's heart pumped faster, making it difficult to stay calm. "Has King Hezekiah asked for my resignation, or is this your idea?"

"As palace administrator, I speak for the king."

"Answer my question, Shebna! Did King Hezekiah tell you to come here?"

"I am trying to spare you the embarrassment of being publicly dismissed."

"That's very kind of you. And I thought you didn't like me."

"You will resign, then?"

"I'll think about it."

"Do not take too long, or the decision will be taken out of your hands."

"Is that a threat?"

"It is a fact." Shebna turned and left.

Eliakim shrank at the thought of being fired, and he wondered if King Hezekiah felt the same way as Shebna. He had taken an oath of loyalty and obedience to King Hezekiah, but was it disloyal to disagree? Should he resign? For his family's sake, he would be wise to do so voluntarily; yet if this was Shebna's idea and not the king's, Eliakim refused to let Shebna have his own way.

He pushed the documents around on his desk without seeing them. He sat deep in thought for several minutes, then finally spread a blank square of parchment in front of him and carefully penned his letter of resignation. He signed it and sealed it with his signet ring, but he had no peace about the decision he had just made. He rolled it up and stuffed it into the fold of his tunic, then put on his outer cloak.

"Where are you going, my lord?" his aide asked.

"I'm not sure."

He pushed past his aide and left the palace, hurrying down the hill toward the city. He walked past the street where he lived, into the older section of Jerusalem with its closely packed houses and tangled, twisting streets. He had to watch his step to avoid the shallow gutters where waste water ran, passing horses and mules straining beneath their loads and children playing games in the dirt. He had walked this route long ago in the dark of night, and it had seemed spooky to a boy of 13. Years later little had changed.

The streets all looked the same, and he wandered in circles for a while, passing the same tethered donkey three times before finally finding the rabbi's modest house. As he stood on the threshold he was struck by a familiar thought he had had before—why would Isaiah, grandson of King Joash, choose to live here instead of among the nobility?

He knocked on the gate and waited. *You will be a father to the house of Judah*, Isaiah had once predicted on this very spot. How astonishing that it had been fulfilled! But perhaps Eliakim's term of office was over now.

He pounded on the front gate again, and Isaiah came to the door. His probing gaze and quiet dignity made Eliakim feel like a tongue-tied boy again. To his surprise, Isaiah bowed.

"What an honor, Lord Secretary. Please come in."

Eliakim followed him inside and looked around. The fire in the hearth had burned out, and a chill had settled over the sparsely furnished house. Isaiah offered him a seat beside a table strewn with parchments.

"How can I help you?" he asked.

Eliakim didn't know where to begin. He struggled to marshall his thoughts. "I've come to ask your advice, Rabbi. Shebna came to me a while ago and said that since I disagreed with all of King Hezekiah's decisions I should resign. I think the king would have told me himself if he wanted me to resign, but I can't be sure. I don't know what to do. I remember how you once prophesied that I would hold this position one day, and I wondered if—"

"You wondered if I'd give you another prediction about your future to spare you the embarrassment of being fired?"

Eliakim stared, then looked away, ashamed.

"Go see a fortune-teller, Eliakim. God doesn't show us the future to spare our feelings."

Eliakim felt like the child he had been years earlier. The silence became uncomfortable. "I'm sorry, Rabbi," he said at last. "May I begin again?" Isaiah nodded.

Eliakim ran his fingers through his hair and drew a deep breath. "When the ambassadors came from Babylon, I advised against making a treaty with them. They said they came to pay respect, but it didn't ring true. I didn't trust them or their motives. I don't know—maybe I was wrong, but I spoke my opinion, and when the king ignored it I did as I was told. And as you know, King Hezekiah signed an alliance with Babylon."

Isaiah nodded slightly. His face wore a look of keen interest as if probing for the truth, and Eliakim knew he would see through any lies or shading of the truth.

"Then today the Egyptians came, and again I disagreed with signing an alliance with them, and—" He stopped suddenly and gazed at Isaiah pleadingly. "Rabbi, I don't understand why you're not speaking out against these treaties like you did once before. You were so opposed to the Ashdod rebellion that you prophesied stripped and barefoot. Yet this time you're silent. Why? Is this different somehow? Are we supposed to join the alliance this time?"

"God's Word hasn't changed."

"Then why haven't you prophesied against this treaty with Egypt? I strongly advised against it today, but I was only one voice!"

"And you think the king would listen if I went stripped and barefoot again?"

Eliakim shrugged helplessly. "I don't know, Rabbi. Maybe he would."

"No. King Hezekiah's pride has drowned out the voice of God. Until that pride is silenced, the king wouldn't hear me if I shouted God's Word from the pinnacle of the Temple. Hezekiah knows what's right. He has God's written Word in the Torah, and he has experience of God's protection from Assyria. But he's chosen to trust in the strength of pagan nations. He wants to be like them. There is nothing I can say that will change his mind. 'Pride goes before destruction,' and when God destroys Babylon and Egypt, we will be destroyed along with those we trusted."

A runner of fear twined itself around Eliakim, clinging to him. "But I don't agree with the king, Rabbi, and it's getting more and more difficult for me to carry out his plans. Maybe I don't belong in the palace anymore. Maybe I should resign."

"Do you believe your advice to the king is what God wants him to do?"

"Yes, I think so."

"And are you afraid to continue speaking the truth? Afraid of what will happen to you?"

Eliakim remembered preparing to die at Gedaliah's hands months earlier. Why did he hesitate now? "Maybe fear is part of it," he said.

"Let me ask you this, Eliakim—do you believe Yahweh put you where you are? And that He did it for a reason?"

"I do," he said quietly. "I know I couldn't have earned such an honor by myself."

"Then who will speak for God if *you* don't?" Eliakim stared. "God put you at the king's left hand, Eliakim. If Hezekiah asks for your advice, give it to him. Yes, you might be humiliated and thrown out of the palace for speaking for God. Are you willing to risk that?"

Eliakim thought of how Isaiah had gone stripped through Jerusalem's streets and felt ashamed of himself. "I would like to be willing, but won't you help me, Rabbi? I can't do this alone."

Isaiah rose and walked back and forth across the tiny room a few times. Finally he turned to Eliakim. "I went to see King Hezekiah after the Babylonians came. I spoke God's Word. He didn't ask for it, but I gave it to him anyway. I'm not certain he understood what it meant. He hasn't asked for my advice this time either, because, as the psalmist has written, 'In his pride the wicked does not seek him; in all his thoughts there is no room for God.' I have the Word of the Lord for Hezekiah. It's right here." He gestured to the pile of scrolls on the table. "You may read these if you'd like to, Eliakim. They say the same thing you're telling him."

"Then why won't you share them with the king? Please, Rabbi. I can't challenge him all alone."

Isaiah stared at the scrolls scattered on the tabletop for a moment, deep in thought. "Confronting kings with the Word of God isn't new for me, Eliakim. I've had plenty of practice." He smiled fleetingly, then sighed. "I'd just hoped . . . Hezekiah has tried so hard to do what is right . . . I'd hoped I would never have to do this . . . opposing him like I did his father."

"But you'll do it? You'll prophesy to him?"

Isaiah nodded sadly, and Eliakim felt as if he could breathe again. "Thank you, Rabbi."

"No, don't thank me, Eliakim. Unfortunately, my words will do no good. King Hezekiah will not heed them."

15

The banquet with the Egyptians ended very late, and the strain from the elaborate affair left Hezekiah too tense and edgy to sleep. As he passed the deserted harem on his way to his rooms, the familiar longing for Hephzibah tugged at him. She would always soothe him and help him wind down after a day such as this one, and a painful, lonely ache filled his soul in the place Hephzibah had once filled. He turned away from the harem, forcing himself not to dwell on what he had lost.

Forgetting Hephzibah had proven to be a hopeless task. It would have been easier to forget his own name. She filled his thoughts throughout the day and tormented his dreams at night. He would try to busy himself with the daily tasks of his life, but her image would return to him in unguarded moments, stopping him like a sword thrust through his gut. When he arose in the morning he would resolve that this would be the day he would forget her. He would start all over again. He would erase her from his mind. But slowly, silently, before he was even aware of what was happening, she would slip back into his thoughts, and the devastating sorrow would engulf him once more. A continual wail of mourning filled the background of his days, a cry that couldn't be silenced. She was gone. He would never see her again.

Sometimes he wondered what Hephzibah's days were like. Did she think of him a million times too? Did she feel the same gnawing, churning anger and frustration at the hopelessness of it all? Was she sorry for what she had done? Did she suffer as he did? He would never know. Never.

He went through the daily routine of running the kingdom on instinct, certain that his grief remained hidden. No one knew the torment he lived in or the searing pain he felt each time her face appeared in his mind. He hated her for what she'd done.

Get on with your life. Forget her. He recited the little speech to himself whenever something would remind him of her, and sometimes he thought he was beginning to get on top of his grief, beginning to forget her. Then he would recall something she'd said, something she had done that had made him laugh, or he would see her empty place at the banquet table again as he had tonight, and his sorrow would swallow him alive. When would it stop hurting so much? When would the pain go away?

He hurried back to his own chambers, but when he opened the door he was surprised to find several lamps lit and a warm fire burning in the brazier. He was even more surprised to find a woman standing in front of the fire. *Hephzibah?*

Hezekiah shook himself. Hephzibah was gone. He would never see her again. This woman was very young, the age Hephzibah had been when they had first married. And she was tall and long-limbed, not dainty and petite like his wife.

"Good evening, Your Majesty." She dropped to her knees shakily, bowing with her head to the floor, and he recalled how awestruck Hephzibah had been at first. He took a few steps closer and waited.

"You may rise," he said impatiently. She raised only her head and he studied her features in the lamplight—dark brown eyes in an oval face; a fine, straight nose; skin the color of honey; a soft, sensuous mouth. She was a lovely woman but not as beautiful as—. He caught himself making the comparison and hated himself for it.

"What's your name?" he asked to break the uncomfortable silence.

"I am Abigail, daughter of Joah."

"You mean, Joah the Levite? My scribe?"

"Yes, Your Majesty."

"Sit down, Abigail, and tell me why you've come." He sank down wearily on the couch, suddenly aware of how tired he was.

When Abigail sat down beside him, Hezekiah stared at her, amazed by her boldness. "What can I do for you?" he asked again.

She smiled. "Nothing, Your Majesty. I am here for you . . . that is . . . if you want me."

Hezekiah looked around the room for the first time and realized that his valet and the other servants were gone. A tray of refreshments, a flask of wine, and two goblets lay spread out on a low table. He and Abigail were alone.

He saw, then, how carefully she had been chosen for him—beautiful, yet physically the opposite of Hephzibah. She was the daughter of an important family with a God-fearing father and was probably well-versed in the tiniest letter of the Law. He would never find Abigail bowing down to an idol. Yet Hezekiah felt angry for Abigail's sake, angry with whoever had arranged all of this.

"Shall I pour you some wine, my lord?" she asked.

"All right." Her hand shook as she poured wine and handed it to him. He set the goblet down without tasting it. "Abigail—'a spring of joy.' It's a lovely name for a lovely woman."

"Thank you," she said with lowered eyes.

"Tell me something, Abigail. Who arranged for you to come here?"

"What do you mean, my lord?"

"You must realize that I wasn't expecting you to be here . . . that this . . . that you . . . that it's all a surprise to me."

"Yes. They told me you might send me away."

"That's what I'm wondering. Who told you? Who made all these arrangements? Was it my palace administrator, Shebna?"

"Yes, Your Majesty." She searched his face, anxiously. "Are you angry?"

In a way he *was* angry. Shebna had no right to interfere in his personal life—to simply decide that he needed a woman and then send one to his chambers. But he couldn't summon enough emotional energy to be angry. Ever since his illness, Hezekiah had felt very little emotion at all, walking through each day in a flat, gray haze. Maybe Shebna was right. Maybe he needed a wife. And his nation certainly needed an heir to the throne, a son to take his place when he died.

"No, Abigail," he said at last. "I'm not angry."

She looked so worried that he instinctively drew her into his arms to console her. But as he felt her heart beating rapidly against his chest, he wondered if it was fair to Abigail to ask her to be with him like this. Would he ever be able to stop comparing her to Hephzibah and see her for herself? Even if she bore him a dozen sons, would he ever love her as he once loved Hephzibah? Or trust her completely, with his heart and soul? Many years ago his grandfather had said that a wife deserved all of her husband's love and devotion. Abigail certainly deserved that, but Hezekiah wondered if he could give it to her. He released her and held her at arm's length.

"Abigail, look at me. I need to ask you something, and I want you to be honest with me."

"Yes, my lord?"

"Is this what you want, to come to my bed, to be part of my harem? Or are you here out of obedience to your father and Shebna?" She lowered her eyes. "Please, Abigail. I'm not trying to trick you. I need to know that this is something you want."

As he waited for her to answer, he thought of Hephzibah again, of the risk she took in sneaking out of her house to catch a glimpse of the man she would marry. He knew her strong will and daring had been part of her, part of the reason he had loved her so much. He wanted to close his mind against the pain and the memories of Hephzibah that Abigail forced him to relive, but he couldn't seem to do it.

"Is this what you want?" he asked again. "Living here in the palace harem won't be a normal life for you. Don't you want a husband and a family—a life like other women?"

"I would obey my father, no matter who he told me to marry. He knows what's best for me." She gave the standard, predictable answer, what everyone expected her to say.

"Yes, yes," he said impatiently, standing up, "but is it what *you* want? You have a mind . . . opinions . . . desires, don't you?"

"Yes, I have desires."

"And what are they?" He saw the uncertainty in her eyes.

"You may tell me, Abigail. Your words will never leave this room."

She didn't answer at first, and when she finally spoke it was slowly, hesitantly. "For as long as I can remember, ever since I was a child, you have been the king of Judah. I've watched you from the Women's Court as you stood on the royal dais at the Temple. My father—the entire nation—respects you because you are such a great king. Year after year we've waited for the announcement of the birth of your heir. But it has never come. All your people grieve for you."

Hezekiah wondered where this long, rambling speech was leading, but he forced himself to be patient with her. "Your Majesty, all my life, all I have ever desired is to have a husband and children. I would be content to marry an ordinary man or maybe a Levite like my father. But you must understand that to be chosen . . . to be honored with the privilege of bearing the king's son . . ." She stopped, and he saw tears in her eyes. "There are many women who would envy me because I am here with you."

"Abigail. Do *you* want to be here?"

She stood and reached out to touch his face tenderly, as if to assure herself that he was real, that she wasn't dreaming.

"Yes," she whispered. "I can't believe that I am." Her gesture and words moved him. He hadn't known such tenderness since his last night with Hephzibah.

Hezekiah felt the stirring of desire for the first time since the fire. But at the same time he knew the terrible pain that accompanied love. He feared he might hurt this gentle girl the way Hephzibah had hurt him.

"Thank you for your honesty, Abigail. Now I owe you the truth as well. Before you decide that this is what you want, you need to understand that I'm not certain I can ever love anyone the way I loved—" He couldn't say Hephzibah's name. "—the way I loved my first wife. Could you live with that, Abigail? You're so young. Could you live the rest of your life with me, knowing I might never be able to say the words 'I love you'?"

She bit her lip, trying not to cry, but a tear slipped down her cheek just the same. "It . . . it doesn't matter."

She moved into his arms, and as he felt the warmth of her embrace, smelled the sweetness of her scent, his longing for Hephzibah was almost more than he could bear. He took Abigail's face in his hands and kissed her hair, her forehead, her lips. But God forgive him—in his heart he was kissing Hephzibah. When Hezekiah realized what he was doing, he stopped and released her from his arms.

"No, Abigail. It *does* matter. I can't do this to you. I'm sorry."

She stared at him in fear and confusion. "Have I done something wrong?"

"No," he said sadly, "you haven't done anything wrong." Suddenly Hezekiah's grief gripped him so powerfully he had to turn away to hide the tears stinging his eyes. "You are a beautiful, desirable woman, and I'd like nothing more right now than to have you stay with me tonight. But it wouldn't be fair to you. You could give me pleasure, help me forget my grief for a while, even give me a son to take my place someday. But I have nothing to give you in return."

"Yes, the honor of being your wife . . . of living here . . ."

"Honor and prestige and wealth and privilege aren't important in the end. They don't last." He turned to her again. "Relationships, love—nothing can replace them; don't you see? I have the honor and respect of all my countrymen, even of other nations, but it doesn't mean a thing."

She stared at him in silence with tears falling down her cheeks. How could he make her understand?

"Abigail, did you have another suitor? Someone else who loved you and wanted to marry you?"

"Yes . . . but to be married to the king, to give birth to your heir, is—"

"Don't trade a chance at happiness for a title or prestige. It's not a fair exchange. And right now, a title is all I could give you. Maybe in time I'll be ready to love again. Maybe someday I could give you something in return—"

"But I could—"

"Don't you understand, Abigail? When I kissed you a moment ago—I was kissing someone else."

He saw by her expression that she finally understood. And in spite of his efforts not to, he knew he had hurt her deeply.

"I'm so sorry," he said. "You're hurt because you think I'm rejecting you. But someday, when you find a husband who loves you as much as you deserve to be loved, you'll understand why I sent you away. I pray that you'll be grateful."

She looked up at him, her eyes shining with tears. The pain in them was gone, replaced by pity. "But you deserve to be loved too, Your Majesty."

She was a very beautiful woman, and Hezekiah ached inside with the need to be loved, the need not to be alone anymore. He quickly rang for his valet before he changed his mind, before his own selfish needs caused him to ruin Abigail's life.

"Take her home," he told his servant; then he turned his back so he wouldn't have to watch her go.

He was alone again, and his sorrow and grief seemed greater than before. He needed Hephzibah to rub the tension from his aching shoulders and neck, to fill the empty place in his heart. But she was gone forever. He stood before his window staring at the outline of the Temple on the hill.

He had served God faithfully for more than a dozen years, upholding the Law, governing his nation by it. And God had fulfilled His end of the covenant in return, blessing his country, granting him honor in the sight of other nations. God had given him every promised blessing except one—an heir. But as Hephzibah had so painfully pointed out, God had made that promise to David, not to him. And God would keep it too—through Hezekiah's brothers and their sons.

How easily God's Word could be misread and misinterpreted, just as he had misread God's command to marry one wife. *Do not return to Egypt* . . . Maybe he had misread that law too. Maybe it had nothing to do with joining an alliance.

The door opened, and Hezekiah's valet returned, interrupting his thoughts. "Did you take the young woman home?" he asked.

"Yes, Your Majesty. Would you like anything else?"

It seemed to Hezekiah that his valet looked at him strangely, and he wanted to explain to him why he had sent Abigail away; he wanted to tell him that just because he was the king and could have anything or anyone he wanted, it didn't give him a license to use people for his own selfish needs. But the valet wasn't waiting for an explanation. Hezekiah hadn't answered his question.

"Yes, I'd like one more thing. Ask Shebna to come here." While Hezekiah waited, he watched the stars and the thin, gauzy clouds that raced across the sky like a bridal veil. He felt tired, but it wasn't the type of fatigue that sleep would cure. When he heard his door open, he turned around.

"Two things, Shebna. First, I've decided to sign a treaty of alliance with Egypt. You will go as my envoy, but you will make no concessions to them. I will sign as Pharaoh's equal or not at all."

"Yes, Your Majesty. I can be ready to leave right away." He broke into a broad grin, showing his straight, even teeth.

For some peculiar reason, Hezekiah suddenly remembered when he was a child and had met Shebna for the first time. His smile had seemed false. *Your eyes aren't happy,* Hezekiah had told him. He searched Shebna's eyes again and saw that they still didn't seem happy, in spite of the fact that he was the second most powerful man in the nation, that he was getting his wish for a treaty, that his advice had been heeded instead of Eliakim's. He wondered why not?

"And second, don't ever send a woman to my chambers without consulting me again."

Shebna's grin vanished. "She did not please you, Your Majesty?"

"I'm sure she would have pleased me a great deal if I'd let her stay, but that's not the point." He saw Shebna's confusion and searched for a way to explain it to him. "Shebna, you've had the same concubine for many years now. Does she bring you pleasure?"

"Yes, and she has also given me four sons."

"Then why haven't you married her?"

"What for? I am content without marriage."

"Indeed—what for?" he said softly. "'The Lord God said, "It is not good for the man to be alone. I will make a helper suitable for him."' And the Torah also says, 'A man will leave his father and mother and be united to his wife, and they will become one flesh.' There's so much more to marriage than pleasure or sons, Shebna. It's a sacred covenant, a mutual covenant, for the benefit of *both* partners. It's like—"

The blank look of incomprehension on Shebna's face stopped Hezekiah. A wall of unbelief separated him from Shebna, and for the first time Hezekiah realized how different they were, how far apart they'd grown over the years. Hezekiah's faith led him to live for God, not for himself; Shebna had no one to please but himself.

"Never mind," Hezekiah sighed. He sank down on his couch, shaking his head wearily. "That's all, Shebna. You may go."

Shebna didn't move. "I am sorry if I have offended you, Your Majesty. I was only trying to be a friend to you. I thought the girl might help lift the burden of sadness you have carried for so long."

"I know. And I appreciate it. But maybe I'm just not ready to let go of it yet." And for the first time Hezekiah admitted to himself that in spite of all that Hephzibah had done to him, he still loved her. Maybe he always would. Their hearts were joined together in a miraculous, inexplicable way, and no matter how hard he tried, no matter how much he willed it, he would probably never be able to completely forget her, never stop loving her. And "never" was a very long time.

16

The hot sun glared off the paving stones as Hezekiah stood on the palace steps, watching his servants load the caravan with gifts for Pharaoh Shabako. Within minutes, sweat poured down his face and neck, gluing his tunic to his back. He wiped his brow, pushing his damp hair off his forehead.

Eliakim stood beside him, his opposition to the Egyptian treaty clear from his grave silence. In the courtyard below, Shebna strutted before the growing crowd, issuing last-minute orders to the servants. When General Jonadab finished inspecting the Judean soldiers who would accompany the delegation, he climbed the stairs to where Hezekiah and Eliakim stood.

"I can't tell you how pleased I am that you've decided to purchase Egyptian chariots and horses, Your Majesty. They will be a much-needed addition to our arsenal."

Hezekiah nodded vaguely. He didn't want to think about the Egyptian horses. He wanted to get this over with.

"Are you sure you don't want to come along, Eliakim?" Jonadab asked, grinning. "I'll let you ride your favorite horse. It'll be like old times, riding together."

"No thanks, General." Eliakim's usual boyish grin had disappeared. Jonadab looked perplexed.

"I thought this was a happy occasion, Your Majesty. Why all the long faces?"

Yes, why the gnawing uneasiness that churned in Hezekiah's stomach? He had made a reasonable decision about this alliance based on facts and sound advice, but for some reason he couldn't escape the feeling that he had made a mistake.

"We'll celebrate when you return and the treaty is signed."

"Of course, Your Majesty."

They watched in silence as Shebna finished issuing orders and bounded up the steps. "Everything is ready, Your Majesty. We are ready to leave whenever—oh no! What does *he* want?"

Hezekiah watched uneasily as Isaiah pushed his way through the crowd, elbowing people aside, making no effort to mask his disapproval. He stopped at the bottom of the steps and gazed up at him.

"What do you want?" Shebna shouted.

"'Woe to the obstinate children,' declares the LORD, 'to those who carry out plans that are not mine, forming an alliance, but not by my Spirit, heaping sin upon sin . . .'"

Hezekiah moaned. "What's he doing? He's condemning me here? In front of all these people?" The crowd had fallen silent, listening with rapt attention. Isaiah's voice carried clearly across the courtyard and echoed off the palace walls.

"'Who go down to Egypt without consulting me; who look for help to Pharaoh's protection, to Egypt's shade for refuge.'"

Hezekiah hurried down the stairs. The stiffness in his scarred leg made his descent awkward, but he had no time to disguise his limp. He had to stop Isaiah from denouncing his policies in front of all these people.

"Don't do this to me," Hezekiah pleaded in a low voice. "Please, Rabbi. Not in public like this. You don't understand. You don't have all the facts—"

"'But Pharaoh's protection will be to your shame, Egypt's shade will bring you disgrace.'"

It seemed like a bad dream to Hezekiah—the prophet shouting to a rebellious king before an astounded crowd. He remembered standing beside his father near the aqueduct on the road to the Washerman's Field the day the prophet had confronted Ahaz. He remembered Isaiah's warnings in the Valley of Hinnom and how the prophet had pleaded with Ahaz and the rebellious people to stop their sin of idolatry. Now Hezekiah stood in his father's place. Now the prophet directed his angry words and accusations of sin and rebellion at him. Helpless frustration made Hezekiah want to lash out at Isaiah, just as his father had lashed out, but he choked back his anger.

"Not out here, Rabbi, please. Can't we go inside and talk about this?" Isaiah's voice rose even louder in volume.

"These are a rebellious people, deceitful children, children unwilling to listen to the Lord's instruction. They say to the seers, 'See no more visions!' and to the prophets, 'Give us no more visions of what is right! Tell us pleasant things, prophesy illusions. Leave this way, get off this path, and stop confronting us with the Holy One of Israel!'"

"Guards!" Shebna shouted as he bounded down the stairs. "I've had enough of this man!"

"No, Shebna," Hezekiah said wearily. "Let him have his say. Trying to silence him will only make things worse." He turned his back on Isaiah and the caravan to Egypt and slowly limped up the palace stairs, mortified to receive the same condemnation as his father. But Isaiah continued to shout behind him.

"Because you have rejected this message, relied on oppression and depended on deceit, this sin will become for you like a high wall, cracked and bulging, that collapses suddenly, in an instant. It will break in pieces like pottery, shattered so mercilessly that among its pieces not a fragment will be found for taking coals from a hearth or scooping water out of a cistern."

When Hezekiah reached the top step, Eliakim stopped him. "Shall I call off the caravan, Your Majesty?"

Hezekiah turned around and faced the crowd again. The soldiers, servants, and townspeople watched him curiously. Everyone waited for his response. Hezekiah shook his head.

"No, Eliakim—we can't call it off. We can't be the only nation that doesn't join the coalition, or they'll turn against us. We need this treaty. Our national security depends on it."

He had spoken too quietly for Isaiah to hear his words, but the prophet began to shout again as if he had. "In repentance and rest is your salvation, in quietness and trust is your strength, but you would have none of it. You said, 'No, we will flee on horses.' Therefore you will flee! You said, 'We will ride off on swift horses.' Therefore your pursuers will be swift! A thousand will flee at the threat of one; at the threat of five you will all flee away, till you are left like a flagstaff on a mountaintop, like a banner on a hill."

Hezekiah's breath quickened as he fought back the angry words he wanted to hurl at Isaiah. They felt like gravel in his throat. He longed to curse the prophet for confronting him publicly like this, for criticizing his decisions without listening to the facts, for making him feel like a wicked, rebellious king—like his father. He *wasn't* like his father. He had followed God's Law to the letter. He had been faithful to His covenant. Isaiah was wrong. But Isaiah was never wrong.

"Doesn't Yahweh have a *good* word for me, Rabbi? After all that I've done for Yahweh? After all these years?" He heard the pleading note in his own voice, and he felt like Esau begging for his father's blessing after foolishly squandering his birthright.

Isaiah gazed at him sadly for a moment before answering. "The LORD longs to be gracious to you; he rises to show you compassion, for the LORD is a God of justice. Blessed are all who wait for him!"

Hezekiah felt the tension in the gawking crowd. The soldiers, nobles, and officials waited anxiously to see who would win this confrontation. But Hezekiah knew he couldn't back down. In spite of Isaiah's words, he remained convinced that joining the coalition of nations was Judah's only hope against an impossibly superior foe.

"You don't understand, Rabbi. I *am* trusting the Lord. He's the only God I'll ever worship. But for my nation's sake, I have to join with my neighbors against the Assyrians. I can't ignore what's going on in the world around me. I'm sorry you don't see it that way. And I'm sorry you've decided to confront me in public instead of man to man."

Then, because he didn't want to hear any more of the prophet's words, Hezekiah signaled for the caravan to leave and disappeared into his palace.

◀━◆━▶

"Someone to see you, my lady."

Hephzibah turned and saw Jerusha standing in her doorway. She had come back! In spite of all Hephzibah's efforts to drive her away, Jerusha had come back. Her persistence touched Hephzibah's heart, but she didn't want to be touched.

"What are you doing here?"

"I came back to see you."

"Why?"

"Because I want to be your friend."

"I told you, I don't need your friendship. Or your pity. Why can't you leave me alone?" As she glared at Jerusha, Hephzibah noticed something she had missed the last time—an unmistakable bulge in the front of Jerusha's robe. "You're pregnant, aren't you?"

"Uh—yes. I am."

"How can you come here and parade in front of me like that! I'm barren! Do you enjoy reminding me of my failure? Go away!"

"No, Hephzibah—I'm not leaving. I know what you're doing. You're trying to punish yourself by pushing everyone away, but—"

"I don't have to *push* anyone! They've all disowned me! My servants, my family, even my father and mother. I've disgraced them. They consider me dead. And I wish you would too."

"Have you asked God to forgive you?"

"I don't believe in forgiveness. There's no such thing."

"I was angry at God too, Hephzibah. I blasphemed Him and refused to pray or to believe in Him. But when I asked for forgiveness—"

"You lived happily ever after. Good for you. But that's not going to happen to me. Hezekiah hates me. He isn't going to forgive me. So how can his God forgive me? I won't even ask."

"That's not how it works, Hephzibah."

"Yes, it is. Hezekiah obeys all of God's laws. God listens to him, not to me. God will never forgive me." Hephzibah thought she had long exhausted her tears, but when she remembered the look in Hezekiah's eyes the night he had discovered her betrayal, she covered her face and wept. She wished she could erase the memory of the anguish she had seen in his eyes, his terrible pain as he'd read the words of her vow. She longed to forget, but she couldn't; from the moment she had first met Hezekiah she had loved his beautiful dark eyes most of all.

She heard Jerusha moving around the room, opening her curtains and shutters; then she felt the breeze move across her skin like a caress when Jerusha opened the door to the outside. Hephzibah looked up. A sparrow landed on the threshold, cocked its head as if asking a question, then flew away.

"Come out into the courtyard with me," Jerusha said, extending her hand. "Sit in the sunshine."

Without knowing why, Hephzibah followed Jerusha outside and sat beside her on the bench. The bright sunlight hurt her eyes, and the sound of birds and the wind in the trees seemed deafening. She stared at the door to her room as if knowing her freedom couldn't last. She decided to use Jerusha to learn what she ached to know.

"Jerusha . . . do you ever see my . . . ever see King Hezekiah?"

"I saw him at the Temple this morning."

"How is he?" she whispered.

"Hephzibah, why put yourself through this?"

"The last time I saw Hezekiah he was dying. . . . and it was my fault . . ."

Jerusha touched her shoulder. "The king has recovered completely, Hephzibah. He'll be fine. He's lost a lot of weight, but he's growing stronger and stronger every day."

Hephzibah tried to control her tears, but they spilled down her face. "Do you ever go to the palace? Do you see him there?"

"I went to a banquet last week for the envoys from Egypt."

"How did he look?"

"Hephzibah, don't do this to yourself."

"You don't know! You can't possibly imagine how it feels to realize you'll never see your husband again!"

"I know how it feels," Jerusha answered quietly. "When the king nearly died, my husband's life was in danger too. Gedaliah was going to kill him. Eliakim sent me away so I'd be safe, and I didn't know if I'd ever see him again."

Hephzibah looked away. "If . . . if you really want to be my friend . . . then take me to the palace—let me see Hezekiah through your eyes."

"All right." Jerusha's voice shook. "The envoys came to honor him, Hephzibah, and they brought him magnificent gifts. First the Babylonians came, then the Egyptians—"

"He's a man of great importance . . . yet he loved me! I could never quite grasp it . . . he loved *me* . . . I owned a place in his heart. I wish . . . I wish I had realized how precious his love was. I never would have gambled with it." She wiped the tears that continued to fall, then looked at Jerusha again. "What did he look like that night?"

"He wore the crown of David on his head and a robe of deep purple. When he walked into the banquet room and the trumpets played their fanfare, he looked tall and stately, a man of dignity and stature. The Egyptians seemed small beside him."

Jerusha stopped as Hephzibah began to whisper, continuing the vision from memory. "His beard and hair shone like copper in the lamplight, and his shoulders were broad and straight—I could never take my eyes off him. I loved to watch him from across the room, especially his hands. They're so large and strong, and he can't seem to talk without using them. I used to tell him that if he sat on his hands he'd be speechless. Then he'd laugh. How I loved to hear him laugh! Have you ever heard his laughter, Jerusha?"

"I haven't heard him laugh in a long time, Hephzibah. He carries a burden of grief with him all the time, wherever he goes. He's still mourning his loss. I know that he loved you very, very much. I used to see it in his eyes. I can't look into his eyes anymore, because the pain is so naked and so intense. I'm not telling you this so you'll feel guilty and punish yourself, but so you'll know that the love you shared with him was rare and true and very deep. Hang on to that. Treasure that knowledge. And understand that he still loves you, still grieves for you—for what you both lost."

"But it can never be fixed," Hephzibah whispered.

"No, it can't be fixed."

"Then learn something from me, Jerusha. Don't ever go against your husband's wishes. Nothing is worth that risk."

"*You're* worth it, Hephzibah. In God's eyes and in mine."

"Jerusha! You're not supposed to be here, are you? Your husband would never approve if he knew you were here with me!"

"But my husband is wrong. I came back, because I knew it was the right thing—"

"No! I thought my husband was wrong too, and now I'd give anything to choose differently. Leave, Jerusha, and don't come back! Go home and take your husband in your arms, and never let go of him. Get out!"

"But, Hephzibah—"

"I'll tell the gatekeeper never to let you in again. Now, *go!*" She pushed Jerusha away from her until she finally stood up.

"I'll go. But I want you to know that no matter what you've done in the past, God will forgive you the moment you ask Him to. There's a song the Levites sing at the Temple. I want to tell you the words."

"All right. But then you have to leave."

Jerusha's voice trembled as she recited. "'Praise the LORD, O my soul, and forget not all his benefits—who forgives all your sins and heals all your diseases, who redeems your life from the pit and crowns you with love and compassion . . . He will not always accuse, nor will he harbor his anger forever; he does not treat us as our sins deserve or repay us according to our iniquities. For as high as the heavens are above the earth, so great is his love for those who fear him; as far as the east is from the west, so far has he removed our transgressions from us.'"

Jerusha looked at Hephzibah uncertainly, as if she wanted to embrace her.

"You can believe those words," she said quietly. "I know they're true. I've lived them." She turned and walked from the courtyard.

For Hephzibah it was a beautiful poem—nothing more. No one would redeem her life from this lonely, empty pit. And neither Hezekiah nor his God would ever forgive her for pledging to sacrifice his child to an idol. She rose from the bench and slowly walked back to her room, closing the door behind her.

◈

The house was quiet when Jerusha arrived home, the children still napping. She hung her shawl on a hook beside the door and sank down wearily on the bench to remove her sandals.

"Where have you been?"

Jerusha's heart jumped at the sound of Eliakim's voice. She slowly lifted her head and looked up at him, unsure how to answer.

"Eliakim—what are you doing home?"

She tried to smile as he walked slowly toward her, but he didn't return her smile. Sorrow filled his dark eyes, and she had to look away from him. She remembered Hephzibah's words: *"Don't ever go against your husband's wishes. Nothing is worth taking that risk."* She bent to unfasten her sandal, trying to conceal her guilt, but her hands shook as she fumbled with the straps. Eliakim pulled her hands away and took them in his.

"Jerusha, I came home two hours ago. The servants didn't know where you went. I've been worried."

Please, dear God! I obeyed You—I did what You asked me to do. Please don't let him hate me. O God, I couldn't live like Hephzibah. I couldn't live without Eliakim!

He gently squeezed her hands, and his handsome face blurred as her eyes filled with tears. Why had she defied his wishes?

"Jerusha? Why aren't you answering me?"

"I . . ."

Suddenly Eliakim let her hands slip from his. "God of Abraham," he said in a whisper. "You went back to see Hephzibah, didn't you?"

"I had to."

"Get out of my house!" He spoke so softly she barely heard him, but his words sent a shiver of terror through her.

"Eliakim, no! Listen to me—"

"It's too late for explanations." He yanked her cloak off the hook and shoved it into her hands, hauling her to her feet. "I said get out!"

"Eliakim . . . no . . . no!"

"Didn't I make it clear why you couldn't have anything to do with Hephzibah? Don't you understand that you're compromising my integrity? I'm having a hard enough time hanging on to my job without this!"

"What do you mean?"

"I've opposed King Hezekiah on every major issue for the past six months. Shebna told me that if I can't support the king's decisions, I'd better resign before I'm fired. I was so desperate I went to see Isaiah and begged him to back me up. Do you know what he did? He backed me up, all right. He condemned King Hezekiah in front of the entire city! I feel like a traitor!"

"Eliakim, I'm sorry . . . I didn't know . . ."

"That's why I came home today. The king was so upset at being damned in public that he refused to hold court. I don't know if I even have a job to go back to. And now this! If anyone finds out you've struck up a friendship with Hephzibah—God of Abraham, I don't know what I'll do! Everything's falling apart!"

"I'll explain to the king that you had nothing to do with it . . . that I disobeyed you . . ."

"He's not in the mood for explanations, Jerusha." Eliakim passed his hand over his face and groaned. "God of Abraham—why did you do this to me?"

Why had she done it? Why had she put Hephzibah's needs before her own husband's? She had to think, had to remember why—before she lost Eliakim forever.

"I didn't want to disobey you, but I had no choice. God compelled me to go, Eliakim. Who would speak for Him if I didn't?"

His expression changed as if she'd slapped him. "What did you say?"

"I said, 'Who would speak for God if I didn't?'"

He groaned, then quickly turned and walked away from her, disappearing into the house. A moment later she heard the door to their courtyard slam. Jerusha waited, unsure what to do, her fear of losing Eliakim rising to terrifying proportions. At last she followed him outside to the garden. He sat on the bench with his elbows on his knees, his hands covering his face.

"Eliakim, talk to me! What's wrong?"

"That's what Isaiah said. Those were his exact words: Who would speak for God in the palace if I didn't?"

"Then you know how hard it is to obey God when there's so much at risk, so very much to lose. Going back to see Hephzibah against your wishes was one of the hardest things I've ever done. But I had to tell her that God loved her, that He would forgive her—don't you see?"

Minutes passed as Eliakim sat with his head in his hands, the longest minutes of Jerusha's life.

"Please don't send me away," she whispered. "Please, Eliakim. I love you so much."

He reached for her and drew her to him, resting his face against her body as she stood over him. "I've forced you into the same trap I'm in, Jerusha," he said softly. "But obeying God is always the right choice. Will you forgive me?"

She crouched beside him and answered him with a kiss.

17

Shebna stepped out of the new chariot he had brought back from his trip as ambassador to Egypt and stood with his hands on his hips, watching the workers hew out his tomb from the rocky cliff face. The monument disappointed him. The pyramid on top looked so much smaller than he'd envisioned.

"Careful! You are taking too much off!" he shouted to the mason chiseling it from the bedrock. "I want to be able to see it from up there." He pointed to Jerusalem, across the Kidron Valley from where they stood.

Shebna wanted this monument to be visible from his palace window; he wanted to gaze down on it from the Temple mount during the long, boring services. He'd chosen this prominent spot, the highest on the ridge, to build an imposing memorial to himself, because future generations would pay homage at his grave. It must be a tomb fit for a king.

The project foreman walked forward to bow to Shebna, dusting his hands on his tunic. "It will be the most magnificent tomb in Jerusalem, my lord. Except for the king's, of course."

"But not as magnificent as the tombs of my ancestors. Have you heard of the great pyramids of Egypt?"

"Who hasn't, my lord?"

"The Egyptians know how to immortalize their great leaders." He frowned at the rough pyramid taking shape on top of his tomb, wishing it was larger. Even so, it would be the only tomb that had a pyramid. "You will remember to prepare a large place above the door for the inscription?"

"Of course. It's on the plans you gave me."

"Well, make certain you consult those plans once in a while. Take care you do not make a stupid mistake. You cannot put the stone back once you have chiseled it off."

"I know that, my lord."

"You are building a memorial that will be looked upon for centuries to come, like the tombs of David and Solomon. I helped bring about this age of prosperity and glory in Judah, and—"

The foreman's eyes flickered uneasily away from Shebna's face to a point beyond his left shoulder. "Excuse me, sir, but you have company."

Shebna whirled around to find Isaiah standing beside the new chariot. The rabbi appraised it carefully, running his hands over the blue and gold deities painted on the sides; then he wiped his hands on his thighs as if they had been contaminated.

"Are you looking for me, Rabbi?" He hoped not. He felt wary of this complex man, distrustful of his secret sources of information. Isaiah had an uncanny knack of guessing the future, and he had used it to manipulate King Hezekiah over the years. He seemed to want to control the king, yet he had refused the palace administrator's job when Hezekiah had offered it. Isaiah was a descendant of the house of David—did he want to be king? Shebna couldn't make sense of the man.

"Will you answer a question for me?" Isaiah asked politely.

"I will try."

Isaiah took a step closer, and his stance suddenly became challenging. "What are you doing here and who gave you permission to cut out a grave for yourself here, hewing your grave on the height and chiseling your resting place in the rock?"

"I do not need anyone's permission to take whatever tract of land I please and do whatever I want with it."

Shebna squared his shoulders and lifted his chin, confident in the power and position he held. But much to his amazement, Isaiah suddenly smiled, a fleeting grin of superiority and satisfaction that quickly vanished.

"Beware, the LORD is about to take firm hold of you and hurl you away, O you mighty man."

"Who do you think you are?"

"He will roll you up tightly like a ball and throw you into a large country. There you will die and there your splendid chariots will remain—you disgrace to your master's house!"

"How dare you talk to me that way? I am—"

"I know who you are, Shebna."

"Then you know that I have played a key role in shaping this nation and bringing about this age of prosperity."

"Yahweh brought about this age of prosperity—not you."

"I have educated the king and advised him from the very beginning of his reign—"

"And now you will bring about the destruction of everything he has built." Isaiah took another step closer, and his eyes bored into Shebna's. "Woe to those who go down to Egypt for help, who rely on horses, who trust in the multitude of their chariots and in the great strength of their horsemen, but do not look to the Holy One of Israel, or seek help from the LORD . . . He will rise up against the house of the wicked, against those who help evildoers."

"I have heard enough! You know nothing about government. What right do you have to criticize my decisions? This alliance with Egypt will be Judah's salvation if Assyria—"

"The Egyptians are men and not God; their horses are flesh and not spirit. When the LORD stretches out his hand, he who helps will stumble, he who is helped will fall; both will perish together."

"Myths and lies! King Hezekiah's only weakness is that he continues to believe in your myths and lies. And my single failing as his teacher is that I have been unable to convince him to reject these childish superstitions he clings to. But now, with these treaties, I have begun to change his thinking. At last he is beginning to understand the need for alliances with other nations. And when he finally discards your worthless, outdated laws, it will be the crowning achievement of my term of office as palace administrator!"

The self-satisfied smile on Isaiah's face flashed again—swiftly, fleetingly. "This is what the Lord, the LORD Almighty, says: 'Go, say to this steward, to Shebna, who is in charge of the palace: . . . I will depose you from your office, and you will be ousted from your position. In that day I will summon my servant, Eliakim son of Hilkiah—'"

"Never!"

"'I will clothe him with your robe and fasten your sash around him and hand your authority over to him—'"

"Liar! That will never happen!"

"'He will be a father to those who live in Jerusalem and to the house of Judah. I will place on his shoulder the key to the house of David; what he opens no one can shut, and what he shuts no one can open.'"

"Not Eliakim! *Anyone* but that self-righteous—"

Shebna rushed toward Isaiah, angry enough to strike him, but the rabbi calmly turned his back and walked down the path toward the Washerman's Field. A string of curses poured from Shebna's mouth, but Isaiah showed no sign that he had heard them. Trembling with fury, Shebna climbed into his new chariot again.

"Take me back to the palace," he told the driver. But the pride in his new vehicle that Shebna had felt earlier had vanished, leaving the journey up the steep ramp to the city bumpy and uncomfortable. He feared Isaiah's words as he feared little else.

Hezekiah stared at the letter in his hands, wishing he could crumple it between his fists and toss it into the flames. "It certainly didn't take our allies very long to make their first demand," he said.

"What is it?" Shebna asked.

"They want us to help the Philistines overthrow King Padi of Ekron."

"Why?"

"He refuses to join our coalition."

"You did promise military support to all our allies," Shebna said.

"I know I did, but I thought I'd be fighting the Assyrians. I never dreamed the treaty would drag me into a civil war among the Philistines. Why can't they solve this themselves? Why involve me?"

"Well, we *are* their closest neighbor—," Shebna began, but Eliakim interrupted him.

"No. They could defeat King Padi without our help. They're forcing us to prove our commitment to the alliance, Your Majesty."

"King Padi expects an attack from his fellow Philistines," Shebna said. "Our army would take him by surprise."

Eliakim shook his head. "The alliance is using us to bait the Assyrians. Padi was appointed by the King of Assyria. We shouldn't provoke him by attacking his puppet king. It serves no purpose except to earn the Assyrians' attention and wrath."

"You are wrong," Shebna said. "If we help the Philistines, it will prove that we are united against Assyria. They would not dare attack a coalition that stretches from Egypt to Babylon."

"You greatly underestimate the Assyrians," Eliakim said. "And our other allies do too."

Shebna started to argue, but Hezekiah stopped him. "Suppose I decide to help them, Jonadab. Can you come up with a plan?"

"We could launch a surprise attack from Socoh. It's the closest military garrison to Ekron."

Hezekiah only half listened as the general spelled out his plans for the conquest of Ekron and the capture of King Padi. Instead, he watched Eliakim, who appeared more and more troubled as the meeting progressed, running his fingers through his hair, shaking his head, staring at the floor. When Jonadab finished, the throne room fell silent.

"I want everyone to leave," Hezekiah said. "Everyone except Eliakim." When they were finally alone, Hezekiah turned to his secretary of state.

"You want my resignation," Eliakim said quietly.

Hezekiah stared at him in surprise. "That's the farthest thing from my mind. I need your advice now more than ever, yet I'm forced to disagree with you again. Frankly, that worries me. Shebna's logic makes the most sense, yet I know he leaves God out of his plans. I don't want to leave God out, Eliakim, but I don't understand why you and Isaiah think God is against this alliance."

"I would never presume to understand God, Your Majesty, or to speak for Him. But you don't need to turn to other nations for help when you can trust Yahweh."

"If I didn't trust Yahweh I wouldn't have the courage to rebel against Assyria and join the alliance."

"But you're trying to do both, Your Majesty—to trust God and still have a backup plan, just in case. Rabbi Isaiah and I believe you were wrong to get involved in the alliance in the first place."

"I know I was." He saw the surprise on Eliakim's face. "It's true. I was wrong. I know that now, but it's too late. I signed the treaty with Babylon in a moment of foolish pride; then I couldn't refuse when Egypt made the same offer. Now I have to help the Philistines. If I don't, I'll be in the same mess as King Padi. The coalition will turn against me."

"I see what you mean, Your Majesty."

"The irony is, I wanted the treaty with Babylon because I wanted to control my nation's future. But now the coalition is making all of my decisions for me. I had more freedom when I chose to place myself in the hands of an infinite God. At least with God there was room for a miracle."

Hezekiah didn't know why he felt the need to explain himself to Eliakim, but he felt more comfortable with him than with Shebna. The long, lonely months with no one to confide in had left him with a full heart and a heavy soul.

"I wanted to be in control, Eliakim—to be able to save myself. When I was a child, my father sent soldiers to the palace nursery for my brothers and me. They carried us away against our wills and sacrificed my brothers to Molech. I watched my father burn them alive in the flames, and I was powerless to save them or myself. Being helpless is such a terrifying feeling that I swore I'd never experience it again. That's what motivates me to make alliances. I want to save my nation and myself from Assyria. I don't ever want to stand helpless before my enemies again. But now I wish I could roll time backward and do everything differently. I wish I had listened to you and never made a treaty with Babylon, but I can't change what I've done. I can't go back in time—only forward."

Eliakim sat with his head lowered, twisting the signet ring on his finger as if he still expected Hezekiah to ask for it.

"I want to follow your advice this time too, Eliakim, but I can't. I just wanted to explain that to you, alone. I have no choice. I have to go to war against King Padi. But I'm going to ask General Jonadab to take him alive and bring him here to Jerusalem."

"Then I don't understand. How can I help you, Your Majesty?"

"Don't be afraid to disagree with me. I value your opinion, Eliakim, even if I can't always heed it."

"Of course, Your Majesty. I'm very honored."

"In the meantime, let's both pray that Shebna is right—that his dream of a coalition of nations will work. And that Assyria wouldn't dare to attack such a united front."

18

The Assyrian warrior Iddina sat in Emperor Sennacherib's palace in Nineveh and stared at the remains of the banquet in front of him. Neither the magnificent new hall nor the lavish meal he had just eaten could subdue his fierce restlessness and discontent. In fact, the scenes of battle and conquest carved in bas-relief on the walls around him had further inflamed his resentment. The emperor had promoted Iddina to four-star general, one of only three in the empire. The other two generals sat at the emperor's table with him. But Iddina had never tested his new commission. After several tedious years of peace, he longed for the intoxication of battle, the feel of the hard ground beneath him at night, the sound of killing, the scent of death.

One panel of wall carvings had particularly disturbed him. It showed King Jehu of Israel bowing in submission before Assyrian emperor Shalmaneser. Seven years ago Iddina had led the destruction and deportation of Israel, but he had never recaptured his Israeli slave girl, Jerusha. The knowledge of his failure, the knowledge that she had beaten him at his own game still haunted him and filled him with rage. He had unfinished business with Israel and with her sister nation, Judah. They worshiped the same god. And Iddina's life would be incomplete until he saw every man, woman, and child in both nations slaughtered and their god defeated.

"How many men have you killed, Iddina?" He turned to the high priest of Assur, seated across from him, and wondered how the man had come so close to reading his thoughts.

"Only men?—or women and children as well?"

"Human beings. A dozen? A hundred? A thousand?"

Iddina decided to use the priest's curiosity to amuse himself and relieve his boredom. He leaned closer. "Do you want to know how many I've killed with my own two hands? How much blood has stained my fingers? Or how many deaths I've ordered—how many I'm responsible for?"

"With your own two hands." The priest looked fascinated and a little afraid.

Iddina smiled for the first time all evening. He fed off others' fear; it nourished him like food and water. He laid his palms flat on the table in front of him, as if putting his hands on display.

"In my youth as a warrior the scribes always paid me well when they took their head count. I usually averaged 200 to 300 skulls in every battle. And I've been in hundreds of battles. My best count was 463 in a single battle against the Elamites." The priest leaned closer, waiting. His breathing had quickened. "Of course, as the emperor promoted me through the ranks, I saw less hand-to-hand combat. He placed me in charge of the tortures for a while—impaling, beheading, flaying people alive. I tortured hundreds of people to death during those years. I've held the severed heads of countless enemy generals in these hands and stared into their vacant eyes, knowing they would never threaten me again."

"Don't you ever wonder about the spirits of all the people you've slaughtered?" the priest asked. "What a mighty host of demons those thousands of souls would make if they came back to you for revenge! Yet I notice you wear no amulets or fetishes against these spirits."

Iddina smiled. He was aware of the stillness at the table as everyone leaned closer to listen. Even Emperor Sennacherib, who had adorned his own neck and arms and ankles with charms against the spirit world, listened with interest. Iddina basked in his superiority over these childishly superstitious people.

"No—I'm not afraid of the power of demons," Iddina answered. He savored the look of shocked surprise.

"Those are brave words from a man who has killed—what would you say—more than 5,000 people? I'm surprised you can sleep at night."

Iddina waited until the nervous laughter around the table died away. "I was only a child when my father died on a battlefield somewhere, fighting for Emperor Tiglath-Pileser. He was never buried, and I spent my youth paying homage to dozens of demigods and demons, hoping to ward off his avenging spirit, hoping my father's abandoned spirit wouldn't avenge himself by cursing my family with illness or some other disaster. I feared that he would glide into our home at night disguised as a demon to terrify my family for not sending him to the spirit world with a proper burial. I built altars in my youth, made offerings of fruit and grain and meat. Sometimes the gods ate better than I did. Appeasing them was my foremost concern. My arms and neck were weighed down with all the fetishes and amulets I'd created."

Iddina paused to sip his wine, and the priest grew impatient with the delay. "Then why do you no longer fear the spirit world?"

"Because now I have defeated hundreds of gods in battle." The priest gasped. Iddina smiled in satisfaction. With the high priest silenced, Emperor Sennacherib himself continued the questioning.

"Are you a god yourself, Iddina, that you claim to have conquered gods?"

"Not at all. In fact, Lord Emperor, you have slain gods as well."

"Really. If this is flattery, Iddina, I like it. Explain yourself."

"It's simple. If you've conquered a nation, you've defeated their gods. Those deities weren't able to protect their people from you. You've proven that you are more powerful than those gods. You needn't fear them."

"Then in your view, I'm not only emperor over all the nations but emperor over their gods as well?"

"Yes. When people are terrified, they turn to their gods for help. If those gods can't save them, they surrender to whatever terrifies them: you, my lord. You've become their god."

Sennacherib appeared pleased. "I like that. But tell me, Iddina—which gods *do* you fear?"

Iddina glanced at the priest. "I worship Assur, ruler of the gods. But I no longer fear him. I've earned Assur's favor by the countless human sacrifices I've made in his name and by the many lesser deities I've defeated for him. Dozens of gods have bowed to Assur's sword, and I've brought their conquered images to his temple and laid them at his feet."

Sennacherib stood and applauded softly. "Well said. But tell me, General Iddina—have you had your fill of killing men and conquering gods?"

"On the contrary, there are still a few gods whose images aren't resting in Assur's temple. As for killing men"—Iddina paused, fingering his wine goblet—"what motivates me isn't seeing their blood on my hands, but the fear in their eyes. Over the years I've grown bored with mere physical torture. Mental torture is so much more satisfying. The human mind can imagine greater fear and pain than my two hands could ever inflict. I prefer to engage in warfare of the mind. I like to study my enemies carefully before my army marches, then exploit their superstitions and fears until they bow at my feet."

"Interesting," Sennacherib murmured. "Very interesting." He slowly paced the length of the table, deep in thought. Iddina could feel the tension in the room. When the emperor finally came to a stop, all eyes were on him. "I've invited everyone to this banquet tonight for one reason: to announce that we're going to war."

Iddina sat forward on the edge of his seat.

"As you know," Sennacherib continued, "my father spent six years building his capitol here in Nineveh, giving our empire six years of peace. But he ignored some of the distant nations in his empire, and now they've grown restive and rebellious. I've invited my three generals to attend tonight so I could choose one of them to be commander in chief of my armed forces. I favored you for this job, Iddina." He gazed at him levelly. "We worked together closely under my father, and I admire your ruthlessness."

Iddina battled to conceal his growing excitement. He wanted this job badly.

Sennacherib smiled. "But after hearing your views on conquering the gods, Iddina, I've changed my mind."

Hidden beneath the table, Iddina squeezed his hands into fists until his fingernails bit into his flesh. His heart hammered with rage, and he wanted to snap the high priest's neck for goading him into sharing so much about himself. He slowly relaxed his fists and cracked his knuckles, one by one, imagining they were the bones in the priest's neck.

"No, Iddina, you won't be my commander, because I believe I've found an even better job for you: my Rabshekah. I'd like a spokesman who fears neither man nor god."

The emperor's propaganda chief! Instilling fear and suspicion, destroying minds! Iddina broke into a slow smile. "It will be a pleasure, Your Majesty."

"Good. I have already consulted with the priests, and the omens for war have been favorable. First, I will attack Babylon. They are the real power behind all the unrest in my empire, so they will be the first to feel my wrath. I will lead my entire armed forces against them in a surprise attack, striking so swiftly and ruthlessly that they won't have time to call on their feeble allies for help."

The emperor's fierce hatred for the Babylonians was well known, and it didn't surprise Iddina to learn he planned to eliminate them first. Iddina imagined the splendor of watching a quarter of a million men march into battle, the excitement of choreographing a relentless siege and attack, the thrill of witnessing mass genocide. He quivered with anticipation.

"When Babylon is finished," Sennacherib continued, "I will destroy her allies one by one and watch my new slaves carry their pitiful gods back here to Assyria. I've decided to save Egypt for last. It is a prize that has eluded my ancestors, and I want it in my empire."

One of the other generals asked for permission to speak. "Aren't you afraid the Egyptian army will come to the defense of her allies? Together they could assemble an army nearly as large as ours."

"That's doubtful. Babylon holds this alliance together, in spite of the tricks she has employed to make me think otherwise. Without her, I predict the others will quickly surrender, especially once my new Rabshekah begins waging his mind warfare on them. That will clear the path to Egypt—and to world domination!"

As they drank a toast to their imminent conquests, Iddina once more studied the battle scenes carved on Sennacherib's walls, especially the one in which Israel's king bowed in submission. He could hardly wait to bring revenge on the Hebrews in retaliation for the girl who had escaped his grasp. She undoubtedly thought her god had delivered her from him. But he would soon defeat all her people and carry her god to Assur's temple in Nineveh. Only then would Iddina be certain that he had won at last.

The emperor held his glass high. "To victory!" he cried.

"To victory!" Iddina echoed.

3

After all that Hezekiah had so faithfully done,
Sennacherib king of Assyria came and invaded
Judah. He laid seige to the fortified cities,
thinking to conquer them for himself.

—2 Chron. 32:1

19

The king of Babylon paced the length of the wharf, casting anxious glances at the cargo ship that stood loaded and waiting beside the canal. Only the sounds of croaking frogs and lapping water disturbed the warm, muggy night. As Merodach-Baladan retraced his steps, scanning the darkened streets, the ship's captain approached him warily.

"Your Majesty, we should cast off soon if you want to reach Basra before dawn."

"Yes, yes—of course. Just a few more minutes. They should be here any—ah, here they are now." Torch lights bobbed toward him in the darkness, and as the figures drew closer, he recognized the pale, worried faces of his secretary of state and prime minister. "I'll be ready to cast off in five minutes, Captain. Kindly tell my officials I wish to speak with them alone."

Merodach-Baladan moved into the shadows at the end of the wharf and waited. A few moments later, the two men edged nervously toward him. "Over here, gentlemen," he called.

"Your Majesty?"

"Yes, it's me. I'm sorry for all this secrecy in the dark of night, but as you'll soon see, it was necessary."

"What's going on?"

"And why are you dressed like a peasant?"

The king glanced down at his coarse tunic, stained with sweat beneath the armpits, threadbare at the elbows. He leaned against a piling and sighed. "Because I gambled and lost. I'm sorry, gentlemen, but our dream is finished."

The prime minister's melancholy eyes filled with apprehension. "What gamble? What on earth are you talking about?"

"The Assyrians are marching toward Babylon. They have more than a quarter of a million troops."

The prime minister swayed as if his knees might give way.

"Obviously we're not ready to withstand such a massive invasion," the king continued, "so I have no choice but to surrender and submit to them."

"What about our allies?" the secretary of state asked, his voice shaking. "Have you summoned them to help us?"

"There won't be enough time. Besides, the Assyrians sent advance forces to seal off our borders. Our allies couldn't get through to help us even if they wanted to."

The prime minister looked as if he needed to sit down, but there was no place to sit. "How could this happen? Wasn't there any warning?"

"None. I gambled that Sennacherib wouldn't go on the offensive for another year, and I lost. I'd also hoped that he might go after our western allies first—or at least split his forces between two fronts—but he's marching his entire army toward us."

"A quarter of a million troops?" the secretary moaned.

"Yes. At least. We've lost, gentlemen. It's over before it even starts. So rather than subject Babylon to a lengthy siege that we can't possibly win—"

"You're giving up?" The prime minister's eyes widened.

The king shrugged. "There's no other choice."

"Did your military advisers agree to surrender?"

"I haven't told them."

"You would surrender without—?"

"We could never mobilize enough men to match the Assyrian forces. Be realistic. They're professional warriors. We're not ready for them. Maybe we'd be ready in another year, but we barely have another *day!*"

The secretary looked as if he were having a nightmare. "So you're giving up? Just like that?"

"What other choice do I have? Should I let them besiege the city until we're pounded and starved into submission? We can't win! Why destroy ourselves?"

"Why are we arguing about it out here in the middle of the night instead of in your Council Room?" the prime minister asked.

"Because I'm leaving in a few minutes. I want to make sure my family is downstream by dawn. I can best serve Babylon by leading the resistance in exile, rather than by being flayed alive by the Assyrians. I've grown quite fond of my skin over the years." Neither man smiled at his pathetic joke.

"What about the rest of us? Don't we deserve a chance to escape?"

"That's exactly why you're here, gentlemen. You've served me faithfully over the years. Now if you're wise, you'll get out before it's too late."

"And all your other officials? You're just leaving them here to die? Without any warning?"

"They'll receive the official announcement in the morning. I just thought that you two—well, I thought you deserved a little more time to make some plans."

"While you're fleeing the country?—very thoughtful," the secretary said bitterly.

"You know as well as I do that the council would have argued for days about what to do. The military people would have wanted to fight, my economic advisers would have dithered about tribute payments, and so on, and so on. While they wasted precious time, the Assyrians would have the city surrounded. No, gentlemen. I don't need to hear all their arguments. I know it's hopeless, and I've made my plans. If you're smart, you'll take advantage of the hours remaining before dawn and make some plans of your own."

The king glanced at the ship's captain and saw him nervously eyeing the three-quarter moon rapidly sinking in the sky. "I'm sorry that my master plan for a New Babylonian Empire didn't work out, but—perhaps we'll meet again someday and start all over again. It's a pity. You're both good men. But we're living in troubled times." They stared at him, unbelieving. "Until then, may the gods go with you both."

The king of Babylon strode down the wharf to the cargo ship and mounted the boarding ramp. The waiting sailors quickly untied the mooring lines and shoved off. Moments later Merodach-Baladan drifted smoothly down the canal, out of the doomed city of Babylon.

—◆—

When King Hezekiah received the news, he called an emergency council meeting with his top officials and military staff. He sat on his throne, studying their troubled faces as they filed in, and remembered sneaking into his father's emergency council meeting as a boy. When Ahaz had faced a crisis of this magnitude, he had decided to sacrifice his sons to Molech to save himself.

"I've received very disturbing news, which has already been confirmed by several sources," Hezekiah began. "The Assyrians have declared war. Emperor Sennacherib is leading the campaign himself in an effort to reclaim his rebellious empire. He was a formidable general under his father, and he's very experienced in battle. He's mobilized more than a quarter of a million troops, along with countless horses, chariots, and siege machines."

"Now you will see the advantage of our alliance, Your Majesty," Shebna said. "Working together, we can—"

"I'm afraid the alliance is already disintegrating. The Assyrians smashed into Babylon in a surprise attack. They were forced to surrender."

Everyone began talking at once, and Hezekiah had to wait until the noise finally died away again. "Babylon is under enemy occupation."

"They were foolish to surrender!" Shebna shouted. "They should have held out under siege until the allies could mobilize and—"

"It would have taken too long. The Assyrians caught everyone off guard. Sennacherib moved quickly, hoping the alliance would be slow to respond, and he was right. We weren't ready."

"Then we had better start mobilizing right away," Shebna began. "We still have all our other allies—"

"No. We don't. Almost half of the alliance has already surrendered to Assyria."

Again the room dissolved into chaos. Hezekiah recalled how the same thing had happened at his father's council meeting so long ago. He had brought his nation a long way since that night. How was it possible that now he was back where he had started? He glanced at Eliakim, who hadn't said a word, and saw him sitting with his head in his hands, staring at the floor.

Hezekiah began speaking again, and the room grew still. "When the kings of Ammon, Moab, and Edom learned that Babylon had surrendered, they caved in as well. They sent tribute to Sennacherib and sued for peace."

"They cannot do such a cowardly thing!" Shebna said. "We have a treaty that says—"

"But they have done it, Shebna. That leaves the Phoenicians, the Philistines, and the Egyptians as our only allies. So the next question is, do we surrender as well, or fight?"

"We should give what's left of the alliance a chance," Shebna said. "Egypt won't surrender, and together we can still mobilize a formidable army."

"I agree. We're prepared for it," General Jonadab said. "We have almost 50 fortified cities defending all the possible invasion routes, and each one is well prepared for a siege."

"Eliakim?"

"We should never surrender Jerusalem, Your Majesty. Yahweh's Temple is here."

"Good. I'm glad we all agree. I have no intention of surrendering. General, what do you predict the Assyrians' next move will be?"

"They'll hit the three smaller countries hard and fast, trying to eliminate us before Egypt comes to our rescue."

"The Egyptians will be quick to respond, as soon as the Assyrians attack," Shebna said. "You will see. I negotiated that treaty myself. I have Pharaoh's word."

Jonadab paced in front of Hezekiah as if eager to do battle. "If I were Sennacherib, I'd divide my forces and send half down the coast against the Phoenicians and Philistines. They will be easy prey in the flat coastal land. I'd send the other half inland, against us. With Egypt's help we can hold them back at the mountain passes."

"Then let's prepare for that event," Hezekiah said. "Mobilize all the able-bodied men in Judah and dispatch them to the garrisons. When Egypt's forces arrive, we'll combine our troops to defend the passes."

"Yes, Your Majesty. I will personally lead the troops into battle, and—"

"No, Jonadab. I need you here to defend Jerusalem. Eliakim's right—it must never fall."

"But that's exactly why I have to be out there in the field—to coordinate with the Egyptians and hold the Assyrians back so they never get this far."

"Are you sure that's a good idea, General?"

"I will use Eliakim's signal towers to stay in touch with you. We only have to hold the Assyrians back until the Egyptian army comes. I know we can do it."

"Very well," Hezekiah said reluctantly. "Eliakim, do all of our fortified cities have ample water supplies for a siege?"

"Yes, Your Majesty. And food supplies too."

"Good. Then I suggest we block all the springs that are outside the walls and build dams to divert some of the streams. Why should the king of Assyria find plenty of water?"

Eliakim's worried face broke into a smile. "I'll assemble a work force immediately."

"The Assyrians will never get close to Jerusalem, much less lay siege to it," Shebna said. "With the combined forces of our remaining allies, we will drive the enemy back to Nineveh."

"Let's hope you're right," Hezekiah said. "Jonadab, before you go, I'd like you to divide the city into military sectors and appoint officers over the people to keep peace."

"Consider it done."

The Assyrian invasion seemed unreal to Hezekiah, as distant and remote as when they had invaded Israel. He had worked hard—reinforcing the walls, safeguarding the water supplies, building a network of garrisoned cities—hoping all these precautions would never be necessary, hoping his nation could continue to live in peace. But the invasion he had dreaded was upon him. He knew he couldn't blame God for his troubles. He had brought this upon himself the day he had signed the treaty with Babylon.

"One more thing—perhaps the most important one," Hezekiah said. "I've called for an assembly at the Temple to pray for victory. May God have mercy on all of us."

When Hephzibah heard the Temple shofars announcing a convocation, she saw the opportunity she had long awaited. She hurried to the work area behind the villa to search for Hoglah, hoping the time she had spent winning the servant's friendship and trust would finally pay off. She found the elderly widow hunched over a scrubbing stone, washing laundry.

"Hoglah, do you know why the shofars are blowing?"

The servant wiped her hands on her apron and bowed awkwardly. "No, I wouldn't know, my lady."

"Listen, Hoglah. You've been a good friend to me, and—"

"Oh, no, my lady. You've been kind to take an interest in a poor old washerwoman like me."

"Hoglah, I need a favor."

"From me? But I have nothing to offer you."

"Yes, you do—trade places with me so I can go to the Temple. I want to see why they're calling an assembly."

"Oh, please, my lady, don't ask me to do such a thing. I support my family with this job."

Hephzibah slipped the bracelet off her wrist and pressed it into the widow's red, chapped hands. "I will pay you very well, Hoglah. And I promise you won't lose your job."

"But I can't—"

"This weighs a full shekel. Think how long and how hard you'd have to work for a shekel. Think how much laundry you'd have to wash. But this can be yours, just for helping me."

Hoglah's eyes revealed her fear. "What would I have to do?"

Hephzibah took her arm, pulling her along. "Nothing—just trade clothes with me. Then wait in my room until I get back. That's all. Pretend to be asleep."

"But if you don't come back, they will blame me, and—"

"I promise I'll come back. Where else would I go? Come on. We have to hurry."

Hephzibah kept Hoglah moving, giving her little time to think or to argue. As soon as they reached her room, Hephzibah peeled off her outer garment and kicked off her shoes. "Undress, Hoglah. Hurry!"

The front of the old woman's garment was cold and wet from scrubbing clothes. As Hephzibah slipped it on, it felt rough and itchy and stank of stale sweat. "You can lie down on my bed," she said. "If anyone comes, pretend to be asleep."

"Oh, please, my lady . . . I can't . . ."

Hephzibah put her arm on the old woman's shoulder and guided her down onto the bed. "It'll be all right, Hoglah. I promise."

Hephzibah closed the door behind her as she left the room, cutting off the sound of Hoglah's tears. She lifted the tattered shawl over her head and bent her shoulders to conceal her face as she shuffled toward the servants' gate. Hoglah's worn sandals flopped on and off as she walked.

"Finished early today, Hoglah?" the old gatekeeper asked as he opened the latch for her. Hephzibah nodded and tried to keep walking, but he caught her arm. "Hey, what's your hurry? Are you mad at me or something?"

"Going to the Temple," Hephzibah mumbled, trying to imitate Hoglah's raspy voice. She clutched a golden earring in her hand for a bribe, but she hoped she wouldn't need it.

"All right. Let me know what the announcement is when you get back."

Hephzibah hurried away, her shoes flopping noisily, and began the steep climb up the hill to the Temple. Unaccustomed to exercise, she longed to sit down and rest when she reached the top but found no place in the Women's Court. Hephzibah tried in vain to push her way through the enormous crowd to reach the wall that separated the women from the men, but the well-dressed Judean women shoved her to the rear.

"Don't you know your place, girl? Stand in the back with the other servants."

"But I can't see—"

"Go on! Get away from here! You stink!"

Disappointment brought tears to Hephzibah's eyes as they forced her to stand near the rear of the courtyard. She was shorter than most of the other women and could view only the backs of their heads. Her longing to see Hezekiah ate away at her heart. She caught momentary glimpses of the royal dais between the bobbing heads and saw Hezekiah's purple and gold robes, but she couldn't see his face from this distance. She tried to remember the feeling of his arms surrounding her, the sound of his heartbeat when her head rested on his chest, the scent of his clothes and hair, but she couldn't. The courtyard swam through her tears. When the trumpets sounded their fanfare, the crowds grew still. Hezekiah's strong, clear voice carried across the courtyards. She closed her eyes in pain.

"Men of Jerusalem, we've now received word that the Assyrians have declared war on our nation. I've made defensive alliances with the nations around us, and they will stand with us against the enemy. Our city is well fortified and well prepared for a siege."

The Assyrians had declared war on Judah! Hephzibah remembered how much Hezekiah loved his tiny country and how worried he had been when the city of Samaria had fallen seven years ago. He would soon endure the greatest trial of his life, but she could do nothing to help him. Even if she knew the words that would console him, she had forfeited any right to say them. Again Hephzibah briefly caught sight of his purple robes between the bobbing heads.

"Be strong and courageous," Hezekiah continued. "Do not be afraid or discouraged because of the king of Assyria and the vast army with him, for there is a greater power with us than with him. With him is only the arm of flesh, but with us is the LORD our God to help us and to fight our battles."

He signaled the Levites, and the sacrifice began. Smoke from the altar curled above the crowd as the music played, but Hephzibah was too far away to understand the words or to feel like part of the worship. She craned her neck, trying in vain to keep the speck of purple in sight through her tears.

Knowing she may never have a chance to escape the villa again, Hephzibah began edging toward the south wall of the Women's Court, hoping to glimpse Hezekiah as he descended the royal walkway on his way back to the palace. She made slow progress, enduring poking elbows and harsh glares as she forced her way through the crush of people, but by the time the service had ended, she had reached the edge of the courtyard. The royal walkway stood 30 yards away. She wasn't allowed to go any closer.

The crowd buffeted her as they filed from the Temple, and she clutched the wall to keep them from propelling her out of the courtyard along with them. As she watched the royal dais, she squinted in the bright sunlight. Hezekiah stood beside Jerusha's husband; then they stepped off the dais together and began their descent to the palace.

For a few fleeting seconds, Hephzibah had a glimpse of Hezekiah as he hurried past. His dark eyes were clouded with worry, his lips tight with anger. He walked with a weary, limping stride, dragging a leg that was stiff and scarred. His head was lowered, his shoulders hunched forward as if wading into a tempest. Then he vanished from sight.

After all the weeks of planning and waiting for this opportunity, it was over. She had seen him. Hephzibah trembled at the magnitude of what she had done to him and what they had lost. She covered her face and wept, sobbing bitterly in the uncaring crowd.

"Hephzibah . . ."

She looked up, startled. A stranger stood on the other side of the wall from her. He had a faded reddish-gray beard and eyes the color of the sky. She wanted to run, but fear froze her feet to the pavement.

"Forgive me, Hephzibah. I'm sorry if I startled you."

"You know me?"

"I'm Isaiah ben Amoz, a distant relative of your husband."

"You're mistaken. I no longer have a husband."

"I know. But I have a message from Yahweh for you and for all of God's people. Yahweh has rejected his bride in anger, just as your husband has rejected you. But neither king will stay angry forever."

"The king will never forgive me for what I've done to him."

Isaiah's voice grew louder, stronger. "'Sing, O barren woman, you who never bore a child; burst into song, shout for joy, you who were never in labor; because more are the children of the desolate woman than of her who has a husband,' says the LORD." People stopped to listen to him, gathering around both of them. Hephzibah lowered her head, trying to hide her face. She wanted to run, but the crowd hemmed her in.

"Please . . . don't . . . ," she said, weeping.

"'Do not be afraid,'" Isaiah continued. "'You will not suffer shame. Do not fear disgrace; you will not be humiliated. You will forget the shame of your youth and remember no more the reproach of your widowhood. For your Maker is your husband—the LORD Almighty is his name—the Holy One of Israel is your Redeemer; he is called the God of all the earth. The LORD will call you back as if you were a wife deserted and distressed in spirit—a wife who married young, only to be rejected,' says your God."

"Please don't offer me false hope. I know God will never forgive me for what I've done."

Isaiah didn't seem to hear her. "'For a brief moment I abandoned you, but with deep compassion I will bring you back. In a surge of anger I hid my face from you for a moment, but with everlasting kindness I will have compassion on you,' says the LORD your Redeemer."

"Please stop—why are you doing this to me?"

"'Though the mountains be shaken and the hills be removed, yet my unfailing love for you will not be shaken nor my covenant of peace be removed,' says the LORD, who has compassion on you. 'O afflicted city, lashed by storms and not comforted, I will build you with stones of turquoise, your foundations with sapphires . . . All your sons will be taught by the LORD, and great will be your children's peace. In righteousness you will be established; tyranny will be far from you; you will have nothing to fear.'"

"No. It isn't true. Hezekiah will never forgive me, and neither will his God!"

She turned and forced her way through the crowd, leaving Isaiah behind, a look of bewildered sorrow in his eyes. When she reached the Temple gate, Hephzibah kicked off Hoglah's floppy shoes and carried them as she ran down the hill through the streets. By the time she reached the villa and hurried past the dozing gatekeeper, her feet were bruised and filthy.

She fled to her tiny cell and tore off Hoglah's clothes, sending the old widow away without a word of thanks. Then she closed the door to the outside and latched the shutters, sitting alone in the darkness. She wouldn't try to leave the king's villa again.

Iddina ducked inside the Philistine temple and paused to let his eyes adjust to the dim light. The stone structure felt refreshingly cool after the dust and heat outside. He found Emperor Sennacherib waiting for him in the inner chamber.

"There you are, Iddina. Congratulations—you're doing a splendid job inspiring fear in our enemies. Most of them are giving up without a fight."

Iddina hadn't seen the emperor since they had begun the western campaign; Sennacherib preferred to follow after the conquest collecting the spoil, while Iddina rode at the forefront, paralyzing the enemy with waves of shock and terror before the first bloody assault. Iddina bowed slightly. "Thank you, my lord. The campaign has gone well."

"Frankly I'm a little surprised that the Egyptians haven't come to help their allies yet."

"They are cowards, preferring to fight close to home."

"But if they had joined forces with their allies, they might have raised an army nearly the size of ours."

"Yes, it was a stupid strategy on their part, Your Majesty."

The emperor picked up a golden chalice from among the pile of sacred temple vessels and waited as his servant filled it with wine. Then he shoved the golden image of Dagon aside and hoisted himself up on the raised platform in the god's place.

"I want you to hear what I've written in my annals, Iddina. Go ahead—read it to him."

"'From the annals of Sennacherib,'" his scribe read, "'Luli, King of Sidon, fled out to sea and died. His fortified cities of Sidon, Zarephath, Achzib, and Acco were stunned by the prevailing arms of Assur, my god, and they bowed at my feet.'"

"And now you can add the story of King Mitini of Ashkelon," Iddina said. "When he saw our forces surrounding his city, he went insane."

The emperor laughed. "All our victories should be so easy! Pour me some more wine," he told his servants, "and tell the soldiers to bring in the Philistine priests."

Two soldiers entered with the captive high priest of Dagon, a distinguished-looking man with flowing white hair and beard. His stout body, dressed in a robe of fine linen, testified to a life of ease and privilege, but he moved in a daze, as if trying to awaken from a bad dream. Iddina laughed as he watched the sweat pour down the man's face like a common laborer's. As a man of power and one of the Philistine elite, the high priest had probably never perspired like this in his entire life. The soldiers brought two other priests in with him, one in his mid-40s, the other in his early 20s. Their chalky faces and jerky movements betrayed their terror.

"Blasphemy!" the high priest cried when he saw Sennacherib sitting in Dagon's place, drinking from the ritual cup.

"But I conquered these gods of yours, so who is superior?" Sennacherib asked. "Why shouldn't I take Dagon's place and drink from his cup? I am obviously more powerful than he."

More soldiers entered and began loading all the sacred vessels and images, clearing the sanctuary while the men talked. The high priest looked confused, bewildered, as if watching his life come apart before his eyes.

"Would you like a moment to say good-bye to your gods?" Iddina asked.

"Where are you taking them?"

"To the temple of Nisroch in Assyria," Sennacherib said. "I have a rather nice collection of all the gods and goddesses I've conquered. Now I can add these to my collection as well."

He hopped down from his seat and strode around the temple, examining the furnishings, signaling to the soldiers who streamed in and out whenever he saw something that appealed to him. Iddina liked working with Sennacherib; he didn't waste time. The emperor could plunder the temple and interrogate these priests at the same time.

"But that's not why you're here, gentlemen. Our next target is your neighbor to the east, the king of Judah. I understand that he's your ally. You can spare yourselves an agonizing death by cooperating with Iddina, my Rabshekah. You simply have to tell him what he wants to know, and he'll let you live."

The high priest looked at the other two. "Don't help them. Die like men, not traitors. They're going to kill us all anyway."

"Whether or not you die isn't what's important," Iddina said. "It's how long it takes you to die." The high priest stared stubbornly as Sennacherib sat down on the platform again.

"I assume you don't want to cooperate then?" Iddina asked.

"I'll do nothing to help you."

Sennacherib sighed, shaking his head. "That's too bad."

Iddina signaled to two of his soldiers, and they gripped the high priest's arms and dragged him from the room. Iddina studied the pallid faces of the other two priests while he waited, feeding off the fear he saw in their eyes. The room fell silent. The torture his soldiers would inflict on the high priest would be horrible, but what took place in these men's imaginations was a much more potent form of torture.

A full five minutes passed without a sound. Sennacherib sipped his wine, looking thoughtful. Iddina stood perfectly still, his arms crossed on his chest, not moving a muscle. Sweat poured down the faces of the two priests, and Iddina could see their knees trembling. The shaking gradually spread through their entire bodies.

Suddenly, quite close by, an agonized scream tore through the silence. Terror gripped the two priests in its power, and they fell to their knees, their legs no longer able to support them.

"I'll cooperate," the younger one cried. "What do you want to know?"

But Iddina simply smiled and cocked his head toward the anguished cries as if listening to beautiful music. Several more minutes passed and the screaming continued, blood-curdling, horrifying, until both priests began to weep. The older priest crawled forward on his knees and gripped Iddina's feet.

"Please . . . please . . ."

"Tell me about Judah's king."

The priest's voice shook as the words tumbled out. "His name is Hezekiah . . . from the dynasty of David . . . he's reigned 14 years . . . he's popular with the people . . . very prosperous . . . a soldier . . ."

"What gods does he worship?"

"One . . . only one God . . . Yahweh. The king is telling the people that Yahweh will deliver them from your hands."

Iddina laughed out loud. "What makes him think Yahweh will succeed when your gods and the gods of all the other nations have failed?"

"I . . . I don't know . . . Yahweh is a powerful God . . . He sent terrible plagues on Egypt centuries ago when they won their freedom . . . and He intervenes in Judah's battles, giving them victory."

"We'll soon see about that," Iddina said. He suddenly remembered how Jerusha had eluded him, and he grew tense with excitement as he neared his goal—he must defeat her God.

"Where is Yahweh's Temple?" Sennacherib asked.

"In Jerusalem."

The younger priest suddenly entered the conversation as if anxious to cooperate, his voice high-pitched with fear. "The people used to worship at altars and high places scattered throughout the country, but when Hezekiah became king he destroyed all the shrines. He makes the people worship in Jerusalem."

"Was this a popular decision?" Iddina asked.

"No, not everyone agreed with it."

"Could I use this to turn the people against their king?"

"Yes, I—I think so."

Sennacherib picked up a small calf idol, handling it like a toy. "Tell us about their God, Yahweh. What form does He usually take?"

The younger priest spoke first. "The Judeans have no image to represent their God. He is—"

"Wait a minute. What do you mean, no image?"

"It's been that way for centuries. Their laws forbid the people to make an image of their God."

Iddina couldn't comprehend anything so foolish, and he felt angry at the Judeans for denying him an image for the emperor's collection. "But how can they worship without a representation of their God?"

"They hold sacrifices to an unseen God. It is the wonder of all the nations, this imageless worship of theirs."

"One God with no image? And they've convinced the ignorant masses to believe in something so vague and foolish?"

"Yes, they—"

The screaming outside suddenly stopped, and Iddina held up his hand for silence. Both priests held their breath, waiting, probably guessing that their high priest was dead. Iddina knew better. He smiled to himself, knowing that the soldiers would revive the man any minute. He waited until the chilling cries began all over again, until the two priests wept uncontrollably, pleading with him between screams.

"Please . . . please . . . we'll do anything you say . . ."

"Tell me," Iddina continued, "is there nothing in Yahweh's Temple that represents this unseen God?"

The younger priest sobbed pitifully, too distraught to answer. He pressed his hands to his ears to drown out the sounds of torture. The older priest struggled through his terror to reply, gasping between his words. "Yes . . . in the Temple . . . they have an ark made of gold. The cover is said to be Yahweh's mercy seat."

Sennacherib nodded at Iddina, pleased. "That'll have to do. If we can't have an image of Yahweh, we'll settle for His throne."

The younger priest looked up. "It's very powerful, my lord!"

"Pardon me?" Sennacherib said.

"Yahweh's ark! It contains powerful magic!"

"Is that so? Why don't you tell us what you know about this magic?" Iddina spoke kindly to the young man, like a father to his son.

"Our ancestors once captured the ark of Yahweh in battle and brought it to Ashdod. They put it here in Dagon's temple, but the next morning Dagon had fallen on his face before the ark."

Sennacherib laughed out loud. "How amusing! We must remember that story, Iddina, and tell it to our priests. Maybe we should put Dagon's image beside Yahweh's ark again and see what happens." He and Iddina laughed together.

The young man's face looked pitifully hopeful. He had made the emperor laugh. Maybe he would be spared. He grinned nervously, his face a death mask. "Wait . . . there's more. Our priests put Dagon back in his place, and the following morning he had fallen a second time. This time his head and hands had broken off and were lying on the threshold. To this day we're forbidden to step on the threshold."

"So Yahweh proved to be more powerful than Dagon," Iddina said.

The older priest jumped in to finish the story. "But Yahweh was very angry with us for capturing His ark. When it arrived in Ashdod, He sent a plague and a pestilence with it."

"What sort of plague?"

"He filled our city and the surrounding territories with rats and afflicted our people with deadly tumors. Thousands of Philistines died of these tumors until our leaders finally moved the ark to Gath. But then the tumors and rats afflicted the people of Gath too. They begged the leaders to get rid of the ark of the God of Israel—so they carried it to Ekron. But when the panic of death filled Ekron, the rulers finally sent the ark away . . . back to Israel . . . with an offering."

"What was your offering?" Iddina asked.

"We made golden images of rats and tumors, one for each Philistine city. Then the plague finally stopped."

"A fascinating story! Did you get that all down?" Sennacherib asked the scribe who was writing furiously. "Rats and tumors. What do you make of all that, Iddina?"

"I think I would like to capture this mysterious ark. Where does Hezekiah keep it?"

"In Yahweh's Temple in Jerusalem. It's in a place that's so holy that only their high priest has ever seen it."

"Interesting," Sennacherib said. "Yes, now I'm certain that I'd like to add this invisible God's throne to my collection. Get it for me, Iddina."

He smiled. "Yes, Your Majesty."

Sennacherib hopped down from the platform. "You have been very helpful, gentlemen. Thank you. And now—"

Outside, the high priest's screaming, which had added an ominous accompaniment to the long tale, suddenly stopped again. The perfect timing pleased Iddina. He waited, bowing his head as if in prayer while the two Philistines shivered and wept. They were probably hoping that their high priest was finally dead, that the torture was over. But Iddina knew that if the soldiers did the job correctly, it wouldn't be over for many long days. He glanced at their faces, savoring their torment. Minutes passed; then the agonized moans began once again.

"There," Iddina said, smiling. "And now I believe it is your turn, gentlemen."

The priests collapsed like rag dolls, whimpering pitifully. "No . . . no . . . please! We told you what you wanted to know!"

"Yes, you're right—I did promise, didn't I? Very well," he told the soldiers. "Make sure you kill them quickly. Don't take more than two or three days, all right?"

"You said we would live!"

Iddina shrugged. "I lied."

21

As twilight fell, General Jonadab slumped against the parapet on top of the city wall and closed his eyes. In a few minutes the sky would turn dark enough to send a message by signal fire to King Hezekiah in Jerusalem. He wished he had better news to tell the king than that he had failed, that the Assyrians would soon demolish his fortified city of Mizpeh. Nothing had gone as Jonadab had thought it would. The defense of Judah, which he had planned and prepared for, had collapsed in shambles. Thousands of Assyrians had poured through the mountain passes into Judean territory. Without reinforcements, the Judean army could only huddle inside their fortifications and wait for the Egyptian army's help.

The wall beneath Jonadab shook with the rhythmic pounding of a battering ram. Like a thudding heartbeat, it never ceased day or night. He felt the wall shuddering, weakening with each powerful blow. In the waning light he watched his aide approach, skirting along the top of the wall, bending low.

"How much more pounding do you think this wall can take?" the man asked, crouching beside Jonadab.

"Not much more. Is the millstone ready?"

"They're bringing it now. Are we going to throw it off after dark?"

"It's our only chance. The Assyrians keep the battering rams too well protected in daylight."

"Their archers are deadly, sir."

"I know. I'm tired of watching row after row of our finest soldiers fall every time we peer over the wall to take aim. No more."

Jonadab's troops had suffered such devastating losses that he had finally ordered them not to return the enemy's fire. The Assyrians stood below in orderly rows, archers in front, artillerymen with sling stones behind. Each row fired, then knelt to reload in routine, lethal fashion.

"The flaming torches didn't work?" his aide asked.

Jonadab shook his head, his face grim. "The Assyrians were ready for them. They doused the flames before the battering rams even caught fire. Listen—hear that?" In the silence between each pounding blow, the clear sound of hammer and chisel chipping against stone rang out in the night.

"What is that?"

"They've got sappers working to enlarge the hole the battering rams make. They're right below us. We can't even see them, let alone stop them."

"Persistent, aren't they? What's their hurry?"

Jonadab rubbed his eyes. "From the time Sennacherib made his first strike against Babylon, his strategy has been to move so quickly that the allies don't have time to rescue each other. It's working too."

"Where are the Egyptians? Why aren't they here helping us?"

"I'd give my right eye to know. We could have defended the mountain passes with their help and kept the Assyrians out of Judah. Now they've broken through, and we're no match for them alone."

Jonadab rose to a crouch as a knot of soldiers came into view, rolling and heaving a huge millstone toward him. Then, raising his shield to protect his head, he stood and peered over the wall at the battering ram below him. As he gauged his target, a sling stone whizzed past his head.

"General, look out!"

A second stone bounced off the edge of his shield, smashing into the side of his face. His aide grabbed Jonadab around the waist and pulled him down behind the wall.

"You're hit!"

"No, I'm all right. It's just a nick." But the fist-sized rock had stunned him momentarily, and Jonadab's cheek stung painfully as he wiped away the blood with his fingers. "Roll the stone over here," he said when he had recovered. "That cursed battering ram is right below us. And maybe we can flatten a few of those mongrels with the chisels while we're at it."

They rolled the stone into place, then Jonadab signaled to his archers to line up on either side of him and create a diversion. A hail of Assyrian arrows and stones followed their meager volley, and even in the fading daylight Jonadab saw too many of his Judean soldiers falling under the onslaught.

"OK, heave!" Jonadab put his shoulder to the huge millstone and helped shove it through the embrasure in the wall. Frustration and bitterness fueled his strength. The stone tottered off the edge and disappeared. A moment later anguished cries and the satisfying sound of crunching metal and wood came from below as the stone smashed into its target. Jonadab grabbed his shield and peered over to look. The millstone had crushed the armored section around the workers and broken the battering ram's protruding beam clean off.

"Bulls-eye!" he shouted. "It's out of business for good!" He ducked behind the wall again as a heavy round of arrows and stones pounded into his shield, nearly knocking it from his grasp. "They're not too happy about it, either," he said, grinning. The weary Judeans cheered. But the celebration ended quickly when one of the sweating men who had helped roll the millstone to the top of the wall suddenly stood up. "I've got to see this . . ."

"No!" Jonadab cried. He dove forward to tackle the man around the knees, but he was too late. Two Assyrian arrows had already punctured the man's chest. His friends knelt beside him, cursing and weeping helplessly as he died. "How can they shoot like that in the dark?" Jonadab mumbled.

He watched soberly as the soldiers tended to the wounded and dying archers, aware of the undisturbed stillness now that the pounding had ceased and the wall no longer trembled beneath his feet. But 30 feet below, the faint clang of chisels meant that the sappers had resumed their work, finishing the job that the ruined battering ram had begun. It might take them longer, but those cursed heathens would accomplish their goal.

Jonadab longed to give up, to lie down and recover the three nights of sleep he'd lost. But he had to hold the besieged city as long as he possibly could. He had to hang on until Egyptian reinforcements arrived. Together, they could still drive the Assyrians back.

When all the wounded had been tended, he signaled to his aide, and they crept away. "How is the Assyrian ramp progressing?" he asked.

"Quickly. Much too quickly."

"I want to see it." The two men skirted the top of the wall, crouching low. All along the way Judean soldiers huddled miserably behind the parapet with their weapons lying idly beside them. Many of them—too many of them—wore bandages from earlier skirmishes. They were losing. Everyone knew it. In a matter of hours the Assyrians would breach the walls, and hundreds of thousands of them would pour inside. Outnumbered, the Judean defenders would be slaughtered.

Jonadab's aide stopped when they reached the section of the wall where the Assyrians were constructing their earthworks. "It's right down there, sir."

"Prepare some torches. We'll throw them over the side as a diversion instead of risking more of our archers." His men retrieved bundles of tightly wrapped straw soaked in oil, manufactured by the women and children of the besieged city. When Jonadab gave the signal, the soldiers lit the torches and hurled them over the wall in a steady volley of flames. Then he carefully raised his shield and gazed down at the scene below.

Progress on the ramp had proceeded so quickly that he could scarcely believe it. It was nearly three-quarters finished! He saw laborers scattering to avoid the rain of torches and realized that the Assyrians worked on the ramp even though the sun had set. Under clear, starlit skies and a brilliant full moon, they could work throughout the night. He stared down in angry disbelief until a shower of stones and arrows forced him down.

"Curse them all! How could they make that much progress? Can't we stop them?"

"They keep up a steady covering fire to protect the workers."

"Then fire on the workers!"

"Our men won't do that, sir. The Assyrians are using captured Judean slaves to build the earthworks. We'd be killing our own people."

Jonadab closed his eyes and leaned against the wall. It shuddered beneath him as another Assyrian battering ram pounded into the wall nearby. Exhaustion and despair tore into Jonadab like a pack of wild beasts clinging to his throat. He no longer had the strength to shake them off.

"God in heaven, there must be something we can do . . . we have plenty of food supplies . . . they're showering us with enough ammunition to return fire . . . if we can just hold out a little longer . . ." He rubbed his burning eyes as his voice trailed off.

"Sir, what about the signal fire? Maybe we can find out when Pharaoh is sending reinforcements."

"You're right. Let's go." He hauled his aching body upright and followed his aide along the top of the wall to the signal tower, avoiding the frightened eyes of the soldiers they passed. These boys weren't seasoned warriors like the Assyrians. They were farmers and shepherds, young men barely old enough to grow beards. They should be home plowing their fields and flirting with the serving girls, not facing battle-hardened professionals who outnumbered them 10 to 1. He wanted to weep at the injustice of such a mismatched fight.

As he wearily climbed the stairs to the tower, Jonadab looked up at a perfect twilight sky, slowly fading from deep purple to black. At least he had managed to hold the Assyrians at bay for another day. He silently prayed for one more.

"What's the message, sir?" the signalman asked.

Should he send King Hezekiah the truth? Mizpeh, one of his strongest fortified cities, would probably fall before tomorrow night. And if Mizpeh couldn't hold out against the Assyrians, even with Jonadab commanding its defense, then none of the other fortified cities stood a chance of surviving either—including Jerusalem. Its defenses contained weaknesses too, and in time the Assyrians would find them and exploit them. He remembered Eliakim's warning and knew he had been right—they had greatly underestimated their enemy and overestimated their allies.

Jonadab peered through the narrow slit at the valley below, where fields and vineyards once stood. The shadowy forms of Assyrian tents stretched toward the horizon in every direction, dotted with flickering campfires. Tiny Judah didn't stand a chance. The signalmen waited for his message.

"Tell them—" Jonadab sighed. "Tell them we're still under heavy enemy attack, that we're waiting for the Egyptians—but that we will defend Mizpeh to the very last man."

"Yes sir."

"If you get a reply, I'll be in the command bunker."

A beautiful full moon perched on the horizon, illuminating the city streets as Jonadab climbed down from the wall and made his way to his command post. With so much light, the Assyrians would prod the slaves to continue with the earthworks throughout the night. The battering rams would also hammer relentlessly, with a fresh shift of archers covering for them. Jonadab could feel the pounding blows deep in his gut, even though he no longer stood on the wall.

Sennacherib's lightning campaign would rage all night while the city of Mizpeh huddled in uneasy slumber. Without Egyptian help, he couldn't possibly stop them. Jonadab sank onto the bench behind the plank table in his bunker and rested his head in his hands. He was trying to think of a way to halt the construction of the earthworks without killing Judean slaves when he fell into an exhausted sleep.

He awoke in a daze when his aide shook his shoulder. The light of early dawn filled the bunker along with the sound of heavy fighting.

"General! One of the battering rams has breached the south wall near the gate! They've finished the ramp too! Assyrians are pouring into the city!"

Jonadab scrambled to his feet, unsheathing his sword, willing his stiff legs and groggy mind to move faster. "Divide all the troops! Order them to cover both sectors. Now!" Jonadab's aide blocked his path.

"Sir, it's hopeless. We've already lost."

"If you're not going to follow my orders, then get out of my way!"

"No. I won't let you go out there, sir." He gripped Jonadab's shoulders and held him back. "It's hand-to-hand combat, and we're hopelessly outnumbered. We can't possibly win."

"Maybe not, but I intend to die fighting! Now let go of me!"

"Change out of your uniform, sir. They'll see that you're the commander in chief, and they'll—"

"You're wasting time! Let me go!"

"Listen to me. I've brought you some civilian clothes . . ." Suddenly Jonadab noticed that his aide wasn't wearing a military uniform.

"You miserable coward! My men are fighting for their lives! How do you think they'll feel when they see me in civilian clothes, trying to save my own neck?"

"Sir, the Assyrians always torture high-ranking officers, and—"

"Get out of my way!" Jonadab finally managed to twist free, and he strode to the door, sword in hand. "I've worn this uniform all my life—and if God wills, I'll die in it."

22

→⇒

After sunset King Hezekiah climbed the stairs to the signal tower on the north wall of Jerusalem. As he surveyed the quiet countryside on this chilly spring evening, he found it difficult to imagine the terrible slaughter taking place just miles away near his northern borders.

"Any word from General Jonadab?" he asked the two soldiers standing guard.

"No, Your Majesty. Not yet."

He remembered Jonadab's final message five nights ago—*We will defend Mizpeh to the very last man*—and he breathed a silent prayer for him. The general had been Hezekiah's friend since childhood, and he wished in vain that he had ordered him to stay in Jerusalem. Hezekiah had made too many mistakes in the past few months. He couldn't undo any of them.

"There's the signal, sir."

A pale star of light blinked on the horizon. Hezekiah waited for the translation, his hands squeezed into fists.

"It's from Michmash, Your Majesty. They say there's still no word from Jonadab in Mizpeh, but they presume the city is lost. The Assyrians have moved south to besiege Ramah. Michmash and Geba have prepared for the worst." The light blinked off. Hezekiah waited a few more minutes, but the horizon remained dark.

"Send a messenger to me at once if you receive any word from the general," he said. Then he began the long walk downhill to the palace, wishing he could do more for his friend than carry a useless weight of worry and sorrow. Lately, the news from his allies had depressed him, growing worse and worse. After conquering the Phoenicians, the Assyrians had thrown their forces against the Philistines. His own city of Lachish, governed by his brother Gedaliah, was also under siege. Emperor Sennacherib himself encamped there, using Lachish as his headquarters while his troops finished destroying the Philistines. Then they would likely push deeper into Judah, closing toward Jerusalem from the south as well as from the north, gripping Hezekiah in a stranglehold. He had sent desperate pleas to Pharaoh for the help he'd promised but had received no reply. Against his will, Hezekiah was forced to conclude that little hope remained for his nation's survival. When he reached the wall surrounding the Temple, he paused, looking across the Kidron Valley in the twilight to the Mount of Olives and the rolling Judean hills.

"I lift up my eyes to the hills—where does my help come from? My help comes from the LORD, the Maker of heaven and earth . . ." Hezekiah recited the psalm to himself, trying to draw strength from its promises, to find peace in his heart. *"He will not let your foot slip—he who watches over you will not slumber . . . the LORD is your shade at your right hand; the sun will not harm you by day, nor the moon by night."*

In a few minutes Shebna and his other advisers would meet with him in the Council Room. Hezekiah faced another long strategy meeting filled with difficult decisions; after that, another long, sleepless night as he waited for dawn.

"The LORD will keep you from all harm—he will watch over your life; the LORD will watch over your coming and going both now and forevermore."

"Amen," Hezekiah whispered. "May it be so."

———◈———

Shebna stood in his room at the palace and gazed out the window at his tomb in the valley until darkness fell, wrapping the monument in a veil of shadows. Even the distinctive pyramid on top vanished in the night. He had built it as a memorial to his achievements, but now it served as a reminder of Isaiah's prophecy, a nagging taunt that mocked him. Isaiah had been right once again. The Egyptians had failed them. How could the man have known the future? The source of Isaiah's wisdom remained a frustrating, unexplained mystery.

Shebna had been so certain that intellect and reasoning could provide all the answers. He had relied on his own judgment, staking his entire career on the anti-Assyrian alliance. He had counseled Hezekiah to gamble their nation's future on the promised support from Babylon, Egypt, and the other allies. But now as catastrophic reports poured in, detailing disaster after disaster at the hands of the Assyrians and the slaughter of Judah's allies on the battlefield, Shebna knew his wisdom had failed.

Judah—once a free, prospering nation—would suffer defeat because of his advice. Joining the alliance had drawn the Assyrians' attention and wrath, just as Eliakim had warned it would. Shebna had never dreamed the Assyrians would advance this far, but Judah's fortified cities toppled one after the other as the enemy moved south, trampling and burning the beautiful Judean countryside. According to the reports, the Assyrians were slaughtering Judah's young men—the future of their nation—while women and children who had been free and were prospering just a few months earlier trudged into captivity as slaves.

Shebna was unaccustomed to failure. He had always been in control, victorious. Now his failure was causing the total destruction of his nation and would mean certain death for him. King Hezekiah had trusted him, believed in him. But the king should have listened to Eliakim. Once again, one of Isaiah's predictions would come true—*you disgrace to your master's house!*

Alone in his darkened room, Shebna unfastened the royal sash that symbolized his office and slipped the golden signet ring from his finger.

———◈———

Hezekiah paced restlessly in his chambers when the scribe arrived to summon him. "Your Majesty, your advisers are ready for you in the Council Room."

"Very well."

"But Lord Shebna has asked to speak to you alone first."

"Send him in."

As soon as Shebna walked through the door, Hezekiah noticed that he no longer wore the familiar purple sash of the palace administrator; he carried it folded in his hand. He bowed low, then laid the sash in front of Hezekiah and placed his signet ring and palace keys on top.

"What are you doing, Shebna?"

"I have come to resign."

"Now? In the middle of a crisis?"

"I have no choice. My counsel caused this terrible disaster, and I will offer you no more advice."

Hezekiah groaned and sank onto his couch. He had sustained so many blows in the past few weeks that he should have been immune to bad news by now, but Shebna's resignation stunned him.

"You picked a lousy time to desert me, Shebna. I need you."

"No. You need a palace administrator who has confidence in himself and in his decisions. I have none."

"Shebna—"

"I negotiated the treaty with Egypt. I believed Pharaoh's promise to help us. This is all my fault."

"You don't think help will arrive in time?"

Shebna shrugged. "I do not know, Your Majesty, and I am afraid to guess. The stakes are much too high."

Hezekiah groaned again and rubbed his temples. "Look—in spite of everything that's happened, I still have a great deal of confidence in you. I need your wisdom and experience to—why are you shaking your head?"

"I never dreamed I would admit this, but I have reached the limits of my wisdom. I cannot advise you anymore."

"What?"

"It all seemed so logical on paper—the allies would help each other, we would present a united front to hold Assyria back—but it all fell apart, and I do not know why. I cannot go on."

"Shebna—"

"Accept my resignation. You know that you must."

Hezekiah closed his eyes, remembering the argument between him and his grandfather over Shebna's appointment, remembering how Zechariah had quoted the psalmist: "'Blessed is the man who does not walk in the counsel of the wicked.'" He knew Shebna was right, but it was still a painful decision to make.

"I'm sorry, Shebna," he said quietly.

"So am I."

They gazed silently at each other for a moment; then Shebna pointed to the sash and ring on the table between them. "Who will you give these to?"

"You know there's only one other man who is capable."

"Eliakim." The bitterness in Shebna's voice shocked Hezekiah.

"Why do you hate him so much?"

"You asked me that question a long time ago, and I did not know the answer then, but I think I am finally able to put it into words." He paused for a moment, and Hezekiah noticed how naked Shebna looked, stripped of his pride. Deep shame and humiliation clothed him instead.

"I knew from the beginning that Eliakim's intellect rivaled mine, yet he clings to a superstitious belief in God, leaning on Yahweh for answers like a crippled man leans on a crutch. He believes his own wisdom has limits and that he must ask for God's wisdom when those limits are reached. But I do not believe there is a God, nor that there are any limits to what the human mind can accomplish. And so it became an unspoken contest between us—man with God versus man without Him. Which one of us would prove right?" He looked away, then said in a shaking voice, "It seems I have lost the contest."

"Are you saying you finally believe in Yahweh?"

"I wish I could believe, Your Majesty. I have seen too many coincidences over the years that cannot be denied—but my doubt remains. I am afraid it is part of me."

"You've placed man on God's throne, and now you can't get him off."

"According to your Torah, viewing man as the source of wisdom is a form of idolatry."

Hezekiah hated witnessing his friend's ruin. Shebna's despair and humiliation added yet another weight to the heavy burden Hezekiah already carried.

"If Eliakim accepts the position, I want you to replace him as secretary—I still need you on my council," he said at last.

"Do you really think that is wise?"

"Under the circumstances, I think it's necessary," he said angrily. "You're still an able administrator."

"Very well. Shall I summon Eliakim for you?"

Hezekiah sighed wearily. "All right. Send him in."

After Shebna left, Hezekiah felt utterly alone. Suddenly the prophecy Isaiah had spoken on the palace steps drifted through his mind: *"Till you are left like a flagstaff on a mountaintop, like a banner on a hill."*

Alone. Hezekiah had lost all the people who meant the most to him: his grandfather, his wife, Isaiah, Jonadab, and now Shebna, who had been with him from the very beginning. He thought of Yahweh's promise, *"I will never leave you nor forsake you,"* and he knew he needed a palace administrator who would remind him that the Lord was still his strength. A few minutes later Eliakim entered. Hezekiah recognized an inner reserve of peace and humility in Eliakim's soul that Shebna, with his endless analyzing and rationalizing, had always lacked. The terrible desolation that had filled Hezekiah at the thought of being cut loose from Shebna after all these years began to fade, replaced by a quiet conviction that Eliakim was the man Yahweh wanted at his right hand. But considering the crisis his nation faced, he wouldn't blame Eliakim for refusing to take over the reins of a nation that galloped out of control toward disaster.

"Eliakim, I know I've asked a great deal of you over the years—repairing the Temple, housing the refugees, digging the tunnel, building the defenses of Judah and Jerusalem. You've served me exceptionally well, and I'm very grateful."

"Thank you, Your Majesty."

"What I'm going to ask you now is probably more than I have any right to ask, especially when I consider how I've disregarded your wise counsel these past few months." He picked up Shebna's ring and toyed with it for a moment. "I've just accepted Shebna's resignation. I would like you to replace him."

"God of Abraham—You said this would happen!" Eliakim groped for the nearest seat and dropped into it. He seemed incapable of saying more, so Hezekiah continued.

"We both know that Judah is in serious trouble. So far, none of our allies has been able to withstand the Assyrians, and nothing I can see with my eyes tells me that we will be able to withstand them either. It's a dangerous time to sit at my right hand, knowing what the Assyrians will do to us if we lose. I don't expect an answer now. You may take time to pray if—"

"No, Your Majesty, I don't need any time. I already know God's answer. I've known since I was a boy."

"How is that possible?"

"The year I became of age, Rabbi Isaiah prophesied that this would happen, that one day God would place the key to the house of David on my shoulder. So regardless of our national crisis, I can't refuse God's will."

Hezekiah stared, amazed to learn that Eliakim was indeed God's choice. For some reason he suddenly thought of the two bronze pillars that stood in Yahweh's Temple. Long ago his grandfather had taught him their names: Boaz—in Him is strength; Jakin—Yahweh establishes. And he realized that they were amazingly similar to his name—the Lord is my strength—and Eliakim's name—the Lord will establish. He smiled slightly, certain that his grandfather would also approve of Eliakim.

Hezekiah placed the sash, ring, and keys in Eliakim's lap. "Here. These are yours now." He saw Eliakim's hands tremble slightly as he pulled the secretary's ring off his finger and put on the larger palace administrator's ring in its place. Then Eliakim fumbled with the purple sash and fastened the keys. "Are you ready?" Hezekiah asked.

Eliakim drew a deep breath, then exhaled. "Yes, Your Majesty."

A hush fell over the Council Room as Eliakim entered and took the seat on the king's right hand side. Hezekiah decided Shebna's absence needed no further announcement.

"Once again we face a critical decision," Hezekiah began. "I've heard nothing from General Jonadab at Mizpeh for five nights now.

Since the Assyrians have moved south to Ramah, I'm forced to assume the worst—that Mizpeh is lost and Jonadab is dead." He paused, swallowing an unexpected knot of grief, then cleared his throat.

"Meanwhile, Sennacherib has besieged Lachish and is using it as his base camp. I've been receiving desperate messages from my brother Gedaliah saying he is under a massive enemy assault and fighting for his life. He's not sure how much longer he can withstand such a fierce pounding. If Sennacherib continues to tighten this noose, with forces advancing on us from the north and the south, Jerusalem will soon be strangled in the middle. Neither our military forces nor those of our allies seem capable of stopping the enemy, and the Egyptian army is nowhere in sight. So after much wrestling, I've decided that I'm left with only one option—I will submit to Emperor Sennacherib and pay whatever tribute he demands. It's the only way to save what's left of our country."

A murmur swept through the room, then quickly died away. Eliakim turned to him, frowning. "Your Majesty, pay the tribute if you have to, but you must not agree to surrender the city. The Temple is here. There can be no enemy occupation of Jerusalem."

"I agree. I'll accept the same terms we had during my father's reign. We will be a self-governing vassal state paying annual tribute to the empire. I'll send a delegation to Lachish tomorrow to negotiate the terms of their withdrawal. I'll let everyone know their demands as soon as the delegation returns."

Late into the night Eliakim worked with King Hezekiah to draft a letter to Emperor Sennacherib. It began, "I have done wrong. Withdraw from me, and I will pay whatever you demand of me." They also decided to return the Assyrian vassal, King Padi of Ekron, whom Hezekiah had captured and kept in chains in Jerusalem. As they worked, Eliakim sensed the king's deep discouragement and despair.

Eliakim returned home after midnight. His house was dark, his family and all the servants asleep. He would have to wait until morning to share the news of his promotion. He crept up to his room without lighting a lamp, slipped off his robes, and carefully crawled into bed beside Jerusha, trying not to awaken her. But she stirred, then rolled over sleepily and snuggled beside him.

"Ooo, you're so cold, Eliakim."

"It's chilly outside."

"And your feet! They feel as if you've been wading in a mountain stream!"

"The palace always feels cold this time of year, even with all the braziers burning. I'm sorry I woke you."

"No, your baby is the one who's keeping me awake. He doesn't seem to know it's nighttime. Feel this." Jerusha took his hand and pressed it against her stomach.

Eliakim smiled as he felt the vigorous movement in her womb. "What's he doing in there?"

"I don't know, but I wish he'd stop." As she held his hand in place, Jerusha's fingers brushed the ornate palace administrator's ring. "What on earth is this?" She pulled his hand out from under the covers and held it in front of her face. "This isn't your ring."

"No. It's Shebna's."

"What are you doing with his ring?"

Eliakim recalled the happiness they had all shared the day he'd announced his promotion to secretary of state. Now he had earned the highest position in the land, yet he knew the news would not be celebrated this time. As King Hezekiah had said, it was a dangerous time to be palace administrator.

"Shebna resigned tonight. The king asked me to replace him."

She pushed him away and sat up. "No! You can't accept it!"

"I already have."

"But you know what the Assyrians will do to you if—"

"Yes. The same things they would do to me if I was the secretary of state."

"Why can't you resign too? Why can't we get out of Jerusalem before it's too late."

He tenderly brushed a strand of hair off her face. "Sweetheart, there's no place to go."

"Can't we go back to your cousins' farm in Beth Shemesh?"

"The Assyrians are just a few miles away from there, in Lachish."

"We could hide someplace safe, in the wilderness maybe, or—"

He sat up and took her into his arms, cutting off her words. "Jerusha, the safest place to be is in the will of God. 'A thousand may fall at your side, ten thousand at your right hand, but it will not come near you.'" She shivered, and he hugged her tighter. "Listen— I know that accepting this job is God's will for me, so we don't have to be afraid. 'If you make the Most High your dwelling . . . then no harm will befall you, no disaster will come near your tent.'"

"Eliakim, I'm so scared."

"Please trust me, Jerusha. Right now this is the safest place for all of us to be."

23

"Thirty talents of gold, Eliakim."

"A *ton*, Your Majesty?"

"Yes, and 300 talents of silver."

"God of Abraham—they may as well ask for a million."

Hezekiah stood in his palace treasury with Eliakim, examining the accumulated wealth of his reign. The delegation to Emperor Sennacherib had returned with the Assyrian tribute demands, and they had staggered Hezekiah. Even with full storehouses, he could see that he might not have enough.

"The last time we were in here was with the Babylonians," Hezekiah said. "God forgive me. I was such a fool." A surge of anger swelled inside him, trying to force its way out. It pushed against his lungs, making it difficult to breathe. "I felt so proud of myself when I showed them all these things. 'Look at all I've accomplished! Look at my wealth!' I forgot that it was all a gift from God. And now I'm forced to hand over every last shekel of it."

"Thank God you have it. It will save our nation."

"Yes, I guess so." He walked over to the golden box the Babylonians had given him, decorated with forbidden idols, and he grew so angry with himself that he had to fight the urge to smash the box into pieces. "Why didn't I listen to you? Why did I accept this cursed thing and bring this disaster upon us?"

Eliakim didn't answer. Hezekiah gave the golden ark a shove with his foot. "Pride is an ugly thing, Eliakim. And it has caused the downfall of many other kings before me. I should have known better." With his anger still smoldering, he turned to Eliakim again. "I'm sorry. We'd better get to work."

For more than an hour Hezekiah helped Eliakim tally the weight of the items in the treasury. When they finished, Eliakim stared at his computations, his brow creased in a worried frown.

"It's not enough, is it?" Hezekiah said.

"No. We'll have to levy taxes."

Hezekiah groaned. "I'd hoped I wouldn't have to tax the people for my own mistakes."

"I'm sure they'd rather pay than be annihilated, Your Majesty."

"Of course. You're right."

Eliakim checked his figures again, then looked up. "But that still may not be enough."

"Are you sure?"

"Eleven tons is a lot of silver. And a ton of gold?" He shook his head. "Even if we got a shekel from every man, woman and child . . . there's just not that much gold in Jerusalem except in the—"

"No! I won't strip the Temple!"

"Then we may have to surrender."

Anger raced through Hezekiah like a brush fire, hot and swift. He picked up a silver bowl and hurled it against the wall. "I curse them! They can have everything I own, but I won't give them Yahweh's gold!"

Eliakim touched his arm. "Your Majesty, if we don't pay this tribute, they'll destroy us. Either way they'll get Yahweh's gold. Wouldn't it be better to give it to them now and save the Temple from total destruction?"

As quickly as it had flared, Hezekiah's anger cooled. The fire went out, replaced with the familiar leaden heaviness that wouldn't lift. He was living a nightmare. "Let's get it over with, then."

They trudged up the hill to the Temple in silence. For weeks, now, Hezekiah's life had trudged uphill like this, while he carried a heavy weight on his shoulders and dragged huge stones of grief and sorrow from both of his ankles. Time and events seemed to gallop past him at breakneck speed while he plodded slowly on, unable to keep up. His days and nights had reversed so that he felt groggy and exhausted during the day, then lay wide awake throughout the night, his eyes refusing to close, his mind unable to find rest. When would it end?

The high priest led them to the Temple storeroom, and Eliakim began tallying the weight of the meat hooks, platters, tongs, bowls, and all the other gold and silver utensils used for the sacrifices. Hezekiah remembered coming to this storeroom with his grandfather, staring at the naked shelves after his father had stripped them. "Will this be enough?" Hezekiah asked when Eliakim finished. He prayed that it would be—that he wouldn't have to do what his father had done and strip the holy sanctuary.

Eliakim bit his lip. "There's probably enough silver, but . . . I'm sorry . . . we'll still need more gold."

Cold shock extinguished the fire of Hezekiah's anger. He shuddered as his body went numb all over at the terrible news. "I'm sorry," he told the high priest. "I'm so sorry . . ."

"It can't be helped," the high priest said.

"I never meant for this to happen . . . I . . ."

"I know, Your Majesty. Lord Eliakim, if we strip the gold off the sanctuary doors, will that give us enough?"

Eliakim ran his fingers through his hair as he checked his calculations. "Yes, I think so, God willing."

As they emerged into the courtyard again, the cold and the dampness and the leaden clouds matched Hezekiah's mood. He stared guiltily at the golden Temple doors for the last time. "I remember how excited I was as a child, going to the Temple with my grandfather to see the golden doors," he told Eliakim. "But when I got here they weren't gold after all. They were wood—ugly, scarred wood. I was so angry with my father for stealing them—and now I've done the same thing."

"As soon as the nation gets back on its feet, we can repair them," Eliakim said. "We've done it before."

Hezekiah shook his head. "I've brought our country right back to where I started when my father died. The treasuries are empty, the nation is bankrupt, we're slaves to Assyria, the Temple is defaced and pillaged—even the prophets are speaking out against me."

"It's not the same, Your Majesty. King Ahaz's idolatry caused his downfall, but—"

"There's more to idolatry than worshiping statues, Eliakim. Putting our faith and trust in something other than God is also idolatry. I should have obeyed the Law instead of signing that treaty with Babylon. Now I've lost everything I've worked for these past 14 years."

"There's one thing you can never lose," Eliakim said quietly, "one thing your father never had: your faith in Yahweh. King David sinned too, first with Bathsheba, then when he numbered the Israelites. He suffered the consequences of his sin, but Yahweh didn't forsake him. And He won't forsake you either. As David himself has written, 'The LORD is gracious and compassionate, slow to anger and rich in love . . . The LORD is near to all who call on him . . . he hears their cry and saves them.'"

"If only I'd relied on Him to begin with instead of on the arm of the flesh." Hezekiah felt an ache in the pit of his stomach as he looked at the morning sacrifice burning on the Temple altar. It seemed unfair that an innocent lamb had to die to pay the price for his sin. He turned away and began walking toward the palace.

"I guess we've finally hit bottom, haven't we?"

"Things can only get better, Your Majesty."

"Only because they can't get worse. We'll pay the Assyrians their tribute—then maybe this nightmare we're all living will finally end."

———◆———

The journey over Judah's rugged mountain passes had exhausted Iddina, and by the time he reached Lachish, his mood had turned foul. Why would the emperor waste time summoning him back to headquarters? The besieged city of Anathoth had just fallen, and Iddina had wanted to participate in the slaughter. It was the last city standing in his path to Jerusalem and the Temple of Judah's god.

Iddina found Emperor Sennacherib seated on his ivory throne outside his royal pavilion. A court scribe sat at his feet taking notes while the emperor's artist busily sketched the besieged city of Lachish, which stood on the hill opposite them.

"Ah, General Iddina! You're just in time to tell me what you think of the artwork I've commissioned."

Iddina peered over the artist's shoulder at the detailed drawings of the fortress of Lachish. In the picture, battering rams pounded the walls, portions of the city were in flames, Assyrian archers and slingmen launched a rain of missiles while Judeans tumbled from the walls to their deaths. Soldiers marched the prisoners of war away from the conquered city along with the booty of Lachish. But across the valley the actual city looked nothing like the drawing. The battering rams stood silent, the soldiers idle, and the city gates remained tightly barred. For some reason, the battle had halted without a victory.

"I'm going to have these drawings made into wall murals for my palace in Nineveh. What do you think of them?"

Iddina didn't care about the emperor's foolish art projects. He wanted to know why the siege had been called off and why he'd been summoned to Lachish.

"Nice pictures, Your Majesty," he mumbled.

"Yes, I think so too. And this is what I'm inscribing on the prism to commemorate our western campaign." He motioned to his scribe. "Go ahead. Read it to him."

"'As for Hezekiah the Jew, who did not submit to my yoke, I laid siege to 46 of his strong cities, walled forts, and to the countless small villages in their vicinity. I conquered them by means of well-stamped earthen ramps and battering-rams brought near to the walls combined with the attack by foot soldiers, using mines and breaches as well as sapper work. I drove out 200,150 people, young and old, male and female, horses, mules, donkeys, camels, cattle beyond counting, and considered them booty. Himself I made prisoner in Jerusalem, his royal city, like a bird in a cage.'"

"Would you say that's an accurate description of what we've accomplished, Iddina?"

"Yes, Your Majesty. So far."

"Good. And now that King Hezekiah is finished off, we can move on to Egypt."

"Wait a minute. We haven't conquered him yet. I haven't taken Jerusalem."

"King Hezekiah paid tribute to me three days ago. I asked an exorbitant amount, by the way, and the man actually paid it—30 tons of silver and a ton of gold."

"Is that why you've called off the siege of Lachish?"

"Yes. There's no sense wasting any more energy on this pitiful country. Your forces can join mine for the final assault against Egypt."

"But why are the gates of Lachish still barred? Why haven't they surrendered the city?"

"Those were the terms I agreed to. They paid my enormous tribute demands in exchange for our immediate withdrawal."

"You can't do that!" Iddina wanted to snap someone's neck in frustration. He didn't care about tribute payments; conquering Judah was the goal of his western campaign! He wanted to flatten the entire nation in revenge for Jerusha's escape! Her god was the one he had most wanted to subdue and control! The emperor couldn't quit now—not this close to victory!

Sennacherib gazed at him in surprise. "I've already accepted those terms, Iddina. What's the problem?"

Iddina forced himself to calm down. He could never explain his motivation to the emperor. Personal revenge had no place in military strategy.

"I don't think we should move ahead to Egypt until we're occupying the fortresses of Jerusalem and Lachish," he said carefully. "We're leaving an undefeated enemy at our backs. And Lachish straddles our only line of communication and supply."

"Iddina, I cleaned out King Hezekiah's treasuries. You defeated most of his army. He's not a threat to us. He has nothing left."

"Your Majesty, if he could raise that much tribute so quickly, he probably has a lot more. Did he hand over the sacred articles from his Temple?"

"I don't recall seeing any images—no."

"They don't believe in images, Your Majesty. But Yahweh's golden throne—the one the Philistines talked about; remember?"

"Now that you mention it, I don't think they sent it. The only golden ark I saw appeared to be a Babylonian one."

"Then they must have more gold. Lots more. And they might use it to purchase weapons and mercenaries to attack us from the rear. Besides, we need to conquer *all* the gods, Your Majesty, including Judah's. Hezekiah must surrender both cities as well as his Temple."

"I already accepted his terms of submission."

"*I* didn't accept them! And if you give me a chance, I can force Hezekiah to surrender!"

Sennacherib stared at him curiously for a moment, then broke into a sly smile. "I like you, Iddina. You're a clever, devious man. Very well—take as many troops as you need, and go tell King Hezekiah that I've changed my mind."

"You won't regret it, Your Majesty."

"I think you should arrive at dawn, Iddina. Scare them to death when they're still half asleep. Or better still, at dusk, when they're tired and hungry after a hard day's work."

"With all due respect, Your Majesty, the best time to stun an enemy is right after breakfast, when everyone is awake and out about his business. I want every man in Jerusalem to see our army gathered in force and to hear my demands. They'll quickly realize there's no hope. They'll turn against King Hezekiah and surrender Jerusalem to me in record time."

"Then do it."

"What about Lachish, Your Majesty?"

"Yes, you're quite right. I suppose we should finish what we've started here too."

"After all," Iddina said, grinning, "you wouldn't want those murals on your palace walls to tell a lie, would you?"

24

The instant Jerusha heard the ominous rumbling, she recognized the sound. She had heard it on the morning of her cousin's wedding in Dabbasheth when her world had come to an end, and she had felt it in the cistern beneath her father's house as she had huddled beside her sister. She would never forget that sound as long as she lived.

"Eliakim—they're here!"

"What?"

"The Assyrians! I hear them!"

"God of Abraham—that's impossible." Eliakim struggled to his feet, rocking the breakfast table. For a moment Jerusha glimpsed his fear. Then, as he listened to the horrible rumbling, a change came over him, and his face hardened with determination. She saw his strength and his faith, and she wanted to cling to him as if to a rock in a flood, drawing strength from him. The rumbling grew louder.

"Listen, I have to go to the palace," he said. "Don't wait up for me. I'll probably be late." He bent to kiss Jerusha, just as he kissed her every morning—then he looked into her eyes for a long moment.

"Stay inside, Jerusha. Don't go to the wall. Don't look at them."

"I'm so scared!"

"Everything will be all right." He squeezed her shoulder; then he left.

Jerusha shivered as the rumbling grew louder, and she felt the baby tossing in her womb. Hilkiah wrapped a shawl around her, holding her tightly.

"Trust God, my child. Trust God," he said.

Jerusha tried to calm herself, knowing her fear was upsetting the baby. She began stacking the breakfast dishes, hoping to find consolation in the familiar task, then noticed little Jerimoth and Tirza poking at their untouched food.

"All done, Mama," Jerimoth said.

"No, you're not—you haven't even started. Come on, now." But when she picked up a spoon to feed Tirza, her hand shook. The terrible rumbling continued, growing louder in the background.

"Mama, is that thunder?" Jerimoth asked.

"No, it's people marching. And horses, my little one."

"How can horses make a sound like thunder?"

"It's their hooves. There are lots and lots of them."

"Are you cold, Mama?"

She couldn't stop shivering. "Yes. Just a bit. Let's sit outside in the garden where the sun is warm, shall we?"

"I want to see the horses."

"No, honey. Abba wants us to stay home."

"Can't we go see them for a minute, then come back home?"

Jerusha knew what the Assyrians would do in full view of the people on the wall. She shook her head. "No, love. We can't. Abba will take you to see the horses at the palace stables sometime. I promise."

Jerusha sat in the courtyard, watching her children play, but even the warmth of a thousand suns wouldn't have been able to make her stop shivering.

<hr>

"What's that sound?" Hezekiah asked his valet.

"I don't hear—"

"Shh . . . listen . . ."

A rumbling like summer thunder rolled in the distance in a long, ominous peal, yet the morning sun streamed through the palace window. The unending noise rumbled on, growing louder.

"It can't be thunder . . ." Then suddenly Hezekiah realized what it was, and he bolted to his feet. "No! I paid their ransom!" The small table with his breakfast tray toppled over as he pushed it aside and hurried out the door. He met Shebna in the courtyard outside.

"Is it the Assyrians, Your Majesty?"

"It must be."

"What more do they want from us? We submitted to them. We paid the tribute."

"There's only one thing left. They must want me to surrender the city."

"Will you?"

"Never."

They climbed the steep stairs to the wall overlooking the Kidron

Valley and arrived out of breath at the top. General Benjamin, who had taken over the defense of Jerusalem for Jonadab, soon joined them. Hundreds of soldiers swarmed to the wall to take up their positions, and Eliakim raced up with them, taking the steps two at a time.

"Those filthy liars!" he breathed. "We negotiated in good faith! We gave them a ton of gold! What are they doing here?"

"Dear God in heaven!" Hezekiah cried as he peered over the wall. Below him, thousands of Assyrians crawled across the valley like flies on dead meat. Sunlight glinted off hundreds of thousands of weapons: swords, arrows, shields, and spears. Horses, too numerous to count, churned up the new spring grass and pounded it into mud beneath their hooves. Scores of chariots rolled up the road, their painted spokes spinning and creaking, their banners flapping in the breeze, snapping like whips. It looked as if a dam had burst, flooding the valley with a deluge of enemy soldiers, transforming the green countryside to a sea of black. The sight stunned Hezekiah like a blow to the head, and he staggered against the wall as his knees went weak beneath him.

Assyrians filled the Kidron Valley, then surged up the slopes of the Mount of Olives in an endless wave. On and on they came, more and more and more of them. The sight paralyzed him. The little breakfast he had eaten rolled in his stomach until he felt sick at the unbelievable sight.

"Dear God, this can't be happening!"

There were more Assyrians outside the walls than people inside them, even with all the refugees from the surrounding villages. Yet there was an order and a pattern to the Assyrians' practiced movements, as if they had choreographed this invasion like a ritual dance. Some of the foot soldiers formed into ranks of archers and slingers, aiming their sights at the city walls. Others began pitching tents and corralling horses as if preparing for a lengthy siege. Each of the thousands of men knew his role and took his assigned post with alarming swiftness.

As they worked, they left a narrow strip of green grass between their camp and the city walls, and at first Hezekiah wondered why. Then, as they began carrying tall, sharpened stakes into the clearing, he moaned.

"O God, no!" He gripped the wall to steady himself as they dragged a pitiful band of naked Judean prisoners into the clearing beside the stakes. He recognized all these men; they were his army commanders and the city officials from the fortified cities conquered by the Assyrians. The prisoners had been brutally tortured, some of them blinded; many had no hands or feet.

"God of Abraham! They have Jonadab!" Eliakim cried.

Hezekiah groaned in helpless anguish as the Assyrians impaled Jonadab along with the others and left him dangling beneath the broiling sun to slowly die. At the sound of Jonadab's terrible screams, Eliakim put his face in his hands and wept.

As the cries of the tortured men crescendoed, Hezekiah turned away and saw the devastating effect the grisly scene had on the soldiers watching beside him. They gazed down at the general in stunned shock, many of them weeping openly like Eliakim. When Hezekiah looked down at Jonadab again, his heart twisted inside him. He fought back his own tears as he watched the tortured general writhe in agony.

"We have to do something to help him," he said.

Eliakim wiped his eyes with the back of his hand. "There's nothing we can do. He's dying."

"No, they won't let him die—not yet. They're deliberately prolonging his execution."

"That is the Assyrian way," Shebna said bitterly. "They delight in this warfare of the mind."

"Well, I have to stop to it," Hezekiah said. "General, bring me your best marksman. The least we can do is end Jonadab's suffering and deprive the Assyrians of one of their victims."

"Yes, Your Majesty."

As Hezekiah waited, the agonized screams of the tortured, dying men seemed to fill the valley. That's when he realized how silent the Assyrian troops were. It was almost as if the sound of death was music to their ears, and they stood in hushed reverence, like an audience before skilled musicians. Why else would 100,000 men be able to set up their siege in such disciplined silence? It was part of the terror they sought to instill. Judging by the faces of the men on the wall around him, Hezekiah knew that it was fulfilling its goal.

"Your Majesty, this is Helez, son of Abiel from Bethlehem," General Benjamin said when he returned. "He is our finest sharpshooter."

Helez bowed to the king, then pulled a bow from the quiver on his back and bent to string it. Hezekiah recognized the skill in his smooth movements, but he seemed little more than a boy—a farmer perhaps or a shepherd—hardly a match for the Assyrians' trained professionals. He thought of David before Goliath.

"Listen, Helez," he said, "I need you to put an end to this torture. Those men down there don't deserve to die like this. Can you do it?"

Helez peered over the wall at the carnage. "That's the general!" he cried.

"Yes. And they'll prolong his agony for days."

Helez took a moment to recover. "Your Majesty, he is at the very farthest limit of my range."

"Will you try anyway, son?"

"Yes, my lord."

Hezekiah watched him adjust the tension of his bow, then weigh his arrows carefully. Sweat formed on the boy's brow.

"Take your time, Helez," he said, but as Jonadab's moans echoed off the city walls Hezekiah wanted to cry out, *Hurry! God in heaven, hurry!*

The muscles on Helez's arm tensed as he drew back the bowstring and took aim. Then with a *whoosh* the arrow sped toward its mark. It flew over Jonadab's head and sank into the earth beyond him.

Helez stared at his feet and shook his head. "I'm sorry—"

"It's all right—try again." *Please, God, get it over with.* Jonadab hadn't been blinded, and he might be aware enough to realize what Hezekiah was trying to do. If so, they added to his torture by prolonging it.

Helez wiped the sweat from his eyes and took aim a second time. Hezekiah felt the tension of the men on the wall around him and held his breath. The second arrow fell short of its mark, but this time Helez didn't waste time apologizing. He pulled a third arrow from his quiver, took aim, and fired. A moment later, Jonadab's tortured body hung limply on the stake, an arrow piercing his heart.

"Thank God," Hezekiah breathed. "I'm very grateful to you, Helez. You'll be rewarded."

"What about the others?" General Benjamin asked.

"Yes, for mercy's sake, end their suffering, too, if you can."

Helez walked to the narrow embrasure once more to take sight of his next target. But before he could reach into his quiver for another arrow, Hezekiah heard him cry out. A look of dazed surprise filled the young man's eyes, and his mouth opened round; then he crumpled to the ground. Three Assyrian arrows, not even a finger's width apart from each other, had pierced Helez's heart. Hezekiah's best marksman fell dead, slain in a terrifying display of Assyrian firepower. Once again his knees went weak.

"God of Abraham!" Eliakim whispered.

In the valley below, the Assyrians quickly impaled another victim to take Jonadab's place while Hezekiah stared at the dead boy in astonishment.

"Your Majesty, you must get down off this wall! Now!" General Benjamin grabbed Hezekiah's arm and pulled him toward the stairs. But suddenly a shout rang out from the valley below.

"King Hezekiah!"

He shook free from the general's grip and turned back to the wall. A lone Assyrian warrior dressed in full battle array stood in the clearing before the Water Gate.

"King Hezekiah! I am Iddina, Rabshekah to Emperor Sennacherib of Assyria. Come forward and surrender your city!"

Bitter anger rose up in Hezekiah with frightening strength. He stared down at his enemy as if peering through a tunnel, the borders of his vision erased by his rage. "Come with me, Eliakim, while I tell this pagan I have no intention of surrendering."

Eliakim grabbed his arm to stop him. "Wait, Your Majesty! That's not the Assyrian king. That's only his second-in-command."

"I know. Let go of me."

"There's no reason why you should go out to him." Hezekiah stared, not understanding. "Listen—you're the king of Judah. Since Sennacherib only sent an envoy to represent him, you should do the same. Send me out there to represent you."

"But won't that anger them?" General Benjamin asked.

"It'll probably infuriate them," Eliakim said with a faint smile. "But it'll also let them know that if Sennacherib wants an audience with King Hezekiah, he'll have to come in person."

"You are asking for trouble," Shebna said.

"We're already in trouble," Eliakim replied, gesturing to the troops in the valley. "But King Hezekiah deserves the Assyrians' respect, and I'm going to make sure that he gets it."

Hezekiah admired Eliakim's ingenuity, but his loyalty humbled him. "Very well, Eliakim. Take Shebna and Joah with you. Go find out what Sennacherib's man has to say."

———◆———

The house seemed strangely quiet to Jerusha, the streets ominously still once the rumbling of horses and marching soldiers finally ceased. As the morning wore on, she began to wonder what was going on outside the city walls. Had King Hezekiah decided to surrender? Would the Assyrians lay siege to the city? The unknown seemed much more frightening to her than simply facing her fears, and when she could no longer stand the wait, she decided to go to the wall. She would show Eliakim that she was strong, that she had faith in him and in God. She wanted to face the Assyrians fearlessly, like he did. Maybe then she could stop shivering.

After Tirza fell asleep for her morning nap, Jerusha sent Jerimoth into the garden with one of the servants. Then she left the house and walked through the deserted streets to the wall.

Hundreds of people packed the ledge on top as Jerusha climbed the stairs. She remembered the day she came up here with Eliakim to inspect these defenses, but she never dreamed the horrible day would arrive when the Assyrians would surround Jerusalem. The people seemed oddly quiet, the atmosphere so tense she could scarcely catch her breath. Everyone gazed down into the valley, but Jerusha couldn't get close enough to see.

"Excuse me, I just got here—may I see?"

A Judean soldier turned to face her. "Shhh. The King has ordered the people on the walls to remain silent."

"But what's happening down there?"

"We're waiting for King Hezekiah to come out. The Assyrians have summoned him to appear."

"May I please see? Just for a minute?" The soldier stepped aside to let her through. Jerusha peered over the wall and instantly remembered the horrible years she had tried so hard to forget. Assyrian soldiers swarmed everywhere—hundreds of thousands of them—spreading out across the valley as far as she could see, with horses and chariots and tents too numerous to count. A gruesome fence of impaled bodies stood before the city gates.

It was a scene so familiar to her, yet so horribly different, for now she was one of the Assyrians' helpless victims, trapped inside the besieged city with no hope of escaping the coming holocaust. She had fallen into their trap, and this time she had so much more to lose. She knew too well the terrible slaughter that would take place when Jerusalem finally fell—important men like Eliakim would be tortured and flayed alive; tiny children like Tirza and Jerimoth would scream in vain for their parents until they starved to death. Yet she saw no way to save the people she loved from what would soon come. She stood frozen with terror, gripping the wall to steady her shaking legs. The world spun dizzily, and she gagged, trying not to vomit.

Then, as her eyes swept the horrible panorama before her, she saw him. She would recognize Iddina's arrogant, catlike stance if he stood among millions of Assyrians. But Iddina stood alone, 20 feet in front of the city gate. It *couldn't* be him. It was impossible that he was the Assyrians' Rabshekah. But it *was* him. He had found her. Jerusha began to scream.

"Shhhhh!" The soldier clapped his hand over her mouth and began to pull her toward the stairs.

"Look! Here comes King Hezekiah," someone said, and the soldier turned back to see, dragging Jerusha with him.

The city gate swung open a crack. Three figures emerged from the stronghold. But the one in front, walking forward to meet Iddina, wasn't King Hezekiah. Jerusha recognized the tall, slim body, the tousled black hair, and high forehead. It was Eliakim.

He looked vulnerable and defenseless as he walked toward Iddina, a gentle, scholarly man facing a vicious animal who could snap his neck with his bare hands. Jerusha tried to scream, to warn Eliakim to go back, but all the air had rushed from her lungs as if she had been punched. She couldn't draw a breath. Something broke inside her, and water gushed from her womb and ran down her legs. Then the world turned black as Jerusha fainted in the soldier's arms.

———◆———

"God of Abraham, help me," Eliakim breathed. He walked through the city gate into the open area beyond the walls with Shebna and Joah following behind. The sight of the impaled men was even more horrifying up close, the agony etched on their faces overwhelming. He remembered the foolish fantasy he had once had of wielding a sword at the city gates to defend Jerusha from the Assyrians, and he didn't know whether to laugh or cry.

As he approached the Rabshekah, Eliakim's legs felt as if they might give way any minute. The cruelty and viciousness he glimpsed in the Assyrian's eye made his heart pound crazily as if trying to escape from his chest. Never before had he stood so close to a man so savage, so dangerous. It unnerved him. He hoped his voice would be steady when he spoke. The Rabshekah's voice roared like a lion's.

"Are you King Hezekiah?"

"No."

"Then who *are* you?"

"I am Eliakim ben Hilkiah."

"Where's King Hezekiah?"

"In his palace. I'm his spokesman."

The Assyrian sputtered for words. "Doesn't he know who I am?"

"Yes. He knows you are Emperor Sennacherib's spokesman, just as I am King Hezekiah's spokesman."

Iddina's dark face flushed with speechless rage, and Eliakim knew he had won the first round. He suppressed a smile.

"I refuse to accept surrender from you! Hezekiah must appear before me in person!"

"King Hezekiah has no intention of surrendering."

"What?" The Assyrian charged forward, his face so terrifying that for a moment Eliakim feared he would tear him limb from limb. Eliakim wanted to back away, but he was too paralyzed to move. Iddina halted a few feet from him and suddenly broke into chilling, mirthless laughter.

"King Hezekiah isn't going to surrender?"

"That's right."

"Is the man insane? Either he surrenders peacefully, or we'll tear the city apart!"

"You'll have to take it by force."

"Very well. He'll get his wish. And when we finally break through these walls, you're *mine*, Eliakim ben Hilkiah! I want the pleasure of slowly slicing you into pieces myself!"

Fear chased through Eliakim. Iddina's ferocious face was inches from his own. In the background the screams of the tortured men seemed to grow louder.

"Give this message to King Hezekiah: The great king of Assyria says, 'No one can save you from my power! You need more than mere promises of help before rebelling against me. But which of your allies will give you more than words? Egypt? If you lean on Egypt, you will find her to be a stick that breaks beneath your weight and pierces your hand. The Egyptian Pharaoh is totally unreliable!' And if you say, 'We're trusting the Lord to rescue us'—just remember that He is the very one whose hilltop altars you've destroyed. For you require everyone to worship at the altar in Jerusalem!"

Iddina's knowledge of Judean affairs staggered Eliakim. How had the Assyrians learned all of this? And how did he know to use this propaganda to erode morale? Iddina's proud, mocking voice carried clearly to the top of the wall.

"I'll tell you what: Make a bet with my master, the king of Assyria! If you have 2,000 men left who can ride horses, we'll furnish the horses! And with an army as small as yours, you are no threat to even the least lieutenant in charge of the smallest contingent of my master's army. Even if Egypt supplies you with horses and chariots, it will do no good. And do you think we have come here on our own? No! The Lord sent us and told us, 'Go and destroy this nation!'"

Eliakim shuddered. That was exactly what Isaiah and Micah had been telling the people—that the Assyrians were the rod of Yahweh's judgment. He glanced behind him at the men crowded on top of the wall and knew he had to silence the Rabshekah before he convinced the people to revolt.

"Speak in Aramaic," Eliakim said, changing to that language. "We understand it quite well."

"Yes, do not use Hebrew," Shebna added. "The people standing on the walls will hear you."

"Has my master sent me to speak only to you and to your master? Hasn't he sent me to the people on the walls too? For they are doomed with you to eat their own excrement and drink their own urine!"

The Assyrian was shouting now, his voice haughty and arrogant. He no longer addressed his words to Eliakim but talked directly to the men on the wall in fluent Hebrew.

"Listen to the great king of Assyria! 'Don't let King Hezekiah fool you. He will never be able to save you from my power. Don't let him fool you into trusting in the Lord to rescue you. Don't listen to King Hezekiah. Surrender! You can live in peace here in your own land until I take you to another land just like this one—with plentiful crops, grain, wine, olive trees, and honey. All of this instead of death!'"

His voice was smooth and persuasive, and his soothing tone said *Trust me.* Eliakim didn't dare turn around again to see the effect of Iddina's speech—he feared it was devastating. Surprisingly, the men on the wall remained silent, as King Hezekiah had commanded.

"Don't listen to King Hezekiah when he tries to persuade you that the Lord will deliver you. Have any of the gods of the other nations ever delivered their people from the king of Assyria? What happened to the gods of Hamath, Arpad, Sepharvaim, Hena, and Ivvah? Did they rescue Samaria? What gods have ever been able to save any nation from my power? So what makes you think the Lord can save Jerusalem?"

Iddina's blasphemy sent shivers of rage through Eliakim. This Assyrian had compared Yahweh to worthless idols! Eliakim grabbed the front of his robe and tore it. Iddina gave him a final look of utter contempt and strode away.

Eliakim stood rooted in place. "'Have mercy on us, O LORD, have mercy on us,'" he quoted softly. "'We have endured much ridicule from the proud, much contempt from the arrogant.'" Finally Joah touched his shoulder and motioned for them to go.

None of them spoke as they climbed the hill to the palace. Eliakim kept his gaze straight ahead as he walked, avoiding the eyes of the townspeople watching him pass. He didn't want to see their faces and witness the demoralizing effect of the Rabshekah's words.

"What happened?" King Hezekiah asked when they reached the throne room.

"I told him you wouldn't surrender, Your Majesty. He tried to convince the people to rebel against you, and he offered peaceful deportation in place of famine and war. He said the Egyptians aren't coming to save us."

"Why are your robes torn?"

"He blasphemed God. He compared Yahweh to all the worthless gods of our neighbors and said He wasn't able to deliver us."

Hezekiah closed his eyes in despair and tore the front of his robes. "'O LORD, you have seen this; be not silent. . . . Awake, and rise to my defense! . . . do not let them gloat over me. Do not let them think, "Aha, just what we wanted!" or say, "We have swallowed him up."'"

An atmosphere of deep hopelessness engulfed them all, and Eliakim prayed that the king wouldn't change his mind and decide to surrender. Shebna finally broke the tense silence. "What are you going to do, Your Majesty?"

"You and Eliakim gather the chief priests and go find Isaiah. I want you to deliver a message to him from me. Joah and I will stay at the Temple and pray."

Everyone, including King Hezekiah, changed into sackcloth, and Eliakim led Shebna and the priests down the hill to find the prophet's house. The overwhelming events left Eliakim dazed, the siege happening so quickly he still hadn't recovered from the shock of it. But at the same time it seemed as if weeks had passed since he had eaten breakfast with his family that morning. He glanced at his house as they hurried past his street, hoping that Jerusha had listened to his advice and stayed home.

"Do you know where Isaiah lives?" Shebna asked as they wove through the maze of streets.

"Yes. I've been there before."

By the time all of the chief priests had jammed behind him into the rabbi's tiny house, Eliakim could barely move. Isaiah gestured to a wooden stool.

"Please sit down, Lord Eliakim."

Eliakim dropped down on the stool, grateful to rest his trembling legs and catch his breath. "Rabbi, the king asked me to give you this message." He held out the rolled square of parchment, but Isaiah shook his head.

"Read it to me."

Eliakim unrolled the page and read it aloud. "'This is a day of trouble and frustration and blasphemy; it is a serious time, as when a woman is in heavy labor trying to give birth and the child does not come. But perhaps the Lord your God heard the blasphemy of the king of Assyria's representative as he scoffed at the living God. Surely God won't let him get away with this. Surely God will rebuke him for those words. Oh, Isaiah, pray for those of us who are left!'"

The prophet stared silently at the floor for several minutes without speaking. Eliakim slowly rolled up the parchment and laid it on the table. The room was suffocating with so many men crowded inside it, and the scratchy sackcloth robe made Eliakim squirm with discomfort.

"'O Lord, be gracious to us,'" Isaiah prayed softly. "'We long for you. Be our strength every morning, our salvation in time of distress.'" Eliakim saw that in spite of the 100,000 enemy troops surrounding their city, this great man of God was at peace.

"Why do you say, . . . 'My way is hidden from the Lord; my cause is disregarded by my God'?" Isaiah asked. "Do you not know? Have you not heard? The Lord is the everlasting God, the Creator of the ends of the earth. He will not grow tired or weary, and his understanding no one can fathom. He gives strength to the weary and increases the power of the weak. Even youths grow tired and weary, and young men stumble and fall; but those who hope in the Lord will renew their strength. They will soar on wings like eagles; they will run and not grow weary, they will walk and not be faint."

The prophet's words nourished Eliakim's hope like manna. He felt Isaiah's peace begin to flood through him as well, and he smiled faintly.

Isaiah continued speaking, his voice confident. "Tell your master, 'This is what the Lord says: Do not be afraid of what you have heard—those words with which the underlings of the king of Assyria have blasphemed me. Listen! I am going to put a spirit in him so that when he hears a certain report, he will return to his own country, and there I will have him cut down with the sword.'"

Eliakim's body went limp with relief. God had spoken through His prophet; they had nothing to fear. He knew Isaiah's prophecy would come to pass.

◈

Hezekiah knelt on the royal dais at the Temple with his forehead pressed to the ground, trying to calm himself enough to pray. God was merciful. He had answered Hezekiah's desperate prayers before, allowing him to live. Now he prayed for his nation's life, for his people young and old whose lives would all be lost unless Yahweh intervened.

Once again he stood helpless before an overwhelming enemy, and he remembered Yahweh's promise to him, long ago: *"When you pass through the waters, I will be with you; and when you pass through the rivers, they will not sweep over you."* He closed his eyes and cried out to God in prayer.

"'Save me, O God, for the waters have come up to my neck. I sink in the miry depths, where there is no foothold. I have come into the deep waters; the floods engulf me. I am worn out calling for help; my throat is parched. My eyes fail, looking for my God. Those who hate me without reason outnumber the hairs of my head; many are my enemies without cause, those who seek to destroy me. I am forced to restore what I did not steal.

"'You know my folly, O God; my guilt is not hidden from you. May those who hope in you not be disgraced because of me, O Lord, the LORD Almighty; may those who seek you not be put to shame because of me, O God of Israel. . . .

"'But I pray to you, O LORD, in the time of your favor; In your great love, O God, answer me with your sure salvation. Rescue me from the mire, do not let me sink; deliver me from those who hate me, from the deep waters. Do not let the floodwaters engulf me or the depths swallow me up or the pit close its mouth over me.

"'Answer me, O LORD, out of the goodness of your love; in your great mercy turn to me. Do not hide your face from your servant; answer me quickly, for I am in trouble. Come near and rescue me; redeem me because of my foes. . . .

"'Pour out your wrath on them; let your fierce anger overtake them. May their place be deserted; let there be no one to dwell in their tents . . . I am in pain and distress; may your salvation, O God, protect me.'"

When Hezekiah finally lifted his head and looked around, Eliakim had returned; he knelt in prayer beside him. He waited for Eliakim to finish, almost dreading to ask the question.

"What did Rabbi Isaiah say?"

"It was good news, Your Majesty. Yahweh said not to be afraid of the Assyrians. He is going to cause them to return to Assyria, where Emperor Sennacherib will be slain."

"Do you think that means the Egyptians will come to drive them back?"

Eliakim shrugged. "I don't know. What else could it mean?"

Hezekiah closed his eyes and pressed his forehead to the ground in prayer once more. "'I will praise God's name in song and glorify him with thanksgiving. . . . The LORD hears the needy and does not despise his captive people. Let heaven and earth praise him, the seas and all that move in them, for God will save Zion and rebuild the cities of Judah. Then people will settle there and possess it; the children of his servants will inherit it, and those who love his name will dwell there.'"

Finally, Hezekiah stood and began walking back to the palace with Eliakim. But as they passed the Women's Court, the sound of women wailing as if in deep sorrow and mourning sent shivers through Hezekiah. He stopped to listen. The women of Jerusalem were weeping and praying for their families and for their lives.

"Is the entire city this fearful?" he asked Eliakim.

"Yes, my lord. Morale is very low. The Rabshekah's words . . . the sight of such a powerful army outside our gates . . . they have everyone terrified. General Benjamin had to put some of his own soldiers under guard after they threatened mutiny."

"Then we have to convince them that God is able to deliver them. Come on."

He stepped up to the gate of the Women's Court, and the wailing stopped abruptly when the startled women realized who he was. "Listen," King Hezekiah said. "You don't have to be afraid. I know the King of Assyria has a vast army with him, but there is a greater power with us than with him. He only has the arm of the flesh. But we have the arm of the Lord our God to help us. He will fight our battles for us."

"But what the Assyrian leader said is true," one of the women cried. "No one has ever escaped from them!"

"What will happen to our children?" another wept.

Hezekiah wondered how he could calm their fears and restore their faith; then he recalled how his grandfather had reassured him and strengthened his faith so long ago.

"'The LORD is my light and my salvation—whom shall I fear?'" he quoted gently. "'The LORD is the stronghold of my life—of whom shall I be afraid? . . . Though an army besiege me, my heart will not fear; though war break out against me, even then will I be confident . . . For in the day of trouble he will keep me safe in his dwelling; he will hide me in the shelter of his tabernacle and set me high upon a rock . . . Wait for the LORD; be strong and take heart and wait for the LORD.'"

He saw that his words had calmed them. The women wiped their tears and bowed to him in gratitude. "Come with me, Eliakim," he said, and instead of returning to the palace, they walked down the hill into the city. As they mingled with the frightened people in the streets, a large crowd quickly gathered around them.

"What's going to happen to us?"

"The Assyrians promised they would take us to a land like our own. They'll let us live if we do what they say."

"Your Majesty, why don't you accept the Assyrians' offer and surrender?"

"Yes, please! Before we're all slaughtered!"

"Listen to me," Hezekiah said. "The Torah says, 'When you go to war against your enemies and see horses and chariots and an army greater than yours, do not be afraid of them, because the LORD your God, who brought you up out of Egypt, will be with you . . . to fight for you against your enemies to give you victory.'"

"But the Assyrians have battering rams and siege towers! What if the city walls can't keep them out?"

"'God is our refuge and strength,'" Hezekiah replied, "'an ever-present help in trouble. Therefore we will not fear, though the earth give way and the mountains fall into the heart of the sea . . . The LORD Almighty is with us; the God of Jacob is our fortress.'"

All afternoon Hezekiah walked among his people, calming their fears with words of assurance, soothing them with the psalms of David. Eliakim took over for the king after his voice went hoarse and gave out. Gradually, the two heard less talk of surrender, more words of faith and trust.

"'Do not fret because of evil men,'" Eliakim told one group in the marketplace, "'or be envious of those who do wrong; for like the grass they will soon wither, like green plants they will soon die away. . . . Be still before the LORD and wait patiently for him. . . . For evil men will be cut off, but those who hope in the LORD will inherit the land.'"

"But how can God possibly save us?" someone cried from the crowd. Before Hezekiah could answer, Isaiah suddenly stepped up beside him and rested his hand on Hezekiah's shoulder.

"May I answer his question, Your Majesty?"

His sudden appearance stunned Hezekiah. He hadn't seen Isaiah since their confrontation on the palace steps. "Certainly, Rabbi!" He took a step back and waited as the power of God filled the prophet.

"'Woe to the Assyrian, the rod of my anger, in whose hand is the club of my wrath! . . . When the Lord has finished all his work against Mount Zion and Jerusalem, he will say, "I will punish the king of Assyria for the willful pride of his heart and the haughty look in his eyes. For he says: 'By the strength of my hand I have done this, and by my wisdom, because I have understanding. I removed the boundaries of nations, I plundered their treasuries; like a mighty one I subdued their kings. . . .'"'"

"'Therefore, the Lord, the LORD Almighty, will send a wasting disease upon his sturdy warriors; under his pomp a fire will be kindled like a blazing flame . . . in a single day it will burn and consume his thorns and his briers. The splendor of his forests and fertile fields it will completely destroy, as when a sick man wastes away. And the remaining trees of his forests will be so few that a child could write them down.

"'In that day the remnant of Israel, the survivors of the house of Jacob, will no longer rely on him who struck them down but will truly rely on the LORD, the Holy One of Israel. . . . Therefore, this is what the Lord, the LORD Almighty, says: "O my people who live in Zion, do not be afraid of the Assyrians, who beat you with a rod. . . . Very soon my anger against you will end and my wrath will be directed to their destruction."'"

The crowd stood in hushed silence when Isaiah finished. The Assyrians would be destroyed in a single day. That could only mean the Egyptians would defeat them.

"Thank you, Rabbi," Hezekiah murmured. Then he and Eliakim began the long walk back up the hill to the palace.

———◆———

The light of thousands of campfires twinkled in the darkness outside the city walls when the urgent message came for Eliakim in the Council Room: his family needed him at home.

"Why? What's wrong? Did they say why?"

"No, my lord."

"Go ahead," Hezekiah told him. "There's nothing more you can do here tonight."

Eliakim hurried down the hill, fighting panic. Was something wrong with Jerusha? Abba? One of the children? They had never disturbed him at the palace before, so it must be urgent. He burst through the door and found Hilkiah waiting for him in the front hall.

"What is it, Abba? What happened?"

Hilkiah gripped his shoulders and pushed him down onto the bench by the door. "Sit. Listen to me first."

After all of the stress he had endured that day, Eliakim wondered why his father's pale face frightened him the most.

"Jerusha?"

"She's upstairs. She needs you."

"Just tell me what happened, Abba!"

"She went to the wall."

"Oh, God of Abraham—no!"

"She was watching when you came through the gate. She collapsed."

"But why did she go there . . . I told her . . . is she all right . . . ?" He tried to stand, but Hilkiah forced him down again.

"You have a new son."

"But it's too soon—"

"I know. The baby is very small. And it was a difficult birth. He was positioned backward."

"Oh, no . . . Jerusha! Is she . . . is the baby . . . ?"

"We think Jerusha's all right, but there's no way to tell. She won't let the midwife come near her. She's terrified that someone's going to take her baby away from her."

Eliakim moaned. "She thinks she's back with the Assyrians, doesn't she?"

"We didn't know what to do, Son. I'm sorry."

"Let me see her."

Hilkiah gripped his arm. "Go slowly, Son."

Eliakim bolted up the stairs, then slipped quietly into the room. The bed was empty. He found Jerusha huddled in a ball in the corner, rocking back and forth, making the eerie, keening cry of mourning. The baby lay motionless in her arms, still smeared with dried blood. Eliakim couldn't tell if he was dead or asleep.

"Jerusha?" The keening stopped.

"Stay away from me!" she said in a voice he had never heard before. This was someone else, not his beloved wife.

"Bring me a basin of warm water," Eliakim whispered to the midwife hovering behind him. Then he began to pray. *God, help me. Show me what to do.* He had faced the leader of the most powerful army in the world hours earlier, but now Eliakim was more terrified than he had ever been in his life. He couldn't lose Jerusha. But how could he pull her back?

The midwife handed him the basin and clean cloths, and Eliakim edged slowly into the room. Jerusha clutched the baby tightly to herself, and he saw one of his son's tiny hands fly open, then slowly close again. He was still alive. Eliakim looked down at the floor, avoiding Jerusha's wild eyes, not wanting to frighten her.

"I've brought you some water—to wash him with." She didn't reply. "He should be clean when his daddy sees him. Don't you want his daddy to be proud of what a lovely son he has?"

He talked soothingly as he edged closer, crouching down. He slid the basin of water toward her, then waited. He could hear the soft grunting sound his son made as he struggled to breathe. He had been born almost a month too soon.

"We have a new son, Jerusha—someone for Jerimoth and Tirza to play with. Have they seen their little brother yet? Let's make him pretty before they come in to see him, all right?" He dipped a cloth in the water and wrung it out, then tried to wash his son's arm. Jerusha coiled back, snatching the baby out of his reach.

"Here. You do it, Jerusha. You make our new son all pretty and clean." He pressed the cloth into Jerusha's hand. She looked down at the baby in her arms. Slowly she began to wash him, first one arm, then the other one, then his body and legs. Her eyes shone with tears as she gently smoothed the water over his head. It was covered with curly dark hair like Eliakim's. He watched her study each tiny finger and toe; then she bent to kiss his forehead.

"He's beautiful, Jerusha. I'm so proud of you. Before you know it, he'll be running all over the house like our other two, racing in and out . . . banging doors . . . begging Abba for horsey rides . . ." Eliakim paused to wipe away a tear that had rolled down his face. He hadn't realized that he was crying.

"What shall we name him, Jerusha?"

Suddenly she looked up at him, and her eyes had lost their wild look. She was almost herself again, but still terribly frightened. Slowly, carefully, as if she were a wild bird that might fly away, Eliakim reached out to take her hand.

"I love you, Jerusha."

"Eliakim?" Her voice sounded very small, as if it came from far away.

"Yes, it's me. Can I see our new son?"

She eased her tight grip on the baby, and Eliakim carefully crept closer until he could see his tiny face, red and wrinkly like his other two children's had been. He was frighteningly small and not breathing quite right, but he was alive. Eliakim slid his arm around Jerusha's shoulder as he sat down beside her.

"He's beautiful, Jerusha. And I love both of you so much." For a moment she gazed at him as if he was a stranger; then a flicker of recognition crossed her face.

"Eliakim?"

"Yes, my love."

"Please don't let him take my baby."

"No one is ever going to take my son away from you."

"But he's here . . . I saw him . . . I saw Iddina. And he took my baby once before."

Eliakim felt a chill pass through him as he recognized the name: *I am Iddina, Rabshekah to Emperor Sennacherib.* God of Abraham, it couldn't be! Out of hundreds of thousands of Assyrian soldiers, was he the officer who had captured Jerusha? If Eliakim had known who Iddina was when he faced him that morning, he would have killed him with his bare hands.

He wrapped his arms around Jerusha and their baby and held them close. "We'll name him Joshua—the Lord saves—because no one is ever going to hurt you or our son. We're going to be safe—I promise you. God is going to take care of all of us."

————◆————

Iddina prowled restlessly around the Assyrian camp, reviewing the day's events in his mind. He should be inside the city of Jerusalem right now, not locked outside the gates.

He had assured Sennacherib that he could force a surrender. Now what was he supposed to do? A siege of this mountain fortress would take months. There wasn't time for it. The emperor wanted to move on to Egypt. The surrender of Judah should be over with by now.

He recalled Sennacherib's words: *I made King Hezekiah a prisoner in Jerusalem, like a bird in a cage,* but that wasn't good enough for Iddina. Why hadn't the foolish king of Judah surrendered to him? He had hoped his terrifying speech would cause the citizens on the wall to revolt and couldn't understand their loyalty to Hezekiah under such hopeless circumstances. Iddina had defeated all of Judah's allies except for the Egyptians, and they would prove too weak to help, as Hezekiah would soon see. But what galled Iddina the most was Hezekiah's refusal to answer his summons. He had sent his Rabshekah instead of coming out himself! What a preposterous bluff! Surely he must know he was already defeated. Well, this puny king and his officials would soon experience Assyria's power. They would show the proper fear when he tortured them and staked them to the ground to be flayed alive! Let them cry out to their imageless god then!

Gradually the routine sounds of army camp had a calming effect on Iddina, soothing his rage. The night sky was clear, and the brilliant moon illuminated the valley like daylight. He loved war—the camaraderie around the campfires, the sound of soldiers sharpening their swords against stones, the keen alertness and bravado of young soldiers out to prove themselves.

When he heard the laughter and shouts of soldiers playing a game, he followed the sound to the garbage dump on the edge of camp. Four young soldiers armed with slings cavorted like boys in the moonlight. As Iddina walked closer, the laughter abruptly stopped, and the four men froze at attention. Iddina usually loved the power and fear he inflicted on others, but for the first time he found he missed the companionship of his fellow soldiers.

"As you were," he said, but his presence had unnerved them. "What's going on?"

"We were practicing, sir. Shooting rats." The soldier edged nervously toward a clearing a few feet away and bent to retrieve his prey. Rats were a common sight near the camp dumps, but the one the soldier held aloft by the tail was the biggest Iddina had ever seen. Plump and well-fed, its long, gray tail was as fat as his finger. Its black eyes glimmered like onyx stones in the moonlight, its small gray feet hung slack. Iddina glimpsed two rows of pointed teeth as the soldier flung the rat onto a three-foot-high mound of garbage.

Iddina was about to move on and leave the soldiers to their fun when it struck him as unusual for the garbage mound to be so large after only one day in camp. He walked closer and saw that it wasn't garbage, but a large pile of dead rats. He detected movement in the pile, convulsive twitches of the dead, or perhaps a few rats that weren't quite dead. As he stared, the other soldiers scooped up three more dead rats and tossed them on top. Iddina guessed there were close to 50 rats on the mound.

"How long have you been out here shooting?" he asked.

Their spokesmen cleared his throat nervously as if unsure if he faced rebuke. "Only a little while, sir—since dark."

"You're lying. You couldn't possibly have killed this many rats in such a short time, even if you're excellent marksmen."

"But there are thousands of them around camp, sir. It didn't take long at all."

"We were wondering what kind of filthy people these Judeans were that they'd tolerate this many rats so close to the city," another soldier added.

"Would you care to try for one, sir?" The soldier handed Iddina a square of soft leather with thongs attached to each side. Iddina hefted the sling, remembering the long hours he'd spent practicing in his youth, learning to time the swing, letting go at the precise moment to send the stone hurtling to its mark. He remembered the feel of the loaded sling whirling through the air, the sound it made as it rushed past his ear, the satisfying thud when the stone struck its target. He had spent hours, practicing, planning, concentrating on each step until the sling had become an extension of his arm and the entire process was as natural and uncalculated as breathing. He had become a superior slingman, and he knew he would never lose his skill. When the soldier offered him a stone, Iddina took it.

"Watch the clearing over there, sir." The lad pointed to a patch of moonlight some 30 feet away, where another soldier tossed bits of rotting meat.

In a movement that was breathtaking in its swiftness, Iddina wrapped one of the thongs around his wrist and across his palm, dropped the stone into the sling, and began swinging it above his head. He glimpsed the awe in the soldiers' eyes at his skill. Almost before the meat touched the ground, five huge rats darted from the shadows to fight over it. Iddina had only seconds to release the loosened thong from his fingers and send the stone to its mark. But in the split second when he should have let go, he suddenly recalled the Philistine priests' bizarre story—Judah's unseen God had once sent an army of rats to destroy His enemies.

The unsettling thought caused Iddina's hand to falter, and he released the stone a heartbeat too late. By the time it thudded to the ground, the rats had retreated into the shadows.

There were no cheers from the watching soldiers nor the usual groans after a near-miss. They stood tense and silent as Iddina handed the sling back to its owner. Then he stalked away to his tent.

Late that night Iddina lay on his mat in the darkness, unable to sleep. What bothered him more than the fact that he had missed was the unfamiliar twinge of superstitious fear that had caused it. It was so much like the terror that had haunted him most of his childhood, a fear he thought he had long outgrown. He remembered lying awake like this, terrified of his father's avenging spirit and the demons that would accompany him. He recalled his frenzied offerings to appease the gods, the dozens of spirit houses he had built to pacify them, the amulets and charms he had made to ward off unseen horrors. He had become the bravest warrior, the finest marksman, the swiftest swordsman so that he would never need to be afraid again. He had conquered his fear by conquering the gods of the spirit world and placing their images where he could see and control them. But now he faced an unseen god whose image he couldn't seize and control, a god who sent an army of rats to guard his golden throne in Jerusalem.

As he lay in the darkness, Iddina suddenly felt the warm brush of a furry body move past his face. He froze, listening and alert. Now he heard more of them, skittering across the floor of his tent, gnawing on his leather sandal straps, squealing softly as they fought over a discarded morsel of food. He slowly turned his head and stared in horror at the floor of his tent. It had come alive in the moonlight, a writhing carpet of furry creatures. His skin crawled as if they slithered across his body.

With his heart hammering against his ribs, he slowly reached beside him for his dagger. Another rat glided past his arm. He shuddered as he brushed aside the large rat that perched on top of his dagger, gnawing the leather-wrapped handle grip. He picked up his weapon.

Then with lightning speed, Iddina sat up, crying out with fury as he pitched the knife into the center of the wiggling mass of animals beside him. He heard a flurry of squeals and skittering movements as the rats fled in all directions, brushing over his bare feet and past his legs. Their rotten, feral smell filled his nostrils, making him gag.

In the aftermath of their flight, one high-pitched squeal continued to sound. Iddina lit a lamp and saw the rat that his dagger had pinioned. It struggled futilely for several more seconds before it finally twitched convulsively, then lay still. Iddina stared at it in disbelief. He had never seen a rat so large. Like the others at the dump, it was as plump and healthy as a household pet.

Iddina set the lamp on the floor and pulled his knife out of the rat's body. He wiped the blood off on its fur, then sat cross-legged with the rat in front of him. He had come too far, been through too many battles, to feel like a superstitious child again, but he couldn't ignore the chill of fear that slithered through his veins.

Slowly, reverently, he cut his prey into pieces, setting aside a limp gray foot, the three-inch tip of snaking tail, a clump of bristly whiskers, a piece of jawbone with a row of pointed teeth. Then, as he had done so often as a boy, he fashioned the pieces into an amulet and tied them to a long leather thong. When he finished, he knotted the thong around his neck and slipped the amulet beneath his tunic. Then he crawled back into bed, his hands still sticky with the rat's blood.

Iddina knew he could defeat any god foolish enough to confront him, especially with an army as pitiful as Judah's. But he didn't know what strategy to use against an unseen god who sent an army of rats. *Fight fair, God of Judah!* he wanted to shout. *Fight the way You're supposed to fight, with warriors and weapons—not slithering vermin!*

He left the lamp burning beside the dissected rat to keep the others at bay, but Iddina lay wide awake until dawn, stunned by the unfamiliar strength of his fear.

25

"Your Majesty . . . Your Majesty, wake up . . ." Hezekiah opened his eyes to find General Benjamin crouching beside him, shaking him. "Are you awake, my lord?"

"Yes . . . I guess so . . ." But it took Hezekiah a few moments to shake off the fuzziness of sleep. When he did, he was startled to discover that he had fallen asleep leaning against the parapet on top of the city wall.

For the past five days since the Assyrians had surrounded Jerusalem, Hezekiah had barely slept. The Assyrians hadn't begun to attack the city yet. Instead, they sat in the valley looking up at the frightened people crowded on top of the walls—watching, waiting, playing their deadly game of nerves. The Rabshekah probably hoped his terrifying words would grow and swell in the Judeans' hearts like yeast in a batch of flour, until the pressure of their fear forced them to surrender.

Hezekiah had spent each day fasting, praying, walking among his people, encouraging them to trust God and not to surrender. He had spent the long nights on top of the city wall, unable to sleep, watching for the nightly signal fires, waiting for word that the Egyptians were coming, wondering what was happening to the rest of his nation. Late last night, exhaustion had caused him to fall asleep looking down on the Assyrian camp.

Across the valley, a pale, cold sun struggled to rise behind the bank of clouds that hid the Mount of Olives from view. Hezekiah rolled his head to ease the stiffness in his neck. "Is it time for the morning sacrifice?" he asked, still dazed.

General Benjamin shook his head. "Not yet. But take a look down there, Your Majesty."

Hezekiah slowly pulled himself up until he could see over the parapet. His cramped body ached, and his sackcloth robe was damp with dew. Through the veil of fog that shrouded the valley, the earth had come alive with movement. He watched the swarming Assyrians for several long minutes before his exhausted mind fully grasped what he saw.

"They're leaving!" he said in astonishment. "The Assyrians are leaving!"

"Yes, it looks that way, Your Majesty."

"Praise God!" He slumped against the wall again. "Any idea why?" The general's face looked somber in spite of the good news, and Hezekiah felt a prickle of fear. "Tell me what happened."

"The signal fire from Lachish never came last night. We think the city has fallen."

"Oh no. My brother . . . ?"

"We haven't heard from him. I'm sorry."

Hezekiah moaned. For the past five days he had received urgent messages from Gedaliah telling him that Lachish was under heavy enemy assault again. The Assyrian emperor had lied; he had pocketed the enormous bribe Hezekiah had paid, then renewed the attack on Lachish as well as besieging Jerusalem. But locked behind his own barred gates, Hezekiah had been powerless to help Gedaliah.

"Lachish is lost." He repeated the words, trying to comprehend the defeat of one of his strongest cities and his brother's certain death, trying to understand why Gedaliah and the elders of Lachish had worshiped a pagan sun god, long after the other cities of Judah had returned to Yahweh.

"But it still doesn't make sense," General Benjamin said suddenly. "Why would the Rabshekah and all these troops leave? Why wouldn't Emperor Sennacherib's forces join him here? Unless—"

"Yes! Unless Pharaoh's armies are finally coming!"

"Could it be a trick to get us to open the gates?"

Hezekiah stared into the misty valley, shivering in the wind and the light rain that had begun to fall as he watched the Assyrians withdrawing with orderly precision. "I don't think it's a trick. It must be the Egyptians. And now that they've finally come, we need to pray that they drive the Assyrians all the way back to Nineveh."

As Hezekiah stood on the dais at the Temple a short time later, the morning seemed too gray and dismal to be a day of celebration and deliverance. The men crowding into the courtyard were subdued, as if afraid to believe that the siege was suddenly ending after only five days. Hezekiah found it difficult to comprehend as well. Part of him wanted to leap and shout for joy, but he was still numb and exhausted, still too uncertain about the future and what the Assyrian withdrawal really meant.

As the priest prepared to slay the morning sacrifice, King Hezeki-ah stepped forward. He had arranged to read the liturgy to the people himself.

> *If the LORD had not been on our side*
>   *when men attacked us,*
> *when their anger flared against us,*
>   *they would have swallowed us alive;*
> *the flood would have engulfed us,*
>   *the torrent would have swept over us,*
> *the raging waters would have swept us away.*
>
> *Praise be to the LORD,*
>   *who has not let us be torn by their teeth.*
> *We have escaped like a bird*
>   *out of the fowler's snare;*
> *The snare has been broken,*
>   *and we have escaped.*
> *Our help is in the name of the LORD,*
>   *the Maker of heaven and earth.*

By the time the service came to an end and the sun had started breaking through the clouds at last, the people had begun to compre-hend the significance of their deliverance. Hezekiah was certain that even the departing Assyrians could hear their final shout of praise. He remained on the platform for several minutes, silently thanking God. Then, as he started down the walkway to the palace, he spotted Isaiah waiting for him.

"Praise God, Rabbi! They're gone, just as Yahweh promised!"

"Now that it's over, Your Majesty, I have a humble request to ask of you."

"Yes? What is it?"

"Would you honor me by joining my wife and me for the Passover feast?"

Hezekiah was dumbstruck. "Passover?"

"Yes. The eve of Passover is three days away."

"With everything that's happened, I'd completely forgotten."

"Then would you do me this great honor?"

The rabbi's request was completely unprecedented. Even though Isaiah descended from royalty, it was no small matter to invite the king to your home. Dining at the king's table was a great honor, and for a moment Hezekiah considered reversing Isaiah's offer and inviting him to the palace. But Hezekiah had made no plans for the feast. It would be the first time he would celebrate Passover without Hephzibah. He couldn't bear to face his memories or his loneliness.

"Yes, Rabbi. I would be honored to share the feast with you." He glanced at Shebna waiting for him at the end of the walkway and was grateful that he was no longer palace administrator. Shebna never would have approved of such an unorthodox invitation.

—◈—

"I heard God promise that it would happen, Abba. With my own eyes I saw the Assyrians leave. But I still can't believe that it's true." Eliakim waded through the crowd of worshipers with his father as they filed from the Temple.

"Yes, praise God—praise God," Hilkiah murmured.

Eliakim wished he could run. "I can't wait to tell Jerusha! She'll be so relieved. Maybe everything can get back to normal."

"How is the baby this morning, Son?"

Suddenly Eliakim's joy vanished. "He's the same. Not good. All night long I could hear him struggling to breathe. He's so weak he can barely eat. He tries to suck, then just gives up."

"God of Abraham, heal him," Hilkiah whispered.

"At least now . . . at least with the Assyrians gone . . . I mean, if he dies now . . ."

"You're not expecting him to die!"

"I honestly don't know how he's lived this long, Abba. But I was so afraid that he would die while the Assyrians were still here, and Jerusha would think they'd killed him, and . . . and I don't want to lose her too, Abba. Losing the baby is bad enough."

"Why do you even talk about him dying? Pray that he'll live!"

Eliakim sighed and ran his fingers through his hair. "He's so tiny—and so sick. Do you know he's never even cried? He doesn't have enough strength. It takes all his strength just to draw a breath."

Hilkiah stopped walking and rested his hand on Eliakim's arm. "Do you believe God can heal him, Son?"

"I—I want to believe it, but—"

"But you still remember when your mother died."

"I don't understand why sometimes God answers prayers and other times He doesn't. I *do* believe in miracles, Abba. I've seen too many of them *not* to believe—Jerusha's escape, the tunnel, King Hezekiah's recovery, and how could anyone doubt God when he looks over that wall and sees the Assyrians retreating? God of Abraham, what a miracle!"

"But your son?"

"I'm afraid to ask. I'm so afraid that if God says no again . . ."

"I understand. When your mother died it rocked my faith like a shepherd's hut in a windstorm." Eliakim stared at him. He had thought his father's faith was unshakable, and his confession surprised him. "It's true, Son. But my faith survived the trial, and yours will too. Don't be afraid to ask for a miracle. But at the same time, pray for the strength to accept God's will."

Eliakim draped his arm around his father's shoulder as they started walking again. "I can't wait to take Jerusha to the wall and show her that they're really gone!"

"Amen. Praise God."

When he reached home, Eliakim scooped his two older children up in his arms. "Let's go upstairs and see your mama."

"And baby Joshua?"

"Yes, the baby too. But you have to be very quiet. They might be sleeping." He crept up the stairs, wondering how he would explain it to little Jerimoth when his baby brother died.

Jerusha lay against the pillow with her eyes closed. She held their tiny son nestled in her arms to keep him warm. Her eyes fluttered open as Eliakim and the children stopped beside the bed.

"Mama!" Jerimoth and Tirza both cried at the same time. They squirmed in Eliakim's arms to get down, but he held them tightly.

"Shhh," he warned. "Don't wake the baby."

"Can I see him, Mama?"

Jerusha folded the covers back, and Eliakim watched his children's faces as they studied their new baby brother in awe.

"He's really little, Abba!"

"Well, he's only five days old."

"Was I that little when I was born?"

Eliakim bit his lip. "No, Son. You were much bigger . . . and . . . and much stronger."

"I kiss baby?" Tirza, still a baby herself, stretched her arms out toward her tiny brother.

"Wait until he grows a bit stronger, Love."

"Abba, why does he make that funny noise?"

The baby made a faint grunting sound each time he struggled to exhale. How should Eliakim answer his curious five-year-old, whose questions always seemed to lead to still more questions?

"That's just the way he breathes, Son," he replied, then hurried to change the subject. "Jerusha, did you hear them leaving this morning? They're gone! All of them! The Assyrians are finally gone!"

She didn't smile. Her eyes filled with tears. "But will they come back again?"

He couldn't answer her question. He was afraid to make a promise he couldn't keep. "Listen—if you feel strong enough this afternoon, I can take you to the wall. You can see for yourself. They're really, truly gone!"

"Hug, Mama! Kiss!" Tirza cried.

Both children strained in Eliakim's arms to go to Jerusha, but she hadn't let the baby out of her arms since he'd been born. "How about it, Jerusha? I'll trade you these two for the baby if you want."

He held his breath, waiting for her response. It would prove that she really believed the Assyrians couldn't hurt her. It would tell him if Jerusha would finally be herself again. He set Jerimoth and Tirza down and held his hands out for the baby. Jerusha closed her eyes and gripped Joshua tightly for a moment. Then she kissed his forehead and handed him to Eliakim for the first time.

The baby weighed nothing. Eliakim could hold him in the palms of his hands. The baby's tiny nostrils flared with each breath he took as if that might help him draw in more air. He opened his eyes for a moment and gazed into Eliakim's eyes as if pleading with him, then closed them wearily again.

As his two older children scrambled into their mother's arms, Eliakim turned away to hide the tears that suddenly filled his eyes. He nestled Joshua against his chest and felt his little heart beating rapidly next to his—much too rapidly.

God of Abraham, he prayed, *please heal my little boy.*

◈

"What went wrong?" Emperor Sennacherib demanded. "I gave you five days."

Iddina's fury pressed against his skull, pounding inside his head, longing for release. "They wouldn't surrender."

"Why not?"

Iddina had asked himself the same question for the past five days, but he didn't know the answer. He had asked it one last time as he stood on a rise overlooking Jerusalem, watching his army withdraw to rendezvous with the emperor's troops in Libnah. The roof of the Temple on Jerusalem's highest hill had shone golden as the sun had emerged from behind the clouds. The Temple of Judah's God. The imageless One. The frustration of failure shook through Iddina's body until he wanted to kill someone. He had only failed once before in his life, when he had failed to recapture Jerusha. And Yahweh—her God—was the only one he had failed to conquer. He would return to Jerusalem, Iddina vowed. After Egypt, he would come back, and—

"Iddina?" The emperor waited for an explanation.

"King Hezekiah is relying on Egypt's help," Iddina said. "As soon as we defeat Pharaoh, he'll be ready to surrender."

"Good. I hate loose ends." He rose from his throne and beckoned for Iddina to follow him into the royal compound. He stopped again beside his tent. "Listen—you simply must do something about all these rats. My servants killed five of them in my tent last night. *Five!* Judah is crawling with them—first in Lachish and now here in Libnah. I've never seen anything like it, have you?"

The unfamiliar tremor of fear rocked Iddina again. He fingered the front of his tunic until he found the lump his amulet made beneath it. But he decided not to remind the emperor of the story the Philistine priests had told them.

"The Judeans are a filthy people, Your Majesty. The world will be better off rid of them for good."

"Right now I'm more concerned about these cursed rats."

Iddina shuddered involuntarily. "If I offer my men a small reward for each one they kill, we should be able to exterminate them quickly."

"Good. Do it. Spend as much gold as you need to, but get rid of them."

While his troops began their campaign against the rats, Iddina spent the day digging through the treasures King Hezekiah had sent as tribute, searching for some article of cultic significance that would give him power over Judah's God and His army of rats. But after sifting through tons of silver and gold, Iddina found nothing with an image or even a symbol of the deity. The only ornamented item he found was a golden ark, clearly of Babylonian origin. He rubbed his eyes to ease the pounding behind his forehead, baffled by Judah's imageless, monotheistic religion.

That evening Iddina went to see the Assyrian high priest, unloading his arsenal of anger and frustration on him. "How can Yahweh be the god of war, the god of fertility, the god of the dead—the god of everything at the same time?" he shouted. "And how can Judah's priests inspire loyalty and devotion in the ignorant masses without an idol? Without so much as a symbol?" He saw the priest appraising him curiously, and Iddina struggled to contain his temper and disguise his fear.

"Why does it bother you so much, my lord? Judah is an insignificant country with an obscure religion. Both will soon disappear from the map and from the history books as if they had never existed. A thousand years from now, no one will even remember the name of their god, much less worship Him. But Assyrian religion, her gods—they will endure throughout time."

"Prove it!" Iddina threw the sack he carried onto the ground in front of the priest. The bag writhed as the living creatures inside fought to escape.

"What is that?"

"Judean rats. My men captured three of them alive."

"*Rats?* What am I supposed to do with them?"

"Examine their entrails. See what they portend."

"You must be joking! Entrails of a *rat?*"

Iddina clenched his fists and took a step closer. "Do it!"

"Very well, my lord."

Iddina hovered nearby as the bewildered priests began the ritual, reciting the incantations to the beat of pounding drums, enveloping themselves in billowing clouds of incense. He watched the high priest's face as he sliced open the first rat, and Iddina knew immediately that the omens foretold something terrible. By the time he slaughtered the third rat, the high priest could no longer disguise his horror.

"I . . . I don't understand this . . . ," he mumbled.

"Tell me!"

"But I . . . I can't explain it."

Iddina grabbed the front of the priest's bloody robe, nearly lifting him off his feet. "Tell me what the omens say!"

"They . . . all three of them . . . foretell death!"

"*Whose* death? The Judeans'?"

"No, my lord." The priest's voice trembled. "*Ours!*"

"How? How is that possible? The Judeans don't have an army left!"

"I don't know, my lord."

"Is it the Egyptians? Are they coming to Judah's aid?"

"My lord, these omens are meaningless. Let me do it again with the proper sacrifices, not with vermin. This time the omens will foretell victory over Pharaoh's forces, just as they have before."

But Iddina didn't wait to see what the omens foretold the second time. He faced a God more powerful than any he had faced before, and he didn't know how to fight Him. He withdrew to his tent, battling his own terrible fear, and spent the long night carving golden figures of rats and tumors—as the Philistines had once done—and fastening them by golden chains to his ankles, to his wrists, and to his neck.

26

Late in the afternoon on the eve of Passover, Hezekiah followed the directions Isaiah had given him, through the narrow, winding lanes to the rabbi's house. As soon as the sun set, Passover would begin. But as Hezekiah wandered the unfamiliar streets outside his palace, he regretted accepting Isaiah's invitation. He felt lonely and out of place here, walking among the crowded houses and stinking gutters.

Isaiah met him at the front gate and led him inside his tiny, one-room home. His wife was busy at the hearth, and the fragrant air carried the aroma of roasting lamb. A small wooden table, covered with a homespun cloth, was set with cheap pottery plates and cups. "Welcome, Your Majesty. We are honored to have you as our guest."

Hezekiah looked around at the cooking pots on the hearth, the sleeping mat in the corner, the rabbi's scrolls and tablets piled on a shelf, and the humble, intimate setting made him feel awkward, like an intruder.

"Won't you sit down?" Isaiah gestured to the seat in the middle, while he and his wife took their places at each end of the table. Hezekiah had presided over all of the Passover feasts at the palace since his grandfather had died, but tonight the honor would go to Isaiah as head of the house.

"Your Majesty, don't you think it's fitting that we celebrate our nation's miraculous deliverance at Passover so soon after our own deliverance from Assyria?"

"I'm still overwhelmed, Rabbi. The Assyrians just vanished, and we were spared! Maybe you haven't heard yet, but Pharaoh is finally sending out his forces to rescue us. A huge Egyptian army is marching north from Egypt into battle. That's probably why the Assyrians withdrew."

"Yahweh promised seven years ago that He would deliver you—remember? 'Like birds hovering overhead, the LORD Almighty will

227

shield Jerusalem; he will shield it and deliver it, he will "pass over" it and will rescue it.'"

"Yes. I remember the day you told me that."

"This Passover feast celebrates our physical deliverance from our enemies, but it symbolizes our spiritual redemption as well."

"Our spiritual redemption? What do you mean?"

"It represents Yahweh's eternal plan to redeem our souls from the sin of Adam's fall."

"I've celebrated Passover dozens of times, but I never heard that it symbolizes our spiritual redemption. Will you explain how it does that, Rabbi?"

"Why don't we begin, and I'll explain as we celebrate." Isaiah's wife lit the Passover candles, and Hezekiah bowed his head as she recited the traditional blessing.

"Just as the woman begins our Passover by providing light," Isaiah said, "so it will be that the seed of the woman will begin God's redemption plan, bringing salvation to light. It is written, 'So the LORD God said to the serpent . . . I will put enmity between you and the woman, and between your offspring and hers; he will crush your head, and you will strike his heel.'"

"Is Yahweh speaking of the Messiah?"

"Yes, the Messiah, the promised seed of the woman. The people who walk in darkness have seen a great light; on those living in the land of the shadow of death a light has dawned . . . For to us a child is born, to us a son is given, and the government will be on his shoulders. And he will be called Wonderful Counselor, Mighty God, Everlasting Father, Prince of Peace. Of the increase of his government and peace there will be no end. He will reign on David's throne and over his kingdom, establishing and upholding it with justice and righteousness from that time on and forever. The zeal of the LORD Almighty will accomplish this."

"I don't understand. How can the Messiah—the seed of David—be called 'Mighty God'?"

"Don't you remember what the psalmist has written? 'O Israel, put your hope in the LORD, for with the LORD is unfailing love and with him is full redemption. He himself will redeem Israel from all their sins.'"

"Yes, but—"

"It was revealed long ago, even to our father Abraham when he told Isaac, 'God himself will provide the lamb for the burnt offering.'"

"Was that when Yahweh provided the ram in the thicket? So that Abraham wouldn't have to sacrifice his son?"

"That's right, Your Majesty." Isaiah lifted the flask of wine and filled their three cups. "This wine reminds us of the blood of the Passover lamb that was shed for Israel's salvation. As it is written, 'When I see the blood, I will pass over you.' The four cups of wine we will drink speak of God's fourfold plan of redemption: 'I will bring you out from under the yoke of the Egyptians. . . . I will free you from being slaves . . . I will redeem you with an outstretched arm . . . and I will take you as my own people.'"

He set the flask of wine on the table, and they all bowed as Isaiah prayed over the first cup. "Blessed are you, O Yahweh our God, Ruler of the world, who chose us out of all people and selected us out of all the nations and made us holy through Your Law. Lovingly, O Yahweh our God, You have given us this feast of Passover, this anniversary of our freedom. Blessed are You, O Lord. Amen." Hezekiah raised his cup and drank.

"Tonight we recall our slavery, Your Majesty, so that we can understand the true meaning of freedom. Yahweh liberated us from bondage to man—and from bondage to sin—so that we would be free to serve Him."

Hezekiah looked at Isaiah to see if his words were meant as a rebuke for trusting in the alliance instead of in God, but the prophet held a clay bowl and pitcher out to him, pouring the water over Hezekiah's hands, saying nothing. When they had all washed, Isaiah passed the plate of parsley and a bowl of salt water to dip it into.

"This represents the hyssop our ancestors used to paint the blood of the lamb on their doorposts. The salt represents the tears we shed in Egypt and at the Red Sea."

After they had eaten the parsley, Isaiah took a basket with three loaves of unleavened bread and broke one of the loaves in two, reciting, "This is the bread of affliction our ancestors ate in the land of Egypt; let all those who are hungry enter and eat, and all who are in distress come and celebrate Passover."

He looked up at Hezekiah. "In the same way, Yahweh invites us to partake of His salvation, saying, 'Come, all you who are thirsty, come to the waters; and you who have no money, come, buy and eat! Why spend money on what is not bread, and your labor on what does not satisfy? . . . Give ear and come to me; hear me, that your soul may live . . . Seek the LORD while he may be found; call on him while he is near. Let the wicked forsake his way and the evil man his thoughts. Let him turn to the LORD, and he will have mercy on him, and to our God, for he will freely pardon.'"

"Rabbi, I have difficulty comprehending a God who is so generous—so forgiving."

"We all do, because we are so unlike Him. That's what tempts us to make idols. We want to cast God in our own image." Isaiah poured their second cup of wine and raised his cup. "This represents Yahweh's second promise to us: 'I will free you from being slaves.' If the holy One had not brought our ancestors out of Egypt, we and our children and our children's children would still be in bondage to the pharaohs in Egypt. But Yahweh our God heard our voice and saw our affliction. Blessed be our Holy God."

Hezekiah stared into his wineglass, wondering why he had so foolishly trusted in Egypt for help. Pharaoh's forces had finally come, but much too late for most of Hezekiah's nation. The enemy had destroyed all his fortified cities except Jerusalem.

"Do you know the next part of the ritual, Your Majesty?"

"Yes, Rabbi."

"Then why don't you recite the words?"

Hezekiah cleared his throat. "God's promise of deliverance has been the hope of our ancestors and of ourselves. For not only one nation, but many have risen up against us in every generation to annihilate us. But the Most Holy God, blessed be He, always delivered us out of their hands—"

He stopped, unable to finish, and Isaiah continued for him: "Just as He brought us forth from Egypt, with a strong hand and with an outstretched arm, with great terror, and with signs and wonders."

Hezekiah bowed his head, reciting the next part of the liturgy from memory as Isaiah and his wife echoed the response: "If God had merely rescued us from Egypt, but had not destroyed their gods . . ."

"It would have been enough."

"If He had merely destroyed their gods, but had not slain their firstborn . . ."

"It would have been enough."

"If He had merely slain their firstborn, but had not parted the sea for us . . ."

"It would have been enough."

"If He had merely parted the sea, but had not drowned our oppressors . . ."

"It would have been enough."

"If He had merely drowned our oppressors, but had not fed us with manna . . ."

"It would have been enough."

"And if He had merely fed us with manna, but had not brought us to this land . . ."

"It would have been enough."

"Yes, Rabbi, it would have been more than enough."

"But we know that Yahweh has done so much more. Someday, Your Majesty, on this very mountain the LORD Almighty will prepare a feast of rich food for all peoples, a banquet of aged wine—the best of meats and the finest of wines. On this mountain he will destroy the shroud that enfolds all peoples, the sheet that covers all nations; he will swallow up death forever. The Sovereign LORD will wipe away the tears from all faces; he will remove the disgrace of his people from all the earth . . . In that day they will say, 'Surely this is our God; we trusted in him, and he saved us. This is the LORD, we trusted in him; let us rejoice and be glad in his salvation.'"

"God will swallow up death, Rabbi?" Hezekiah thought of Molech's gaping mouth, swallowing his victims in death. "How is that possible?"

Isaiah set the Passover lamb on the table in front of him for the next part of the ritual, then held up the shankbone. "This is the Passover lamb our forefathers ate, because the Holy One, blessed be He, spared the houses of our ancestors from death. Even so will Messiah—the Lamb of God—destroy the power death holds over us."

"Has Yahweh shown you the Messiah, Rabbi?"

"Yes, Your Majesty."

"Can you tell me what you saw?"

"He had no beauty or majesty to attract us to him, nothing in his appearance that we should desire him. He was despised and rejected by men, a man of sorrows, and familiar with suffering. Like one from whom men hide their faces he was despised, and we esteemed him not.

"Surely he took up our infirmities and carried our sorrows, yet we considered him stricken by God, smitten by him and afflicted. But he was pierced for our transgressions, he was crushed for our iniquities; the punishment that brought us peace was upon him, and by his wounds we are healed. We all, like sheep, have gone astray, each of us has turned to his own way; and the LORD has laid on him the iniquity of us all.

"He was oppressed and afflicted, yet he did not open his mouth; he was led like a lamb to the slaughter, and as a sheep before her shearers is silent, so he did not open his mouth. By oppression and judgment he was taken away. And who can speak of his descendants? For he was cut off from the land of the living; for the transgression of my people he was stricken. He was assigned a grave with the wicked, and with the rich in his death, though he had done no violence, nor was any deceit in his mouth.

"Yet it was the LORD's will to crush him and cause him to suffer, and though the LORD makes his life a guilt offering, he will see his off-spring and prolong his days, and the will of the LORD will prosper in his hand. After the suffering of his soul, he will see the light of life and be satisfied; by his knowledge my righteous servant will justify many, and he will bear their iniquities.

"Therefore I will give him a portion among the great, and he will divide the spoils with the strong, because he poured out his life unto death, and was numbered with the transgressors. For he bore the sin of many, and made intercession for the transgressors."

A tear glistened in Isaiah's eye as he finished. Hezekiah stared at the Passover lamb on the table in front of him and murmured, "But that can't be—I'm not worthy of such a sacrifice. Why would Yahweh do that for me?"

"Because He is your Father. Unlike your earthly father, who sacri-ficed his children to save himself, your Heavenly Father will sacrifice himself to save His children."

"I can't comprehend such love, Rabbi."

"None of us can. If we could, what different lives we would live!" He raised the cup, reciting, "Therefore, we are bound to thank, praise, glorify, exalt, and reverence Him who performed all these miracles for us. He brought us from slavery to freedom, from sorrow to joy, from mourning to dancing, from servitude to redemption. Let us therefore sing a new song in His presence. Hallelujah!"

They sang the Passover psalms together, but as he pondered what Isaiah had told him, Hezekiah knew the words had never meant so much to him before:

> Let the name of the LORD be praised,
> both now and forevermore.
> From the rising of the sun to the place where it sets,
> the name of the LORD is to be praised.
>
> Who is like the LORD our God,
> the One who sits enthroned on high,
> who stoops down to look on the heavens and the earth?

As he sang the last verse of the hymn, Hezekiah suddenly thought of Hephzibah, and he felt the pain of her betrayal shudder through him:

> He settles the barren woman in her home
> as a happy mother of children.

He scarcely heard the rabbi recite the blessing on the unleavened bread and bitter herbs as he stared down at the table, thinking of Hephzibah. When he finally looked up, Isaiah's wife had taken the pots with the Passover supper from the hearth and laid the meal on the table in front of him. He began to eat, as the others were doing, but he barely tasted the food.

"What are you thinking about?" Isaiah asked gently.

Ashamed to confess that he still thought about Hephzibah, an idolatress, he said, "I was thinking of the words we just sang: 'Who is like the LORD our God?'"

"Yes, our God is a God of miracles—the slaying of Egypt's first-born, the parting of the Red Sea, the manna in the wilderness—God intervenes in the affairs of His people precisely when He's needed. No other god does that."

"I know. I've experienced Yahweh's miracles in my life, Rabbi. He saved me from Molech when I was a child, He healed me when I nearly died, and now He has saved Jerusalem from Assyria."

Isaiah nodded. "The gods of the nations around us must be bribed to perform, with sacrifices and rituals and offerings. The people try to earn the attention of their gods through their own good works and to bend the gods' wills to conform to theirs. But our God can't be coerced by good works. We can't earn His favor."

Hezekiah thought back to when he first became king and how he had renewed Judah's covenant with God in order to earn His blessing on his nation. "Is that what I've tried to do?"

Isaiah pierced him with his gaze. "You tried to earn peace and prosperity for your nation with your reforms, but you should have made the reforms out of love for God, not because of what He would give you in return."

Hezekiah stared.

"You tried to earn an heir by following every letter of the Law, marrying only one wife; then you became angry with God when He didn't reward your faithfulness."

"But . . . I thought . . ."

"When you begged for your life, you reminded God of all your good works, as if you could bribe Him to change His mind."

"Rabbi—"

"You've been trying to earn God's favor and blessing all your life, Your Majesty, and you've used the Law and the sacrifices the same way your father used idols to get what he wanted. But you can never do enough or try hard enough to win God's love. No one can keep the Law perfectly. We all fail. As Solomon has written, 'There is not a righteous man on earth who does what is right and never sins.' And the psalmist said, 'If you, O LORD, kept a record of sins, O Lord, who could stand?'"

"Then how—?"

"Yahweh's forgiveness and blessings are free. You already have His love, and you always did. He saved you from Molech long before you did one good work for Him, because He loves you. Not because of anything you did to deserve it, but because you're His child."

"I know I've sinned, Rabbi—I know I have. I never should have put my trust in the alliance. I should have trusted God."

"You made Yahweh your God a long time ago—now you must let Him be the sovereign Lord of your life."

They finished the meal, and Isaiah's wife quietly cleared away their plates. Then Isaiah bowed his head. "Let us say the blessing for our food. 'Blessed be the name of the Lord from now unto eternity. Blessed be He of whose bounty we have eaten and through whose goodness we live. Amen.'" He filled their cups a third time and lifted his up. "This is the cup of redemption, God's promise to redeem us. Just as He purchased Israel's firstborn by the blood of the Passover lamb, even so will the Messiah buy us back, redeeming us from sin with His blood."

Hezekiah drank it, aware of his sin and disobedience, aware that he was unworthy of such a sacrifice. As soon as he set his cup down, Isaiah filled it for the fourth time.

"The final cup is the cup of praise, for Yahweh has promised, 'I will take you as my own people, and I will be your God.' How, then, can we keep silent? How can we fail to praise Him for such amazing love as this?"

Isaiah began to sing the final Passover psalms of praise. As Hezekiah joined him, the words told the story of his own life, his own redemption, and he relived each memory as he sang:

> Not to us, O LORD, not to us
>   but to your name be the glory,
>   because of your love and faithfulness.

Hezekiah remembered how he had accepted the Babylonians' praise for himself instead of rightfully praising God, and he felt ashamed.

> Why do the nations say,
>   "Where is their God?"
> Our God is in heaven;
>   he does whatever pleases him.

> *But their idols are silver and gold,*
> *made by the hands of men.*
> *They have mouths, but cannot speak,*
> *eyes, but cannot see . . .*
> *Those who make them will be like them,*
> *and so will all who trust in them.*

The psalm reminded Hezekiah of the Assyrian Rabshekah's taunting words. But Yahweh was the only God, a God of miracles, a God of love.

> *O house of Israel, trust in the Lord—*
> *he is their help and shield.*

Again, Hezekiah wondered why he had put his trust in other nations instead of in God. He vowed never to do it again.

> *I love the LORD, for he heard my voice;*
> *he heard my cry for mercy . . .*
> *The cords of death entangled me,*
> *the anguish of the grave came upon me . . .*
> *Then I called on the name of the LORD:*
> *"O LORD, save me!"*

Three times Hezekiah had almost died, first in Molech's flames, then by Uriah's hand, and finally during his illness after the fire. But each time he had cried out to Yahweh, and God had given him back his life.

> *How can I repay the LORD*
> *for all his goodness to me?*

Hezekiah knew that if he lived for a hundred years, he could never repay God. They began the final praise song, and Hezekiah sang the words with heartfelt love for God. They were the words of his own testimony:

> *The LORD is with me; I will not be afraid.*
> *What can man do to me? . . .*
> *It is better to take refuge in the LORD*
> *than to trust in man.*
> *It is better to take refuge in the LORD*
> *than to trust in princes.*
> *All the nations surrounded me,*
> *but in the name of the LORD I cut them off.*
> *They surrounded me on every side,*
> *but in the name of the LORD I cut them off . . .*

I was pushed back and about to fall,
but the LORD helped me.
The LORD is my strength and my song;
he has become my salvation.

Hezekiah saw Yahweh clearly for the first time in his life—a God of power and love, a God of salvation. And even though he'd lost everything he'd worked for these past 14 years, he knew that he still had Yahweh's love—and that was enough. If he needed to lose everything to finally see God face-to-face, then it had all been worth it.

"'Now the Passover celebration is complete,'" Isaiah recited, "'even as our salvation and redemption are complete. Just as we were privileged to celebrate it this year, so may we be privileged to do so in the future.'"

"Amen, Rabbi. In the future." But Hezekiah knew that at this moment his nation's future was very uncertain. "How did I stray so far from what was right?" he asked quietly. "When did I begin to sin?"

"Your sin began after you severed your relationship with Yahweh."

"But how, Rabbi? How did I sever it?"

"You became separated from Him by unforgiveness."

"But I made all the right sacrifices; I confessed my sin every day. Which sin wasn't forgiven?"

"Not God's unforgiveness, Your Majesty—yours. The unforgiveness in your own heart."

"You mean Hephzibah?"

"Bitterness not only destroys you but cuts you off from God. How can He forgive us if we can't forgive one another?"

"But how can I forgive her for what she's done to me?"

"What has she done?" Isaiah asked gently. "She put her faith in something other than God. Is that sin unforgivable, Hezekiah? Because if it is, then you have condemned yourself by your own confession. If she can't be forgiven, then neither can you."

"O God!" Hezekiah leaned his elbows on the table and covered his face.

"Hephzibah isn't evil, Your Majesty, only weak and human like all the rest of us. God couldn't stop loving her because of her sin any more than you could."

After a long time, Hezekiah looked up. He tried to speak, but a fierce tightness gripped his throat.

Isaiah stood and bowed slightly. "Thank you for sharing this Passover meal with us, Your Majesty."

Hezekiah nodded mutely as he rose to his feet. He embraced Isaiah briefly, then turned and left.

When Hezekiah stepped outside, the cold, damp air hit him like a pitcher of water tossed in his face. For a moment he felt disoriented, unsure where he was or where he should go. He started walking, but instead of climbing the hill to the palace, his feet carried him down through the twisting streets, out of the old City of David, and into the new section Eliakim had built. The streets were deserted, but through the shuttered windows he saw lamps and candles flickering and heard the faint sound of praise songs as the people of Jerusalem celebrated the Passover feast.

This brief glimpse inside happy homes where families were gathered together made Hezekiah's life seem as barren and desolate as the Judean wilderness. He felt the familiar weight on his shoulders, the burden of loneliness and grief he had carried for so long, but he understood it now: it was a burden of his own making. He had fashioned it himself and fastened it to his own shoulders, making himself a slave to bitterness and unforgiveness. Passover celebrated a time when God saw the burdens of His people and lifted them from their backs, setting them free to serve Him.

Hezekiah had never been to the villa he had built for his concubines, and it took him awhile to find it. When he finally did, the front gate was closed and barred. He saw lamps burning in the gatekeeper's cottage and listened for a moment to the mumble of voices reciting the Passover story. Then he drew a shuddering breath and knocked on the door. Shuffling footsteps approached.

"Who is it?" The gatekeeper's gruff voice let Hezekiah know he wasn't happy about having his meal disturbed.

"It's King Hezekiah."

"Yeah, right! And I'm the Queen of Sheba! Go away, you drunkard! Get out of here before I call the guards!" The footsteps retreated.

"Wait! I *am* King Hezekiah." He pounded on the gate again. "Open the door and I'll prove it."

"Quit your pounding! I won't open the gate to every drunkard who comes along claiming to be—"

"Open the peephole."

After a pause, Hezekiah heard the man fumbling with the latch to the viewing square near the top of the door, muttering angrily to himself. "I don't know who you think you are, disturbing a man's peace in the middle of his meal . . ."

It was too dark for the gatekeeper to see out, and Hezekiah had no torch, so as soon as the little trap door opened he held his hand up to it, displaying his royal signet ring.

"Look. I am the king."

Air rushed into the gatekeeper's lungs with a sharp gasp. Then Hezekiah heard more frantic fumbling as the man removed the bars and opened the locks with trembling hands. "Forgive me! Oh, forgive me, Your Majesty," he stammered. "I didn't know . . . I . . . I couldn't tell . . ."

"Of course you couldn't—never mind," Hezekiah said as the gate finally swung open. He rested his hand on the man's trembling shoulder. "Listen, I'd like—I'd like to see Hephzibah, please."

As the man led him down the walkway to the last door, Hezekiah was grateful that it was dark, grateful that the gatekeeper couldn't see his face and read the emotions battling inside him.

"Here, my lord. This is her room." The gatekeeper started to knock, but Hezekiah stopped him.

"Wait. I'll do it. Go finish your dinner." The man bowed repeatedly as he backed away.

Hezekiah stared at the closed door for a long time, remembering the last time he had walked into Hephzibah's room at the palace. His chest heaved as he relived all the shock and pain he had felt when he found her bowing to a golden idol. But then he remembered his own sin—remembered the golden box from Babylon covered with pagan images, remembered the Babylonians bowing to him and honoring him as the favored one of the god Shamash. He closed his eyes and knocked.

"Come in."

His heart twisted at the sound of Hephzibah's soft, familiar voice. He lifted the latch and opened the door.

By the light of a lampstand he saw her sitting on her bed gazing down at her lyre lying on the bed beside her. She wasn't playing it, but her fingers stroked the frame as if the feel of the smooth wood brought back cherished memories. When she looked up and saw Hezekiah, she cried out. She slid off the bed and fell to her knees to bow.

"No, Hephzibah! Don't! Don't bow down to me!" Hezekiah dove forward, catching her by the shoulders to stop her. "Please don't, Hephzibah. I'm—I'm just a man, can't you see? A sinful man—like any other."

She covered her face and wept.

Hezekiah pulled her up and seated her on the bed again, then knelt in front of her. He could barely speak. He struggled to force out each word.

"I've come to ask your forgiveness, Hephzibah. I had no right to condemn you. I . . . I was so horrified when I saw the sin and idolatry in your heart . . . but now I see that the same sin is in my heart too. I'm as capable of idolatry as you were . . . as my father was . . . as any other person is. I'm sorry, Hephzibah . . . I'm so sorry. Will you forgive me?"

Hezekiah buried his face in her lap and wept, remembering all that he had lost, realizing the terrible consequences of his sin and un-forgiveness—the devastation of his land, the captivity of his people. Gradually he became aware of Hephzibah's hands caressing his shoulders, of her tears falling into his hair as she bent over him.

"No, Hezekiah, . . . no . . . I don't deserve forgiveness."

He lifted his head to look at her, tears streaming down his face. "None of us do, Hephzibah. But God doesn't treat us as our sins deserve." He took her hands in his. "I should have shown you that. I should have shown you my God instead of making you serve a God you didn't know. I only showed you His rules and laws. But God doesn't want us to worship Him out of fear. He wants a relationship with us. He's our Father, and He wants us to learn to love Him with all our heart and all our soul and all our strength. I should have helped you know Him, Hephzibah. Then you would have loved Him. He's a marvelous, wonderful, merciful God, a God of love and compassion and forgiveness. But I never told you that. I never helped you see Him. Can you ever forgive me?"

"But I've wronged you and deceived you—you have every right to be angry with me."

"God will not harbor his anger forever. How can I? My anger and bitterness were killing me, just as surely as my illness was. They poisoned my relationship with God and separated me from His love, just as they separated me from yours. Will you give me another chance, Hephzibah? Will you let me show you this awesome God of forgiveness I worship?"

"I've already seen Him," she whispered. "Tonight—you showed Him to me tonight when you came here. If you can forgive me after the terrible things I've done to you, then I can believe in God's forgiveness too."

Hezekiah stood, pulling her to her feet with him, and clasped her to himself.

God had joined them together. She was part of him. And as he took her face in his hands and kissed her, he felt whole again for the first time in nearly a year. *Man and woman—then God will dwell in their midst.*

"Let's go home," he whispered.

He snuffed out the lamp and closed the door behind them. Leaning close together, clinging to one another, they walked up the deserted streets to the palace.

27

When Hezekiah reached the palace, he was surprised to see torches and lamps burning in the Council Room and throne room. "You'd better wait for me in my chambers," he told Hephzibah; then he hurried down the hall to find out what was wrong.

"Your Majesty!" Shebna said breathlessly. "We have been searching all over for you. I have already summoned Eliakim and your other advisers. A message has arrived from the Egyptian camp. All is lost."

"What?" Hezekiah couldn't comprehend this news.

"Pharaoh's forces met the Assyrians in battle at Eltekeh. The Egyptians were slaughtered, Your Majesty."

"O God! No!" Hezekiah felt as if someone had squeezed all the blood from his body.

"The Assyrians mowed them down like summer hay."

The words of Isaiah's warning not to rely on Egypt's help sprang unbidden to Hezekiah's mind: *"this sin will become for you like a high wall, cracked and bulging, that collapses suddenly, in an instant."* "We have no allies—we're the only nation left," he murmured.

"Yes, Your Majesty." Shebna's face looked like a corpse's. "I am sorry—I never should have convinced you to join the alliance. I never should have promised you Egypt's help. Now you will surely be forced to surrender."

Close to midnight Eliakim returned home from the palace, exhausted. He found his father waiting up for him.

"What happened, Son?"

"The Assyrians crushed Pharaoh's army at Eltekeh."

"No!"

"It's over, Abba. All our allies have been defeated."

The spirit seemed to go out of Hilkiah, and he dropped to the bench near the door. "What's going to happen now? Will the Assyrians come back here?"

Jerusha had asked Eliakim the same question. "I don't know, Abba. No one does." He saw his father studying him.

"But you think they will."

"Yes," Eliakim sighed. "I do."

"God of Abraham, help us!"

"We discussed it all night, Abba. When Sennacherib demanded our surrender the last time, King Hezekiah decided to hold out, hoping the Egyptians would come to our rescue. Now that they're defeated, the Assyrians are sure to come back and demand our surrender again."

"And will the king surrender?"

"I don't know," he shrugged. "King Hezekiah listened to what everyone had to say, but he didn't tell us what he would do."

"What did you advise him to do?"

"I told him we should never surrender. Jerusalem is well fortified and can withstand a lengthy siege. We have plenty of food and a steady water supply. I told him we should wait and trust God."

"Yes. That's good advice." Hilkiah stood and squeezed Eliakim's shoulder. "You look exhausted, Son."

"I am."

"Get some sleep. You're going to have some rough days ahead of you. What a terrible way to end a beautiful Passover celebration!"

Jerusha was asleep with the baby nestled beside her when Eliakim crept into their room. He let his eyes adjust to the darkness, then stood beside the bed gazing at them. The sound of his son's raspy, labored breathing made Eliakim ache inside. He watched Joshua's tiny rib cage swell and shrink with each breath.

What would Jerusha do if he died? How could she survive the loss of a second child? And what on earth would happen to her if the Assyrians came back? He might lose her forever to her fear.

The unknown weighed heavily on Eliakim's heart. All his instincts urged him to protect his family, to shelter and defend them, but he was helpless to do it. He held the second highest position in the land and had enough money to buy anything he needed, but wealth and power couldn't secure a future for his family. Only Yahweh could.

Suddenly a deep stillness filled the room. It took Eliakim a moment to realize why—the baby had stopped breathing.

"No! O God, no!" He snatched him from Jerusha's arms. "Breathe! Joshua, breathe!" he cried, shaking his limp body. "O God, please—

please don't take my son!" In desperation, Eliakim put his mouth over Joshua's and breathed into him. *God of Abraham, please!*

"Eliakim, what's wrong?" Jerusha cried. "Where's the baby?"

After a moment Eliakim put his ear to the baby's face and heard a faint rasping sound as Joshua drew one shaky breath, then another and another.

"The baby's here, Jerusha. I have him. It's all right." He put his hand on Joshua's chest and felt his heart beating weakly. The baby coughed once, then whimpered softly. "Go back to sleep, Jerusha. I'll rock him for a while."

On legs so weak he could barely stand, Eliakim walked with his son, willing the air in and out of his lungs, willing his unsteady heart to keep beating. He wanted desperately to sit down, but if he did he might fall asleep. And if he fell asleep, Joshua might stop breathing again. Eliakim felt utterly helpless.

"God of Abraham, You have power," he prayed. "You can do anything. You're a God of miracles. You can heal Joshua. You can protect us from the Assyrians. You can make Jerusha whole again. There's nothing I can do but turn to You, Lord. You hold all our lives in Your hand. Please help me, Father. Help little Joshua. God of Abraham, help us all."

❖

"Your Majesty, let me go back," Iddina demanded. "I can make King Hezekiah surrender now. His allies are all defeated."

Emperor Sennacherib took another bite of fruit and licked the juice from his fingers. "I admire your zeal, Iddina, but don't you want to rest a day or two after our stunning victory?"

"No. I want to conquer Judah."

"Why worry about it? King Hezekiah's forces are so feeble that—"

"I don't want to risk an attack from the rear once we invade Egypt. Let me finish him off while the Egyptians are still stunned."

"Very well," the emperor said, wiping his hands on a towel. "How do you want to proceed?"

"You remain here, Your Majesty. I'll bring Hezekiah a message from you demanding surrender."

"Write it for me, Iddina. You have a persuasive way with words. How many men do you want?"

"I'll leave 50,000 here with you and take the rest."

"So many? What do you need 185,000 men for? How strong is Hezekiah?"

"The more men I take the more overwhelmed he'll be, and the sooner he'll surrender. I'll rejoin you in a few days, a week at the most. We'll march into Egypt together."

"Good. By the way, your men did an excellent job in their war against the rats. I haven't seen one in a couple of days."

"Good riddance to them."

"Yes, but now my senior officers are complaining that the rats were infested with fleas. Once you killed the rats, the fleas hopped onto all our men."

"That's not my problem."

"Well, I promised them that you'd allow the men to get a good bath before we invade Egypt."

"It'll have to wait, Your Majesty. We didn't find any water outside Jerusalem the last time we were there."

"No water?"

"None, sir."

"Oh, well—I'm sure you'll think of something, Iddina. You're a very resourceful man. Maybe the soldiers can use the Judeans' baths once you're inside the city."

"We'll do that, sir. And now if you'll excuse me, I want to make sure the army is prepared to march at dawn."

Inside the officers' camp, one of the generals showed Iddina his arms and legs, peppered with red welts. "It's these cursed fleas. I'm sick to death of them. Can't we wait another day before we invade Jerusalem so my men have time to wash their clothes and bedding? We're all miserable."

"No. We leave at dawn."

"But everyone is itching like the devil, and—"

"How hard is it to kill a flea?" Iddina shouted. "We're the most powerful army the world has ever seen! You want me to halt the conquest of an empire so you can kill a handful of fleas?"

"No, my lord."

"Be ready at dawn!"

Iddina stormed off before the general could reply and made his way to the priests' camp to seek omens for his final campaign against King Hezekiah. But even though it was early evening, the priests' camp was deserted, the campfires cold, the torches unlit. As he walked around the high priest's tent, he heard a low moan coming from inside. Iddina tossed the flap aside and ducked in. The gloomy tent reeked of vomit.

"Who is it?" the high priest groaned.

"Iddina."

"Please, my lord . . . you have to help me . . ."

Iddina found a lamp and lit it, then carried it to the high priest's bedside. "Get up! My men march to Jerusalem tomorrow. I need omens."

"I already know what the omens will say—and you've got to help me!"

Iddina squatted down and gazed at the priest. His face looked swollen, his eyes bloodshot. He shivered with fever. "What's wrong with you?"

"I don't know."

"Where are the other priests?"

He shook his head and moaned. "Remember the omens, Iddina? I saw them. They foretold death!" He clutched the front of Iddina's tunic. "You've got to help me. I don't want to die!"

Iddina tried to push him away, but the priest grabbed Iddina's hand and thrust it inside his tunic. "Feel this. What is this lump? What does it mean?" His fiery skin burned with fever, but when Iddina felt the hard, egg-sized tumor in the priest's armpit, he recoiled in horror.

"No, don't leave me!" the priest cried. "Help me! Don't leave me here to die!"

But Iddina had already fled from the tent. He found another priest lying in the next tent, moaning feverishly. He held a light near the man's side and stared at the enormous dark tumor under his arm. When he found a third priest vomiting blood, Iddina fled to the safety of his own tent.

He sat in the darkness for a long time, wondering what to do, unable to deny the paralyzing fear he felt. He had conquered Yahweh's army of rats, but now the plague of tumors had begun. His final showdown with Yahweh would come tomorrow. Yahweh possessed powerful magic, and Iddina had no priests to help him ward off this magic. He knew that he had a host of various gods on his side, but was this Judean god stronger than all of them? He had wrestled with that question for seven years, ever since Jerusha had escaped.

Doubt and fear haunted Iddina. Was it only a silly superstition planted by the Philistines? Had there really been more rats than usual, or had he imagined it? Was the fact that three priests were sick with tumors a mere coincidence? He would learn the answer tomorrow. He would settle once and for all the question of which god was superior. Tomorrow he would convince King Hezekiah to surrender, and by tomorrow night he would be inside Yahweh's Temple. He would confront Yahweh and conquer Him and carry away His golden throne.

Iddina grabbed a parchment scroll and began composing the emperor's letter, demanding King Hezekiah's unconditional surrender.

28

By the light of early dawn Hezekiah gazed at his wife, sleeping beside him. Soon he would have to think about the Assyrians again and about his nation. He would have to face the fact that his enemy had destroyed all his allies, that only his nation remained. He would have to decide what to do. But for now, he studied the contours of his wife's beautiful face as she slept, savoring the miracle that God's forgiveness had accomplished in their lives. After a while Hephzibah stirred and opened her eyes. When she saw him leaning on his elbow, gazing at her, her eyes filled with tears.

"Don't cry," he said, wiping them away. "We've both shed too many tears already."

"I must be dreaming—and I don't want to wake up."

"It's not a dream," he said, kissing her.

When the first shofar sounded the call for the morning sacrifice, Hezekiah reluctantly rose and began to dress. "It's time for me to go."

"My lord, would it be all right if I went with you?" He turned to look at her in surprise. "I want to thank God," she said. "I want to learn about Him—and about what I'm supposed to do."

"Yes, of course." He pulled her into his arms.

"When I was all alone in the villa, your secretary's wife came to see me. Jerusha offered me her friendship when everyone else abandoned me. And she talked to me about your God, about His forgiveness." Hezekiah listened in quiet amazement. "I was in so much pain that I wasn't very kind to her. I refused her friendship and pushed her away. If it's all right with you, could your servants take me to see her? I want to thank her."

"Go this morning if you'd like. Eliakim isn't my secretary anymore—he's my palace administrator. My most trusted adviser."

As Hezekiah climbed the hill to the Temple, he found himself wishing once again that he had listened to Eliakim instead of Shebna. If he had, how differently things might have turned out.

———◆———

"Jerusha? Are you awake? I brought you some breakfast." Eliakim set the tray of food on a table and sat down on the edge of the bed beside her.

"Thanks. I'll finish feeding the baby his breakfast first. Is the sacrifice over already?"

"I just got back." Eliakim tried to watch his son struggle to suck and breathe, but he had to look away. He recalled his panic last night when Joshua had stopped breathing and his own terrified prayer as he had breathed life back into him. This morning the baby still fought to live, and Eliakim decided not to tell Jerusha what had happened, just as he had decided not to tell her the Egyptian army had been defeated.

Jerusha caressed his hand. "You look so tired. How late were you at the palace last night?"

"I don't know. I got home sometime during the second watch, I think." Exhaustion numbed Eliakim. He had stayed awake all night making sure their son had continued to breathe.

"Why so late?"

"Lots of decisions to make. I have to go back in a few minutes. I'm sorry. When things get back to normal, maybe we can—Jerusha? What is it? What's wrong?"

She heard the ominous, thundering rumble moments before he did. She cried out in terror and struggled to get out of bed, her eyes wild with fright, her entire body trembling the way it had the day she had collapsed in the palace courtyard.

"God of Abraham . . . no . . . please!" he whispered as he tried to take her in his arms.

"He came back for me! Iddina came back! He's going to take my baby!"

"Jerusha . . . stop . . ."

"He's going to kill you and our children just like he killed my mother and father! He found me again! I led him here—to you!"

"Shh . . . that's not true . . ." Eliakim tried to hold her and calm her, but she fought him off. He backed away, afraid she would crush the baby in her arms. The rumbling of Assyrian horses and chariots grew louder, closer. Eliakim knew he had to go to the palace. He had to prevent the king from surrendering Jerusalem. But how could he leave Jerusha?

"Jerusha, listen to me, please . . ."

"I should have stayed with Iddina. I never should have come here. I know what they'll do! I know all the terrible things—!"

"Stop it! Listen to me! I promise you that Iddina won't hurt you. He won't hurt our children. He'll never set foot inside this city—I swear it to you. Don't you trust me?" She didn't answer. She lowered her head and sobbed. Eliakim took her by the shoulders, shaking her gently. "Jerusha, look at me! Do you trust me to protect you from him?"

She finally looked up. "I want to," she whispered.

"I will protect you! I swear it!" Eliakim didn't know how he would keep his promise, but he meant every word of it. He released her and raced into the hallway, shouting for the servants—"Where's my father?"

"He already left for the marketplace, my lord."

"Send someone to get him. I need him to stay with Jerusha while—"

"Eliakim, I'll stay with her."

He leaned over the railing and was startled to see Hephzibah standing by his front door.

"Hephzibah . . . ?" He couldn't imagine how or why she was there.

"Please, let me take care of her." And without waiting for his reply, Hephzibah hurried up the stairs and walked past him into the bedroom. Jerusha's weeping edged toward hysteria as Hephzibah went to her.

"Jerusha, it's me, your friend Hephzibah."

"They came back for me! They came back!" Jerusha stood beside the bed, frantically searching for a place to hide.

"Jerusha, look at me—I'm free! I'm out of my prison. God helped me escape, just like He helped you. Here—sit down on the bed beside me." Jerusha sat hesitantly on the edge of the bed as Hephzibah took her hand. "Will you teach me that psalm you recited, Jerusha? It was so beautiful, and I want to learn the words. How does it begin?"

Eliakim heard Jerusha draw a shuddering breath. "'Praise . . . praise the LORD, O my soul . . . and forget not all his benefits . . .'"

"Yes, that's the one. Will you teach it to me?"

"My baby . . . please don't let Iddina take him . . ."

"Can I see him, Jerusha? Oh, he's beautiful! So tiny and precious. A gift from God."

"Iddina took my baby before, and—"

"Could I hold him? I don't have any children of my own. My baby died before he was born. May I hold him, just for a moment?"

Eliakim stared in amazement as Jerusha tenderly laid Joshua in Hephzibah's arms. He knew his wife still balanced dangerously on the edge of despair, but so far Hephzibah was holding her back, preventing her from falling. He had once forbidden their friendship; now he thanked God for it.

"Oh, look at him," Hephzibah whispered. "He's so sweet." Then she looked up at Eliakim. "My husband needs you, Eliakim. Go. I'll stay with her until you come back."

⬥

Hezekiah leaned against the top of the city wall as he watched the Assyrians pouring into the Kidron Valley once again. They had brought many more soldiers than the last time—thousands more—with horses and chariots and enough swords, bows, shields, and spears to fill the palace armory to the ceiling. He felt shaken, as if he were trying to stand still in the midst of an earthquake. He could do nothing but brace himself as the world tumbled in around him.

"They're surrounding the entire city this time," General Benjamin told him. This invasion was the same as the last one, except magnified in intensity and power. Dazed, Hezekiah watched them stream endlessly into the valley and set up their camp. Then, as if reliving a nightmare, he saw them drag tall stakes into the clearing in front of the gate. He shuddered at what was coming.

"Dear God, please . . . make them stop . . . ," he whispered. Again, he recognized the pitiful Judean prisoners being prodded forward; they were the elders of Lachish. Hezekiah gripped the wall and moaned when he saw his brother Gedaliah.

He felt the shock of Gedaliah's pain shudder through him as they impaled him, screaming, before his eyes. Hezekiah forced himself to watch, feeling as helpless as when he'd watched his other brothers die in Molech's flames, and he hated the Assyrians as much as he'd ever hated Molech.

"Shall I find another sharpshooter, Your Majesty?" General Benjamin asked.

Hezekiah remembered how Helez's young life had ended so tragically. "No. I can't ask one of my men to risk his life again. Gedaliah will die anyway. Nothing we do can save him."

"It is hopeless, Your Majesty," Shebna said. "We may as well surrender. No city has ever withstood an Assyrian siege and—"

"Shut up, Shebna!" Eliakim shouted as he raced up the stairs two at a time to join them. "Keep your fear to yourself, or get down off the wall!" Shebna backed away, giving his place at the edge to Eliakim. Hezekiah was relieved to see him.

"King Hezekiah!" a voice suddenly shouted from the valley below. The arrogant Rabshekah had come forward again, standing with his hands on his hips, challenging him. "King Hezekiah! I have a message for you from Emperor Sennacherib!"

"I'll go," Eliakim said.

"Take Shebna and Joah—"

"No. Let me go alone this time."

◆

Eliakim saw a chance to keep his promise to Jerusha. He could make certain Iddina never hurt her again. But he didn't want to endanger Joah and Shebna.

"Let me go alone this time, Your Majesty."

"Are you sure—?"

"Yes."

"Very well," Hezekiah said after a moment.

Eliakim quickly started down the stairs with General Benjamin following to supervise the guard at the gate. When they reached the bottom, Eliakim stopped.

"Let me borrow your dagger."

"My dagger? What for?"

"Self-defense." The general hesitated, studying him. Eliakim thought of his friend General Jonadab and unconsciously fingered the scar on his throat. Jonadab would have guessed why Eliakim wanted a weapon and would never have given it to him.

"You're not going to do something foolish, my lord?"

"No. Of course not. You're wasting time. Give it to me."

Reluctantly, the general pulled his dagger from its sheath and handed it to him. It felt strange in Eliakim's hand, cold and menacing, and much heavier than he had expected. The general had finely honed both edges until they were paper thin and lethally sharp. Eliakim tucked it carefully under his belt on the left-hand side, hidden beneath his outer robe. Then he hurried through the gate.

Iddina stood 100 yards away, waiting for him. As Eliakim walked toward him, his hatred rapidly grew until it was almost out of control. He wanted to run forward and plunge the knife straight into Iddina's heart for what he had done to Jerusha. Iddina had raped and humiliated her. He had killed her first child. He had murdered her father and mother. Eliakim's tiny son had been born too soon and would likely die because of Iddina. He had tortured Eliakim's friend Jonadab. For all these reasons, Iddina deserved to die.

But Eliakim resisted the urge to run. A double row of Assyrian warriors stood behind Iddina with swords and spears in hand. Eliakim would take his time. He would listen to the emperor's message. Then he would say, *And I have a message for you . . .* He would reach inside his robe, as if to remove a scroll, but he would take a step closer and plunge the knife into Iddina's chest.

Eliakim knew he was committing suicide. He would never make it the 100 yards back to the city gate alive. But he wasn't afraid. Iddina would die. Nothing else mattered. He would keep his promise to Jerusha. She would never have to fear Iddina again.

Thou shalt not kill.

The words of the Torah suddenly startled Eliakim, echoing through his mind as clearly as if his father had spoken them in his ear. He felt the unfamiliar weight of the dagger pulling his belt down on his left side. It slapped gently against his hip as he walked.

But the Torah also said, *Show no pity: life for life, eye for eye, tooth for tooth.* Eliakim silently repeated those words to himself instead as he strode forward.

Iddina stood poised like a cat ready to pounce. He looked a few years older than Eliakim, but his muscular body was lean and deadly, armed with a warrior's reflexes. Eliakim knew he would have to move very fast. He couldn't let his face reveal his intentions. *Life for life . . .*

Eliakim stopped three feet from him, closer than the last time. Iddina's eyes glinted dangerously, but Eliakim stared into them without flinching.

"You again," Iddina growled.

"You were expecting King Hezekiah? Sorry to disappoint you." His voice remained calm, his anger and hatred under control. "What's your emperor's message?" Eliakim took a level stance, bracing himself for another onslaught of lies, directed toward the men on the wall like the last time. When Iddina suddenly reached inside his robe, Eliakim nearly backed away in fear. But Iddina produced a scroll and calmly handed it to him.

"From Emperor Sennacherib," he said.

Eliakim quickly recovered his balance. The time had come. He could feel his heart thudding wildly. He accepted the scroll with his left hand, then reached inside his own robe with his right hand and gripped the dagger handle. "And I have a—"

"Eliakim!"

He froze when he heard his name.

"Eliakim . . . help me . . . !"

He looked away from Iddina for a moment and noticed the row of impaled bodies behind him. The closest victim, the one imploring him in a pain-racked voice, was Prince Gedaliah. He'd been horribly mutilated, and the agony in his voice gave it an inhuman quality.

"Please . . . I beg you . . . help me!"

Gedaliah had once been his bitter enemy. The prince would have surely killed Eliakim if King Hezekiah had died. But now Eliakim's heart flooded with compassion for him. No human being deserved to suffer like that.

"You have *what?*" Iddina asked impatiently.

Eliakim's hand tightened on the dagger handle.

"Eliakim . . . please . . ." The voice of his former enemy shivered through Eliakim. Then suddenly, he heard the voice of Yahweh, speaking to him through His Torah once again:

It is mine to avenge; I will repay.

"I have—," Eliakim repeated, his heart leaping. He stared defiantly into Iddina's eyes for a long moment, then slowly uncurled his stiff fingers and released the dagger from his sweating palm. "—I have faith in Yahweh my God, that He will destroy you and deliver you into our hands."

Then he turned and strode back to the city, reciting softly to himself, "O LORD, the God who avenges, O God who avenges, shine forth . . . pay back to the proud what they deserve."

———◆———

Eliakim held the scroll out to Hezekiah. "Emperor Sennacherib sends you this message, Your Majesty." His confrontation with the Rabshekah had been briefer than the last time, with no shouts or threats from the Assyrian, but Eliakim looked pale and badly shaken.

"Are you all right?" Hezekiah asked.

"I—I'll be fine."

"Read the message out loud, Eliakim."

His hands shook as he unrolled it. "'Don't be fooled by that God you trust in. Don't believe it when He says that I won't conquer Jerusalem. You know perfectly well what the kings of Assyria have done wherever they have gone; they have completely destroyed everything. Why would you be any different? Have the gods of the other nations delivered them—such nations as Gozan, Haran, Rezeph, and Eden in the land of Telassar? The former kings of Assyria destroyed them all! What happened to the king of Hamoth and the king of Arpad? What happened to the kings of Sepharvaim, Hena, or Ivvah?'"

"The emperor is right, Your Majesty," Shebna said. "All our allies are destroyed. Perhaps if we surrendered peacefully they would allow us to—"

"Shut up!" Eliakim shouted.

The two men had tried to compromise and work together for years, but they remained bitter enemies. And suddenly Hezekiah knew that his own faith and his own pride were bitter enemies as well. He had been wrong to think he could appease both sides of himself all these years. Only one side could win.

"Sennacherib is right," Hezekiah said, as he stepped between them. "We're outnumbered. Outmaneuvered. We have no allies to save us. So according to all human reasoning, according to all that Shebna taught me, all that my mind and eyes tell me, it's hopeless. I may as well give up."

"No! You can't—!" Hezekiah held up his hand to silence Eliakim's protests.

"But Shebna wasn't my only teacher. My grandfather taught me that when I only trust in what I can see with my eyes, I'm committing idolatry. He taught me that faith in Yahweh is beyond the comprehension of our minds and our senses. So in spite of how hopeless it looks, Sennacherib needs to understand that I'm *never* going to surrender. Yahweh's Temple is inside this city. It's God's holy dwelling place on earth. My ancestor, King David, once confronted an enemy who was bigger and more powerful than he was, and I'm going to tell this Goliath outside our city gates the same thing David told him: 'You come against me with sword and spear . . . but I come against you in the name of the LORD Almighty, the God of the armies of Israel, whom you have defied. This day the LORD will hand you over to me . . . and the whole world will know that there is a God in Israel. All those gathered here will know that it is not by sword or spear that the LORD saves; for the battle is the Lord's.'"

Shebna stared at him, too stunned to speak. "Give me that letter," Hezekiah said. "I'm going to bring it before the Lord."

Eliakim walked beside him as he climbed the stairs to the Temple, and once again Hezekiah thought of the two bronze pillars, Jakin and Boaz. Yahweh was his strength. Yahweh had sworn to establish King David's throne forever. Hezekiah chose to believe.

Suddenly he noticed Shebna and the other officials trailing behind them, and he stopped. "Now that all hope for man's help is gone, Shebna, maybe you can begin to hope in God. But if you still hold unbelief in your heart, then stay out of this Temple. That goes for the rest of you too. The time for empty ritual, the time for making a pretense of faith, is long past. Yahweh is judging the idolatry in all our hearts. That's why the Assyrians have ravaged our land. Only the faithful will be left standing. If you can't pray in faith, if you can't believe in Yahweh's power and sovereignty, then go back to the palace."

He quickly turned and kept walking, unwilling to watch Shebna and some of the others retreat in shame. Hezekiah walked past the royal dais, past the great bronze altar where the morning sacrifice slowly burned, and knelt on the steps to the sanctuary, between the bronze pillars. He spread Sennacherib's letter on the stairs in front of him and looked up at the doors to the holy place. They were wooden, not golden, and Hezekiah remembered his sin. He knew he could approach God only by grace, not because he deserved any blessings from Him. He bowed his head to the ground.

"I believe in You, Yahweh, not in what I see. And I believe Your Word. I believe Isaiah's promise that You will shield Jerusalem and deliver it, that you will 'pass over' it and rescue it."

He stopped, remembering what else Isaiah had told him at the Passover feast. The prophet had talked about God's eternal plan for redeeming mankind, buying them back from the curse of Adam's sin. The Messiah would be the seed of David—Hezekiah's seed—and his life would be a guilt offering. God himself would redeem Israel from all their sin. Great was the love of his Heavenly Father. Hezekiah bowed his head again.

"This isn't about me, Lord, it's about You—Your plan, Your will for Your nation. What happens to all of us doesn't matter as long as it brings glory to Your holy name. I don't care if I suffer and die, as long as I play my small part in Your unfathomable plan. At last I know You, Lord, and I trust You. You're a holy God of love and forgiveness. You're my Father and my God. I want the world to know of Your love and grace and power and forgiveness. 'Hear, O Israel! Yahweh is our God—Yahweh alone!'

"O Lord God of Israel, sitting on Your throne high above the angels, You alone are the God of all the kingdoms of the earth. You created the heavens and the earth. Bend low, O Lord, and listen. Open Your eyes, O Lord, and see. Listen to this man's defiance of the living God. Lord, it is true that the kings of Assyria have destroyed all those nations and have burned their idol-gods. But they weren't gods at all; they were destroyed because they were only things that men had made of wood and stone. O Lord our God, we plead with You to save us from his power; then all the kingdoms of the earth will know that You alone are God."

As he knelt before God with his forehead pressed to the pavement, Hezekiah had no idea how many hours had passed. But when he felt a hand on his shoulder, he lifted his head.

"I'm sorry for disturbing you, Your Majesty," Eliakim said, "but this message just came for you. It's from Rabbi Isaiah."

Hezekiah took the scroll and unrolled it, reading the words silently:

"This is what the LORD, the God of Israel, says: Because you have prayed to me concerning Sennacherib king of Assyria, this is the word the LORD has spoken against him . . .

> *Who is it you have insulted and blasphemed?*
> *Against whom have you raised your voice*
> *and lifted your eyes in pride?*
> *Against the Holy One of Israel! . . .*

> *But I know where you stay*
> *and when you come and go*
> *and how you rage against me.*
> *Because you rage against me*
> *and because your insolence has*
> *reached my ears,*
> *I will put my hook in your nose*
> *and my bit in your mouth,*
> *and I will make you return*
> *by the way you came.*

> *This will be the sign for you, O Hezekiah:*
> *This year you will eat what grows by itself,*
> *and the second year what springs from that.*
> *But in the third year sow and reap,*
> *plant vineyards and eat their fruit.*
> *Once more a remnant of the house of Judah*
> *will take root below and bear fruit above.*

"Therefore this is what the LORD says concerning the king of Assyria:

> *He will not enter this city*
> *or shoot an arrow here.*
> *He will not come before it with shield*
> *or build a siege ramp against it. . . .*
> *I will defend this city and save it,*
> *for my sake and for the sake of David my servant!"*

When he finished, Hezekiah handed the scroll to Eliakim. "Read it," he told him.

Then Hezekiah bowed his head to the ground once again as the tears came, and he praised his holy God.

———◆———

Iddina headed for his tent after he had delivered Sennacherib's message to Eliakim. He had planned to shout to the people lined up on the wall as he had the last time, instilling fear in their hearts, inciting them to rebel against their foolish king. But he felt strangely weak and dizzy, and he lacked the strength to shout. He would wait to see if Hezekiah surrendered voluntarily first. He had plenty of time for frightening speeches.

As he walked to his tent, Iddina noticed that an eerie stillness had spread throughout the camp. He had trained his men to set up their siege in silence in order to instill terror, but this silence seemed different. Usually he could feel the tension in the men as they stayed alert with expectation. But today the soldiers seemed lethargic and dazed. They stood at their posts or sat in front of their tents listlessly. Maybe they were battle-weary. Perhaps he should have allowed them to rest for a day after their victory over the Egyptians.

Iddina felt lethargic as well. His head swam, and sweat poured off him as if he stood under a blazing sun, but the weather was cloudy and cold, just as it had been for weeks. A jolt of alarm shot through him when he remembered the dying priests' strange tumors.

Iddina detoured to his officers' tents. He would order his men out of this stupor and put a spark back into his troops. But Iddina found the officers' camp deserted. It looked as if it had been hastily thrown together. He opened the flap to the first tent he came to and hurried inside. The smell of vomit overpowered him.

"Captain? Where are you?"

The man answered with a moan. He lay sprawled on the floor a few feet from his sleeping mat.

"What's the matter with you?" Iddina turned him over and saw the same symptoms he had seen in the three priests—swollen face, bloodshot eyes, shivery with fever. "Answer me, Captain! What's the matter with you?"

The officer replied in a jumble of feverish words that made no sense. Iddina squatted beside him and raised his arm, searching for tumors like those he had seen on the priests. He found none.

"Food poisoning," Iddina said aloud. "You must have eaten spoiled meat. It's happened to troops in the past and no doubt it will happen again. In 24 hours you'll be well again, in time to accept King Hezekiah's surrender and march into the city." The captain groaned and rolled away from Iddina to vomit.

He found his other officers sick inside their tents as well. None of them had tumors in their armpits. Relieved, Iddina returned to his tent. His own aide looked droopy and listless.

"Call me if there's any answer from King Hezekiah," he told him. Then Iddina sank down on his sleeping mat. The sensation of sweating and shivering at the same time felt very odd. Suddenly the food poisoning struck him too, but he fought the urge to vomit. He probed his armpits. They were tender, but he found no tumors.

"I'm not afraid of You, God of Judah," he mumbled as he drifted to sleep against his will. "The gods who have brought me victory over all the nations will soon bring me victory over You as well."

Iddina slept restlessly, his sleep filled with feverish nightmares. When he awoke and saw the sun lying low in the west, he felt a surge of terror. How had he slept so long? He wondered what had awakened him, then heard a trumpet sounding in the distance. He crawled to the door of his tent. It came from the highest point in the city, from Yahweh's Temple.

"You won't defeat me," he said aloud. "I'm not afraid of You." But as he shivered in the late afternoon shadows, he felt an intense anxiety he couldn't explain. His heart hammered rapidly in his chest for no reason at all.

He pulled himself to his feet and staggered to the nearest tent, the ground whirling and spinning beneath his feet. The movement made him nauseous. He found the commander in chief of the Assyrian army shivering on his pallet.

"Who's there? Is that you, Shamshi?"

"No. It's Iddina."

"Where's Shamshi? I need him."

"Probably sick like the rest of us."

"Am I going to die?" Iddina saw terror in the commander's eyes. He had never seen it there before, in spite of all the battles they had fought together. "What . . . what are you doing?" the commander cried as Iddina probed his armpits. No tumors. Iddina sank to the floor, weak with relief.

"You're not going to die," Iddina said, trying to convince himself. "It's food poisoning. It'll pass in a day or two."

As he groped his way back to his own tent, Iddina looked out over the camp. It was so quiet he could hear the moans of the impaled men, halfway across the valley. He saw no movement anywhere. He couldn't stop trembling, and he wondered if it was from his fever or his terrible fear. Something wasn't right. How could the entire camp be so still? He wanted to shout and awaken everyone, to scare away the demons that lurked behind all the tents, waiting for him, but he lacked the strength.

He felt another wave of nausea, even though he had eaten nothing all day. His stomach should be empty. But Iddina couldn't stop himself from being sick. Afterward he felt weak and shivery. But when he saw the huge quantity of blood he had spewed up, he crawled into his tent and fainted.

29

"It's been quiet down there all day, Your Majesty," Eliakim said. "When do you suppose they'll start their assault?"

Hezekiah stared down at the deathly stillness in the valley. "Probably as soon as they get it through their heads that I'm not going to surrender." He sat with Eliakim and General Benjamin, huddled beneath heavy robes to ward off the evening chill.

"Are you sure you don't want a fire, Your Majesty?" the general asked.

"I'm sure. I don't want them to know how many soldiers we have guarding the walls." *Or how few,* he said to himself.

"Don't you think it's odd that they're not building any campfires either?" Eliakim asked. "They built fires the last time they were here."

"Yes, very odd, especially considering how cold it is." Hezekiah stuck his hands into his armpits to warm them.

"I wonder if it's mind warfare, like Jonadab talked about."

Hezekiah shrugged. "I don't know, General. It might be."

"Listen—my men will stand watch during the night, Your Majesty. There's no need for you to stay up. Why don't you and Lord Eliakim go inside and get some sleep?"

"I wouldn't be able to sleep anyway." Hezekiah had walked among the people after the evening sacrifice and sensed the tension and fear barely hidden beneath the surface. He had detected fear even among many of his soldiers. No one could guess why the Assyrian troops hid inside their tents out of view, and the mystery heightened everyone's terror. If the tension inside Jerusalem grew much worse and fear took control of a few persuasive men, Hezekiah knew the ensuing panic could start a stampede to open the gates and surrender. He would stay awake all night with his soldiers. He and Eliakim would walk the streets again, if necessary, calming the fears of his people.

As darkness fell, the night grew quiet and still. Not a sound stirred from the Assyrian camp. Even the night birds and insects seemed silenced by the unbearable tension in the air. Aside from nervous whispers among his troops, the only sounds Hezekiah heard were the dying moans of his brother and the elders of Lachish, growing fainter all the time.

———◆———

Vivid, terrifying images haunted Iddina's feverish sleep, peopled by the host of demonic creatures he had feared throughout his childhood. "No! Leave me alone!" He cried out in delirium as his fever climbed steadily higher, but the legions swarming around him refused to depart.

Shortly before dawn he awoke when someone entered his tent. "Who's there? Who is it?" He sat up fearfully, expecting to see Death's messengers arriving for him. Instead, he saw two soldiers looting his tent. "What are you doing?" They backed away in terror.

"There's death in the camp!"

"It's everywhere!"

"We came to see if you—"

"No! I'm *not* going to die!" Iddina tried to stand.

"But all the others are dead."

"We're leaving this camp . . . those of us who are left . . ."

"Wait! Come back! Take me with you!" But they quickly fled from the tent, and minutes later Iddina heard pounding hoofbeats fading into the distance.

He pulled himself to his feet and tried to walk, but a fierce pain stabbed him in the groin. He groped for the source and felt a huge tumor at the base of his legs. Iddina couldn't remember ever weeping in his life, but suddenly he began to sob.

"You can't kill me, Yahweh! I have more power than You do!" The terrible pain in his groin dropped him to his knees. He couldn't control his hysteria as he crawled to the nearest tent, dragging himself across the rocky ground. He found the commander in chief of Sennacherib's army lying dead. Blood poured from his ears and nose and mouth. Iddina lifted the dead man's tunic and saw the huge black tumors in his groin.

"I'm not afraid of you, Yahweh," he wept as he crawled from tent to tent. They were all the same. All his senior officers were dead. All of them had tumors; some in the groin, some in the armpits, a few at the side of the neck. It was just as the Philistine priests had said, just as the two looters had said—Death had stalked the Assyrian camp during

259

the night. Iddina saw his footprints everywhere. Soon Death would come for him.

"No! You can't kill me like this! I'm a warrior! Kill me in battle! Let me die an honorable death!" Iddina heard laughter ringing in his ears, demonic laughter as the hosts of enemy spirits came to claim him. He couldn't let them take him yet. He had one more god to conquer—Yahweh.

As the sun rose, Iddina crawled toward the clearing where he had confronted Eliakim. Once again he would demand King Hezekiah's surrender. He would pour terror into the Judeans' hearts with his words. He would convince them that their unseen god could never save them.

The morning breeze swiftly blew away the damp clouds, and the weather promised to be bright and hot at last. Iddina saw a flash of sunlight glint off the Temple roof, and it seemed as if Yahweh laughed at him in triumph. Iddina raised his fist in the air.

"I conquered hundreds of gods! I hold power over a host of deities! Do You think an invisible God can—?" But Iddina never finished his challenge. As blood gushed from his mouth and nose, he collapsed in the clearing outside Jerusalem's gates.

◆

Heavy clouds had hidden the moon and stars from view as Hezekiah watched atop the city wall all night, silently reciting the psalms of David to bolster his faith and stay awake.

> Deliver me from my enemies, O God;
> protect me from those who rise up against me.
> Deliver me from evildoers
> and save me from bloodthirsty men. . . .
> See what they spew from their mouths—
> they spew out swords from their lips,
> and they say, "Who can hear us?"
> But you, O Lord, laugh at them;
> you scoff at all those nations. . . .
>
> I will sing of your strength,
> in the morning I will sing of your love;
> for you are my fortress,
> my refuge in times of trouble.

In the pale light just before dawn, Hezekiah detected a flicker of movement in the Assyrian camp. He stood up, straining his eyes to see in the darkened valley below. As he watched, a dozen Assyrian soldiers ran from tent to tent as if to rouse the others from their slumber. But no one seemed to stir from their efforts. After several minutes he saw movement near the horse paddocks. The handful of soldiers saddled some of the horses, then mounted and galloped out of the valley, quickly disappearing in the low-hanging clouds.

"What do you make of all that?" Hezekiah asked the soldier standing watch beside him.

"I can't even guess, Your Majesty."

Several minutes passed, and the shadowy valley remained still. Slumped against the wall beside him, Eliakim suddenly stirred from his sleep and sat up. "I'm sorry . . . I didn't mean to fall asleep . . ."

"It's all right. Everything's been quiet."

"What time is it?"

"The last watch. Almost dawn."

Eliakim pulled himself to his feet as Hezekiah told him about the soldiers who had ridden away.

"It certainly seems strange," Eliakim agreed.

"I stayed awake all night, and I never saw a watch fire or a torch or even an oil lamp," Hezekiah said.

"How can they keep predators away from the camp without watch fires?"

"Something is very odd, Eliakim. Let's walk a bit." Cold and cramped from his all-night vigil, Hezekiah began a slow circuit of the top of the city wall with Eliakim, stopping to talk to his unit commanders along the way. The enemy encampment completely surrounded Jerusalem, but with the exception of the Assyrian horses, they saw no sign of movement or life.

As the sun rose higher, Jerusalem began to stir. Hezekiah smelled the smoke of early fires and heard the faint grinding of handmills. Serving girls walked through the streets toward the Pool of Siloam with their jars on their heads. But outside the walls all was quiet.

It took Hezekiah and Eliakim almost two hours to complete their circuit and return to where they had started. By the time they stood overlooking the Kidron Valley once again, the sun had risen over the Mount of Olives, chasing away the chilly clouds.

"Was that body lying down there before, Your Majesty?" Eliakim pointed to a figure sprawled facedown in the clearing where the Rabshekah had stood a day earlier.

"I don't know. It was too dark to see when we started."

The Assyrian horses whinnied, pacing restlessly in the paddocks. "They'll need water," Hezekiah said. "Especially once the sun gets high." The Assyrian camp remained motionless. A quiet surge of hope swelled inside Hezekiah.

"Do you suppose it's a trick?" Eliakim asked. "To get us to open the gates?"

"We'll wait and see."

Soon word began to spread through the city that nothing moved in the Assyrian camp, and people hurried to the walls to see. As they packed the ledge, gazing in wonder at the scene below, no one spoke above a whisper, as if awed into silence themselves. The only sounds Hezekiah heard as he stood watching and waiting were the joyous chorus of birds in the olive groves and the distant sound of frightened horses as they capered nervously in their corrals.

◈

"Lord Emperor?"

"Get back! Stay away from me!" The servant froze in the doorway of Emperor Sennacherib's tent. "What is it now? More sickness?" The linen cloth the emperor held over his nose and mouth muffled his voice.

"Worse!"

"Tell me."

"A dozen soldiers just rode in from your camp outside Jerusalem, and—"

"Has King Hezekiah surrendered yet? Or are the Judeans fighting back?"

"Your Majesty, this handful of soldiers are the only survivors!"

"Handful! Where are the others?"

"It's a disaster of unbelievable proportions! A plague has spread throughout the entire camp, and—"

"What about my commander in chief? My officers? My Rabshekah?"

"They're all dead, along with your entire army! One hundred eighty-five thousand soldiers!"

"May all the gods preserve us!" Sennacherib clutched the cloth to his mouth, murmuring incantations to the gods as he dropped into his chair.

"It was the same sickness as here, my lord. All the men had fevers and tumors."

Sennacherib trembled as fear rocked through him. He had to get out of Judean territory, away from Yahweh, the God of plagues and pestilences. The stories of the devastation He had inflicted on Egypt centuries before were legendary, but the emperor had never believed in them until now. Nor would he have believed the Philistines' superstitious story of rats and tumors if he hadn't witnessed this plague with his own eyes. Yahweh's power was beyond his comprehension.

"I was so close!" he suddenly cried. "I could have conquered Egypt. I could have succeeded where my father and grandfather failed. How . . . Why . . . Are you certain they're all dead?"

"Yes, Your Majesty."

"I had the most powerful army the world has ever seen! How could the gods fail me like this? How could they let the God of Judah defeat us all?" Sennacherib's anger and frustration brought him close to tears, but he couldn't allow his servant to witness his distress.

"Break camp," he said suddenly. "Right now. Right away. We'll take whatever men are left. The healthy ones. Make sure none of them are sick."

"Where will we go?"

"If what you say is true . . . if my army is destroyed . . . then I have no choice. I'll have to return to Nineveh."

"What about the men who are sick and dying?"

"Leave them."

"But—"

"Don't you understand? We have to get out of Judean territory now! Away from the wrath of their God! Harness my chariot! Hurry!"

Alone in his tent, Sennacherib raged at the injustice of it all. He had defeated nations far more powerful than Judah—Babylon, Moab, a huge Egyptian army. How could he return home in defeat, conquered by King Hezekiah of Judah? He thought of all the golden images he had deported to his temple in Nineveh, but the unseen, imageless God of Israel had defeated him in the end. Sennacherib covered his face in anger and despair.

—◆—

As the sun climbed higher in the sky, the morning wind carried the stench of death to the top of the wall. A half-dozen vultures began making slow, sweeping circles over the valley.

"Your Majesty, it's been hours," Eliakim said. "Nothing has moved down there. Let me go out and investigate."

"Are you sure you want to do that, Eliakim?"

"Yes. I'm not afraid."

"I'll go too," the general said, "with some of my men."

"Take volunteers. No one should go out unless he wants to."

Excitement crept through Eliakim as he descended the stairs and waited for the soldiers to open the city gate for him.

"You're not armed, my lord. Do you want my dagger again?" General Benjamin asked.

"No. I won't need it." Eliakim knew Yahweh had worked a miracle. He jogged across the clearing toward the Assyrian camp, his legs trembling with anticipation. When he reached the body lying facedown, he kicked it over with his foot. Trails of dried blood ran from Iddina's ears and nose and mouth. His wide eyes stared sightlessly.

"Oh, thank God . . . thank God . . . ," Eliakim murmured. Yahweh had done it—He had avenged Jerusha more wonderfully than Eliakim could have ever imagined. He looked for something to take to Jerusha, something to prove that Iddina was dead, and spotted the dagger tucked in Iddina's belt. He remembered Jerusha's story of the night she had nearly ended her life with that dagger. He pulled it from Iddina's belt and carefully tucked it into his own.

Suddenly Eliakim heard a soft moan and looked up. Gedaliah dangled above him on the stake.

"General Benjamin! Come over here," Eliakim shouted. "Help me take him down." Gedaliah cried out in agony as they lifted him off the stake and laid him on the grass. "Do you have any water we can give him?" Eliakim asked.

"He won't live, my lord," the general whispered as he untied a skin of water from his belt.

"I know. But we can still ease his suffering. Tell your men to take the others down too." He raised Gedaliah's head and poured water between his parched lips.

"Eliakim . . . ? You came back . . . ?"

"The siege is over, Gedaliah. The Assyrians are all dead. Yahweh destroyed them during the night." The prince sighed and closed his eyes.

Eliakim stood and began to jog toward the Assyrian camp. Under the hot sun, the stench of death nearly overpowered him. He needed to look in only three or four tents to know what he would find in all the others. All the Assyrians were dead. Hundreds of thousands of them.

He turned around and ran back toward the gate, shouting to King Hezekiah and the men on the wall above him as he ran. "They're dead! Yahweh sent the angel of death! The Assyrians are all dead!"

The cheer that went up from the city made Eliakim's ears ring. He was breathless when he reached King Hezekiah on the wall. He bent over with his hands on his thighs, panting.

"Plunder the Assyrians' weapons and chariots," the king ordered his soldiers. "Then burn all their tents and the dead bodies." He turned to Eliakim, his voice hoarse with emotion. "Well, I guess I didn't need to buy Egyptian horses after all. Yahweh sent more horses than I can possibly use!"

"Your Majesty . . . may I go home for . . . I have to tell . . ."

"Yes! Certainly, Eliakim! Go!"

He took off at a run again, never slowing until he burst through his front door. He took the stairs two at a time and was stunned to see Hephzibah still sitting on his bed, gently rocking his son. Jerusha looked shaky, but she was all right.

Eliakim could barely talk. He carefully pulled Iddina's dagger from his belt and laid it in Jerusha's hands. "Look!"

"That's Iddina's!"

"Yes . . . he won't need it anymore . . . he's dead." She stared at it, wide-eyed, as if afraid of it. "I saw him with my own eyes, Jerusha. He's dead. They're *all* dead. The entire Assyrian army. Yahweh worked a miracle!"

Hephzibah touched his sleeve. "Eliakim. Yahweh worked another miracle last night. Here." She laid Eliakim's tiny son in his arms. Joshua's breathing was smooth and even.

"God of Abraham!" he whispered. Suddenly the baby opened his eyes. He gazed up at Eliakim for a moment; then his miniature face puckered. And for the first time in his short life, Joshua let out a gusty wail.

—◈—

As Hezekiah looked down from the wall at the miracle Yahweh had performed, he wondered if Moses could have felt more joy when the Red Sea swallowed the Egyptians. "Praise our God, O peoples," he said aloud, "let the sound of his praise be heard; he has preserved our lives and kept our feet from slipping."

The shofars began to sound from the Temple hill, trumpeting in joy and triumph. It was still Passover week, the celebration of Yahweh's deliverance in the past. Now they would celebrate His deliverance in the present, witnesses to God's salvation power. Hezekiah climbed down from the wall to join the joyful pilgrimage to the Temple.

When he reached the lower gate, he found Shebna waiting for him. He looked like such a weary old man that Hezekiah barely recognized him at first. His back sagged beneath the weight of his body, and his stubbled chin trembled when he spoke.

"Your Majesty, I . . . I see it with my eyes . . . but I . . ." Then much to Hezekiah's surprise, Shebna began to weep. In all their years together it had never happened. Hezekiah rested his hand on his friend's shoulder, fighting his own tears.

"We tried so hard to figure out a way to save ourselves, didn't we, Shebna? Weapons, . . . fortresses, . . . armies, . . . alliances. We worked for 14 years, but all our efforts failed. We were helpless. But what we were powerless to do, Yahweh accomplished in a single night! They're all dead! The entire Assyrian army! Hundreds of thousands of men! They can never threaten us again. Can you comprehend that? I—I don't think I can." Hezekiah brushed a tear from his eye with the heel of his hand.

"Your Majesty, I beg you. Let me stand in the Court of the Gentiles today. Please."

"Do you believe in Yahweh, Shebna?"

"I cannot deny this miracle . . ."

"If you're coming to seek God, I know you'll find Him. But don't come to the Temple for any other reason."

Shebna looked into Hezekiah's eyes. "Will you help me, Your Majesty? Will you help me believe?" Hezekiah squeezed his shoulder and nodded.

"Come on."

As they passed the Women's Court, Hezekiah saw Hephzibah kneeling in worship. He was so overwhelmed with gratitude and praise he could no longer stop his tears. He knelt on the royal platform and closed his eyes, praying silently. "O Lord, let me praise You with my life. Let me live in faith and obedience to You." Then he fell on his face before God as the praises of the Levites rang from the Temple hill in triumphant song:

> In Judah God is known;
> his name is great in Israel.
> His tent is in Salem,
> his dwelling place in Zion.
> There he broke the flashing arrows,
> the shields and the swords, the weapons of war. . . .
> You are resplendent with light,
> more majestic than mountains rich with game.
> Valiant men lie plundered,
> they sleep their last sleep;
> not one of the warriors
> can lift his hands.
> At your rebuke, O God of Jacob,
> both horse and chariot lie still.
> You alone are to be feared.
> Who can stand before you when you are angry?

From heaven you pronounced judgment,
  and the land feared and was quiet—
when you, O God, rose up to judge,
  to save all the afflicted of the land. . . .

Surely your wrath against men brings you praise,
and the survivors of your wrath are restrained.

Make vows to the LORD *your God and fulfill them;*
  let all the neighboring lands bring gifts to the One to be feared.
He breaks the spirit of rulers;
  he is feared by the kings of the earth.

Acrid smoke from the funeral pyres drifted up to Hezekiah, carried by the wind. The scent of idolatry reminded him once again of Yahweh's promise, spoken by Isaiah years ago: *"When you pass through the waters, I will be with you; and when you pass through the rivers, they will not sweep over you. When you walk through the fire, you will not be burned; the flames will not set you ablaze. For I am the* LORD, *your God, the Holy One of Israel, your Savior."*

Yahweh had brought him through the flood to prove His strength and faithfulness. He had taken Hezekiah through the fire to finally purge all the idolatry from his heart. As Isaiah had prophesied, a remnant from the house of Judah would "take root below and bear fruit above." Hezekiah could start anew, his sins and his foolish pride forgiven. Someday, from Hezekiah's own seed, Yahweh would send the Messiah; and this great day of salvation from Assyria would be only a shadow of the eternal salvation the Messiah would bring.

With a heart too full to speak, Hezekiah lifted his hands toward heaven in praise to his holy God.

Epilogue

Emperor Sennacherib stood in the temple of Nisroch with his two sons and gazed at the dazzling golden idols arrayed on the platform before him. He had conquered all these gods. The people who had once bowed down to them now bowed to him. He was "Sennacherib the mighty king, the powerful king, King of Nations, King of Assyria." His artisans had inscribed those words on the walls of his royal chamber, and he never grew tired of reading them.

As his eyes ranged over the images, Sennacherib noticed a gap between the god Baal and the goddess Asherah, as if one idol was missing. He thought of Yahweh, the imageless God of the Judeans, and the hair prickled on the back of his neck. All of his finest officers, the fiercest and best-trained army in the world, slain overnight. He shook his head to erase the memory.

Yahweh's golden throne belonged in that vacant spot. Sennacherib had failed to retrieve a symbol of the deity, but he had conquered King Hezekiah and his God. Hezekiah had paid the bribe Sennacherib had demanded. The Assyrians had defeated almost 50 of Hezekiah's fortified cities and deported their people.

"I did defeat you," he mumbled aloud. "You have no power over me."

"What did you say, Father?" his son Sharezer asked. He stood a few feet behind Sennacherib.

"Nothing. I wasn't talking to you."

I'm talking to You, Yahweh. He stared at the vacant place again. *If You have so much power, why didn't You kill me along with all the others? Why am I still alive and reigning as emperor of the world? If You're really more powerful than all these other gods, then strike me dead right now!*

Sennacherib stood with his hands on his hips, staring defiantly at the place where Yahweh's throne belonged. When several seconds passed and nothing happened, no lightning bolt from the sky struck him dead, Sennacherib began to laugh.

"You see?" he said aloud. "I did defeat Him. I defeated all of the gods!" He whirled around to face his two sons. "Yahweh—"

Sennacherib never finished his boast. His two sons, Adrammelech and Sharezer, rushed toward him, plunging their knives into his gut, spilling his bowels on the temple floor. Then they fled from the temple of Nisroch, leaving Sennacherib to die alone with his conquered gods.

———◆———

"May I see her now?"

The midwife bowed to him. "Yes, and congratulations, Your Majesty."

Hezekiah still couldn't comprehend the amazing news. He had a son. Yahweh had given him an heir.

Hephzibah looked weary and flushed. She lay propped against her pillow holding a tiny mound of blankets in her arms. Hezekiah sat down on the bed beside her and kissed her.

"How are you?"

"Tired. But I never dreamed I could be so happy. Look at him." Hephzibah shifted the bundle in her arms, and Hezekiah stared at his son's pinched, ruddy face in alarm.

"Is he all right?"

"Yes," she laughed. "He's strong and healthy. And he shouts like a king when he's hungry."

"But he looks so—" Hezekiah didn't want to say it, but the baby looked too scrawny to survive the night.

"Hezekiah, haven't you ever seen a newborn baby before?"

"No, I guess I haven't."

"He's a strong, healthy boy who will grow to be as tall and handsome as his father one day."

"Have you thought of a name?"

"I would like to call him Manasseh, because Yahweh has helped me forget all my sorrow."

"Then that's his name—Manasseh." Outside the window, shofars began to sound from the Temple wall. "Listen—do you hear that? The priests are announcing to the nation that an heir has been born at last. The throne of David will continue through all the generations, just as Yahweh promised."

"Would you like to hold him?"

"Hold him? Is it all right?" He was so tiny—Hezekiah was afraid he would crush him.

"You'll do fine," she smiled. "He won't break." She lifted Manasseh into Hezekiah's arms before he could reply. The bundle felt soft and warm. This sweet-smelling, vulnerable little child was his son! Hezekiah's heart filled with love for him, but it amazed him to think that what he felt was only a shadow of the overwhelming love Yahweh felt toward His children.

Manasseh opened his eyes and looked up at his father, blinking in the light. "Listen carefully, Son," Hezekiah said. "I'm going to teach you your very first lesson. And you must never forget it, because it's also the most important lesson you'll ever learn: 'Hear, O Israel! Yahweh is our God—Yahweh alone! And you must love Yahweh your God with all your heart and with all your soul and with all your strength.'"

---

*So the LORD saved Hezekiah and the people of Jerusalem
from the hand of Sennacherib king of Assyria
and from the hand of all others. He took care of them
on every side. Many brought offerings to Jerusalem
for the LORD and valuable gifts for Hezekiah king of Judah.
From then on he was highly regarded by all the nations.*
—2 Chron. 32:22-23

*Hezekiah trusted in the LORD, the God of Israel.
There was no one like him among all the kings of Judah,
either before him or after him. He held fast to the LORD and did
not cease to follow him; he kept the commands the LORD
had given Moses. And the LORD was with him;
he was successful in whatever he undertook.*
—2 Kings 18:5-7

*Hezekiah rested with his fathers and was buried on the hill
where the tombs of David's descendants are.
All Judah and the people of Jerusalem honored him when he died.
And Manasseh his son succeeded him as king.*
—2 Chron. 32:33

Scripture Credits

Scripture quotations from *The Living Bible* (TLB) are found on the following pages (see page 4 for copyright information): 205, 206 (third, fifth, and seventh full paragraphs), 207-8 (carry-over paragraph), 251 (last paragraph), 253 (last paragraph).

Paraphrased verses by the author are found on the following pages: 13, 30, 76 (ninth paragraph), 83 (third and seventh paragraphs), 85, 89 (second full paragraph), 114 (fourth full paragraph), 115, 253 (fourth full paragraph), 271.

All other Scripture quotations are from the *New International Version*® (NIV®). See page 4 for copyright information.